The Death of Reality

*How the blending of corrupt politics with linguistic
theory have threatened science by undermining our
culture's capacity to perceive reality.*

Books by Lawrence Dawson

Fiction

Locust and Wild Honey

Non-Fiction

The Death of Reality
Four Dimensional Atomic Structure
The Quantum Dimension

The Death of Reality

How the blending of corrupt politics with linguistic theory have threatened science by undermining our culture's capacity to perceive reality.

Lawrence Dawson

THE PARADIGM COMPANY

Boise, Idaho

The Paradigm Company, Inc.

3500 Mountain View Dr.

Boise, Idaho 83704

208-322-4440

First 2nd Edition Printing 2015

Library of Congress Cataloging-in-Publication Data

Dawson, Lawrence, 1944-
  1st Ed. The death of reality: how a conspiracy of fools has
laid claim to the destiny of a nation / Lawrence Dawson.

p. cm.

2nd Ed. ISBN 978-0941995368

1. United States--Social conditions.
HN57.D32   1997   96-48496
306' .0973--dc21   CIP

To

**The editors and journalists in the nation's
underground press.**

Men and women who have labored for truth with neither
recognition nor financial reward. The unsung heroes of a
generation.

Acknowledgments

I am indebted to the following people for the present work:

Peter Watt who, in many ways, is a coauthor of this book, having spent many hours with me in discussion of its major thesis.

My wife Meg who lived with me during its completion and provided counsel both for the ideas contained in the book and for the working psychology of its author.

Doctors Edward Krug and Arthur Robinson, men of science who provided information in their own writings and valuable insights in personal communications.

The 300 plus publications which made up the substance of the *American Information Newsletter* and alerted the author to the depth of information suppression currently practiced by the American media.

Contents

.

FOREWORD TO 2015 EDITION

Why the 2015 edition is better suited to the book's major thesis

When this book was first issued in the last decade of the last century it was considered by some to be a political polemic; as a tool to further favored political causes. If this were true, why reissue the book in 2015 when those causes are now stone cold? It is being reissued precisely because the political issues covered in the book are "stone cold." Now, the larger purpose of the *Death of Reality* might be considered objectively.

This book was never about politics. It was about the way that the infusion of our culture by the social-linguistic philosophy of Ludwig Wittgenstein had allowed a political movement to reinvent reality. In the mid ' 90's, political passions were too close to the issues chosen to exemplify the corruption and the book had to oppose a counter-tide of political prejudices. Since most of those issues have cooled in 2015, that tide of political prejudice has receded, allowing a more reasoned examination of the issues.

The issue is even more critical in our day, because the practice of Wittgensteinianism threatens to undermine science itself. Our culture does not recognize that fact. In 1995, F.S. Rowland shared the Nobel Prize in Chemistry for a mathematical hypothesis which alleged that chlorine oxides such as those contained in the refrigerant freon threatened atmospheric ozone.

Environmentalist at the time were seeking the banning of freon and were using Rowland's hypothesis towards that end. However, by objective scientific standards, Rowland's hypothesis had been disproved through experimentation.

Nonetheless, Rowland received the Nobel because none of the contradictory experiments could or would be reported in the scientific press.

It could only be reported in "alternative" scientific journals unrecognized by academic science. Any opposition to Rowland's hypothesis, even from science itself, was seen as "anti-environmentalist." That may no longer be true as environmentalists have gone on to a new *"issue du jour"* in man-made global warming.

In retrospect, we can now reexamine the Rowland fiasco, outside the pressure of political passions, and see what threat it might place upon the factual practice of science. It shows a willingness to impose artificial socially-constructed reality in place of the scientific method. It is an application of Wittgenstein's thesis that we cannot know objective reality as all our concepts of reality are socially generated. Wittgenstein simply cannot coexist with objective science.

That *The Death of Reality* is actually a critique of Wittgenstein's social linguistics and not a political polemic was acknowledged in the pages of the British journal *Philosophy Now*, in 2003. The thesis of the book was attacked by Professor Anthony Flew who was a graduate student under one of Wittgenstein's disciples, Gilbert Ryle, and who was "privileged to have studied The Blue Book and The Brown Book in typescript before the publication of [Wittgenstein's] Philosophical Investigations." *

Flew is one the last living academics with a direct connection to Wittgenstein himself. His defense of Wittgenstein's commitment to objective reality falls well short of the mark. If anything, his article shows the confusion which Wittgentsteinian thought can impose upon an otherwise fine mind.

* *"The Death of Reality by Lawrence Dawson; Anthony Flew scorns Lawrence Dawson's attack on Wittgenstein"*; Philosophy Now, Issue 39, December 2002/January 2003

Foreword (1996 edition)

This book is dedicated to a single proposition. A conspiracy of fools has laid claim to the destiny of this nation. They are merrily laying an axe to the root of Western culture, thinking that all humanity will live harmoniously among the shattered and fallen dead-wood. They have been at it for thirty years, and all they have produced is barbarism.

The amazing thing about all this is that so few have noticed what has occurred. The evidence was there for all to see: in the total collapse of sexual morality and the loss of family loyalty, in the generation of American women who have slaughtered their offspring with a cold-blooded ruthlessness, in the primitive styles of the youth which seem more natural to a jungle or a pirate's lair, in the casual killing by inner city youth, symbolized by the random and anonymous "drive by" shootings.

Something has short-circuited the ability of many Americans to comprehend what has happened to them. The relations between the sexes are degenerating to promiscuous loneliness, bitter hostility and superficial pretensions. They do not see this because they think of it as "liberation" from social constraints.

A massive crime against the next generation is committed. It requires that a woman first execute her best instincts, her natural desire to nurture and protect her young. They do not see what it means because they have become entangled in an unnatural belief. They think of it as sustaining the pleasantries of their lives and their freedom of action.

The children who do survive the abortion gauntlet are left to stumble without guidance. They are encouraged to "experiment" and to trash their own heritage. Left without direction, they have reinvented savagery. This is not recognized because primitive styles are considered "innovative" and vulgar actions are considered daring advances.

The rapid victory of decadence and cultural anarchy since the '60's is a phenomenon which has occasioned much comment from groups resisting the new "values", especially from Christian and conservative circles. The advocates of the decadence, however, have immunized themselves from such criticism primarily by a method which has seldom been noticed or commented upon by the critics. The decadence is defended by a type of mental aberration which neutralizes such criticism.

This aberration consists of a systematic denial of reality. The negative consequences of the decadence are ignored by the simple expedient of treating such facts as if they were only the opinions of the detested "right wing." When critics, for example, point out that sex education in government schools only increases pregnancy and abortion rates, those facts are considered "irrelevant" because they are put forward by the "Christian right." Similarly, the correct observation that AIDS in the U.S. is largely a homosexual venereal disease is called "homophobic." People are publicly required to accept the illusion that the AIDS infected are "innocent" sufferers who in no way contributed to their own infections. We are expected to disavow all reason and reality by mentally holding the absurd position that the homosexual AIDS patient was "randomly" struck and that his disease does not reflect on his sexual conduct. Reality dies in a conspiracy of foolishness. This is the great thesis of this book.

It is our contention that the moral decadence has been politically inspired, and this is the reason that its defense is political in nature. Both the acceptance of the decadence and its defense are considered principles of party. By aligning what are essentially moral failures with a political ideology, specifically the leftist ideology, a powerful weapon for the defense of moral turpitude has been invented. It allows immorality to parade in the false cloth of respectability, as a "victim" requiring the protection of "noble" political sentiment.

Such an alliance, however, begins to expose the left for what it is, as the organizer of debased sentiments, as a kind of "new Mafia" which profits from vice and human failure. It thrives by offering ideological "protection" against the claims of reality. It offers such "protection" to immoralists, to artists who cannot or will not perform by authentic esthetic standards, to the envious, to cultural rebels, to dissenting minority groups of all kinds, to disbelievers and heretics, to those of unnatural affections and ambitions, and most recently, to its own bastard children, to the neo-primitives and pagans of its own making.

It is not our purpose, however, to examine the dark motives of the left. Rather, we wish to probe the method by which it provides such "protection." It has embarked upon a rigorous campaign to make certain elements of reality "untenable" in the interest of the above mentioned "clients." The measure of its success in this is the degree to which the very idea of reality has become "untenable" in our current society. People have begun to live in pink-clouds and fantasies, a state which they neither recognize nor can associate with any reason or cause. It is our purpose to expose the condition, its extent and its cause.

Brief comments should be addressed to the origins of the current work. The problem of a general deficiency in "reality appreciation" was brought to the current writer's attention from two unconnected sources. For the last six years, he has edited a newsletter, the whole premise of which was that information was being systematically censored from the established media due to a shared ideological commitment. Using over 300 "underground" sources, the *American Information Newsletter* revealed as many as fifty major stories a month most of which never saw the light of day in establishment media outlets. Month after month, it became slowly but painfully obvious that the media were censoring facts to establish an "alternative perception of reality" which favored an ideological clientele. Not only was the media proven to be ideologically monolithic, but it was shown to be quite willing to use that monopoly to distort reality. Much of the information contained in this book came from the *AIN* and its sources.

A second well for this work had been opened decades previously, while the current writer was a graduate student at Columbia University. During the "days of rage," that is during the '60's when left-wing politics turned that university into shambles, he discovered a relatively obscure philosopher whose peculiar version of chaos was becoming the latest fashion among left-wing students. That philosopher was destined to provoke a "revolution within the revolution."

That philosopher's name is Ludwig Wittgenstein, and he is still largely unknown by the general public. But he is as surely the father of contemporary unreal thinking as Darwin was of the hardened atheism of modern scientism.

Wittgenstein gave a novel interpretation to language and in the process rendered it useless as a tool to describe or discover objective reality. Words became soft and malleable, their "meanings" shifting in every wind of fashion. Wittgensteinian language made the world indistinct and unknowable, truth as nonexistent. All reality was only a personal perception.

For a time, the current writer became a "true believer" and that belief became a form of madness. His words no longer held reality. His perceptions of the world—perceptions which he had once trusted—were rendered false and unreliable. The very language which he had once believed to have been firmly anchored in objective reality became something else. "Reality" became a private organization of linguistic "meanings," a kind of artificial order one imposed upon an essentially chaotic and unknowable world. Language according to Wittgensteinianism only gave the impression of reality, and that impression was false.

For the last thirty years, the current writer has seen Wittgensteinianism slowly filter into the popular culture. He saw it in the increasing tendency of people to give artificial and self-serving meanings to words, to shift "meanings" to make the world appear to be something they "preferred," rather than something which possessed an autonomous reality of which they disapproved. Perverse sexual addictions became "orientations," and most recently the word "gender" has been shifted in meaning to incorporate such addictions. The word is no longer biologically defined, but has taken on an artificial, socially-preferred "meaning." The elimination of an unborn child is now called "choice," thus associating it with freedom. This is a radical meaning shift in the concept of "freedom." It now means the right to take something that belongs to another person, in this case, his life and existence. Many other examples are given in the following work.

It is our thesis that a brew mixed in hell is eating away the nation's ability to perceive objective truth, to appreciate factual reality. A corrupt political ideology has been melded to an equally corrupt philosophy of language to give an historically unprecedented power to the lie.

Lawrence Dawson
Cana, August 1996

1. The Politics of Unreality

"In the postmodern, post-everything world view, there is no objectivity or truth. Everything is relative. Nothing is better or truer than anything else. Knowledge is politically constructed, an extension of power." U.S. News and World Report, August 7, 1995

Let me propose an absurdity. In this case, however, it is an absurdity which actually happened. The scene is upper Manhattan, in a West Side subway station servicing a poorer, but mostly white working class neighborhood which borders Harlem. This detail is significant to the story I am about to relate. It is later afternoon, but the subway platform is not yet crowded with the commuters who will soon pour out of every arriving train. Still, the pulse of city life is quickening and there are increasing numbers of people awaiting the downtown train on the platform.

A young black man descends the subway stairs, avoids the token booth, leaps over the turn stile and begins awaiting the train with a nonchalance bordering on insolence. His acrobatic avoidance of the fare, of course, has not gone unnoticed. A grim-faced clerk in the glass-encased toll booth picks up a phone. Within minutes a transit cop arrives, and a hurried conference with the toll clerk identifies the young man. The identification is not difficult. The target is sticking out like a sore thumb, first because he is the only black on the platform, and second because the other passengers are giving him a wide berth out of a New York visceral fear of might-be predators.

The cop approaches the young man. Everything is clear. Everyone saw the young man leap the turnstile. Everyone is offended by the act. But this open-and-closed reality is about to change. In a well-drilled, authoritative voice this burly cop—perhaps twice the size of the youth—informs the offender that he is under arrest. Does the kid bolt? Not on your life. Instead, the kid looks up and puts his face as close to the cop's as he can. He begins poking his finger at the cop and screeching, "You're in trouble, man. Now, you're in deep trouble." The kid's act of "offended innocence" was good. He projected a perverse moral assurance that he had done nothing wrong but saw plenty wrong with the cop's attempt to arrest him.

The incredible aspect to this otherwise trivial occurrence was the onlookers' reactions. They began to give credibility to the kid's self-serving theatrics, gave credibility to it in direct contradiction to their own eye witness, and the cop wilted before their responses. The cop's well-drilled authoritative demeanor disappeared before increasingly disapproving eyes in the crowd. These were the same people who had watched the kid leap the turnstile and, only moments before, had avoided him as a scofflaw and possible threat to them personally. The cop didn't use the handcuffs he had taken out to facilitate the arrest. Instead, he began gingerly and hesitantly trying to direct the kid toward the exit by nudging his arm. The kid complied, screaming at the cop all the way out. It appears he was never arrested but simply let go after exiting the platform.

I offer the following postulation for your consideration. The people on that platform had willingly adopted an unrealistic point of view with respect to this scene which had unfolded before their very eyes. An apprehended lawbreaker was transformed in their minds into a victim of "racial injustice." This transformation occurred without the slightest supportive evidence and in direct contradiction to the witness of their own eyes. "Reality" for them spontaneously became a different thing than they factually knew it to be. The kid had uttered magic. He had taken a clear and apparent event, one with no ambiguity at all, and turned it into something else again. He had thrown a collective mental switch in a random crowd of people who had been preprogrammed to react as he wanted by New York culture. People who had witnessed a small crime, in a city where massive crime has instilled a deep dread in its populous, simply suppressed their immediate knowledge of that crime. They suppressed reality in favor of a trained sentiment. The perpetrator became a possible "victim" by evoking culturally-programed images of himself as a "victim of racism" and thus overrode recognition of the justice in his arrest.

The significance of this event was not the absurd irony of a culprit successfully making the attempt to arrest him seem like the crime. The real significance was that the absurdity actually occurred, that a group of people randomly thrown together actually were willing to short-circuit their mental facilities, suppress the evidence of their own eyewitness and actively support a hastily constructed social-myth, indeed even help construct that "alternative definition of reality," if you will.

That little scene was observed by the current writer well over a decade ago, and since, we have seen the liberal cultural myth that blacks are "perpetually victims," hence "perpetually innocent," move from freeing a black fare-thief to freeing a black celebrity who savagely murdered his white ex-wife and her current white lover with a serrated butcher's knife. In the latter case, as with the former, a portion of the population has deliberately ignored the evidence of their reason in favor of a belief in the "perpetual victimhood" myth which blacks currently enjoy. It is this self-mutilation of reason and truth, not the fact that liberal-dominated culture is breeding a new, sinister form of racial injustice, which is significant in both these cases.

What is going on here? What has convinced a people that it is safe to desert an accurate appreciation of factual reality without suffering the consequences usually associated with insanity? Is there really an "impulse to unreality" abroad in the land?

Most will agree that our willingness to, at least, "acknowledge reality" is socially influenced. Nobody badmouths the Pope at a Catholic dinner party or Fundamentalists at a Baptist potluck. But this is not the same thing as accepting a "socially-generated reality." "Socially-generated reality" is the belief in the "actuality" of something often contradicted by objective facts because a social group in which someone desires membership expects that belief.

A socially-generated reality should not be confused with the unproven beliefs which define most religious faiths. A socially-generated reality is a statement about the world which can be subjected to objective testing to see if it is true or not, but which is immune to such testing because it is a socially-accepted belief. It is accepted as true regardless of what the facts prove and, often, in direct contradiction to them. The young black man who jumped the turnstile became a "victim" of the transit cop by the process of socially-generated reality. It was a "fact" which stood in direct contradiction to the evidence. This new "reality" was generated by a socially-determined belief, a belief which created a spontaneous sense of community among those in a subway crowd.

We now begin to see that the apparently trivial event which opened this chapter may not be all that trivial. A promiscuous urban culture has created a new type of human character, one which is willing to desert factual reality in favor of a politically-defined sentiment as a substitute reality. We will call this trend the politics of unreality.

The politics of unreality is a step beyond what might be called the politics of deception. Political forces that rule by deception hide the truth from the people. Political forces that rule by unreality don't even bother. Reality is made "operative" or "nonoperative" by political opinion. The people themselves become active defenders of the lie. Like the New Yorkers who called a black criminal a "victim" because that sentiment rewarded them while witnessing the truth didn't, the people consciously and willingly participate in the deception. Reality becomes "what we want it to be," not "what I observed it to be." They no longer distinguish between want and fact, between a "reality" which is preferred and the reality which is. They move from becoming externally deceived to becoming self deceived. These are the frightening first signs of authentic totalitarianism beginning to root in the United States.

Reality is What We Want it to Be

That there is a Politics of Unreality abroad in the land is easy enough to prove. It is apparent, for example, in the environmental movement. Draconian regulations ultimately banning the use of freon in refrigeration have been forged at a huge social cost, especially to the poor. It is alleged that escaping freon from refrigeration units is destroying a stratospheric ozone layer. It is said that this ozone layer protects us from low frequency ultraviolet radiation from the sun, and that if it is lost we will be subjected to massive increases in skin cancer and other radiologically-induced disorders. This is presented as a "collective threat," and it is claimed that the "selfish wills" of individuals to keep their personal comfort must be surrendered to the "good of the whole." This socialist idea is ALWAYS present in environmentalist claims, specifically that individual freedom of action must surrender to the "good of the whole."

The ozone scare is especially poignant because, as we shall see, it clearly illustrates that appreciation of objective reality can be replaced by what might be termed "politically-generated formula thought."

The belief that stratospheric ozone is threatened by organic chlorine compounds (CFCs), such as freon, has been accepted as "truth" by both the media and the politicians. Further, it is alleged that unless something is done about human destruction of the ozone layer a new plague will strike the earth. On November 4 of 1991, *Newsweek* told its readers, "In April the U.S. Environmental Protection Agency announced...more cases of UV-induced cancer—an extra 12 million cancer cases among Americans over the next 50 years." In February of that same year, *USA Today* told the nation that a report from the United Nations Environment Program predicted serious health effects from ozone depletion. The newspaper approvingly quoted a Greenpeace spokeswoman as saying that "Ozone depletion is now so serious ...that it now amounts to a threat to the future of all life on earth."

What are the facts supporting these dire predictions? We find out there are no "facts" as such. We find that the very idea of ozone depletion was politically generated, that the alleged "cause" of this depletion has been changed to fit political needs of the moment, and that scientists have been fired and research projects shut down to prevent their results from contradicting the belief in "ozone depletion." In short, from the very first the belief in "ozone depletion" was a politically-generated formula not a factual discovery.

The nature and history of the "ozone scare" has been outlined by Dr. Edward Krug in his newsletter *Environment Betrayed*. Krug is probably the nation's premier environmental scientist currently debunking green pseudoscience. In that capacity, he has appeared on the op-ed pages of the *Wall Street Journal* and on the CBS television program *60 Minutes*. He has identified the origins of the "ozone scare," and it wasn't some relatively obscure scientist making a lonely discovery.

The "ozone scare" began as a tactic invented by the environmentalist movement to stop production of the supersonic transport plane (SST) being contemplated in the early '70's. The SST was made the alleged "threat" to the stratospheric ozone layer. First, it was said that water vapor in the plane's contrail would decompose to hydroxyl and deplete the ozone layer. When this didn't create the desired public reaction, a second SST "threat" to the ozone layer was invented. Water was simply too "natural" to make a good heavy in this eco-fiction. Krug states, "The preconceived conclusion that SSTs are 'bad' was retained and the SST water vapor bogey man was replaced. The excuse this time—oxides of nitrogen (NO_x) emitted by high flying SSTs will erode the ozone shield (Johnston, 1971)."[1] Ultimately, the nitrogen oxide "ozone threat" succeeded in stopping production of the SST.

The greatly beloved American heretic Ralph Waldo Emerson once said that foolish consistency was the hobgoblin of little minds. The eco-movement would never be accused of being "little minded" by Emerson's standards. It might even be said that they have managed to take "big mindedness" to new heights of absurdity. They couldn't let the eco-fictions they had made of hydroxyls and nitrogen oxides die a decent death and slip ever so quietly into public forgetfulness. They actually resurrected the culprits as "eco-heroes." Green VP Al Gore's book, *Earth in the Balance,* now called those nasty hydroxyls "natural detergents" which cleansed the atmosphere. In 1984, with the newest CFC "bogey" targeted on the ozone-depletion radar screen, *Nature* magazine characterized those once-killer oxides of nitrogen as "defenders" of the ozone shield from the new CFC nasties.

The greens weren't going to lose a bop, neat and keen racket such as "ozone depletion" simply because they had knocked a multi-billion dollar aircraft out of the sky. In the 1984 *Nature* article, the US Academy of Science was cited to prove that increases in oxides of nitrogen gases in the atmosphere protected ozone from the CFCs. "[Fortunately a]tmospheric concentrations of ...N_2O have been observed to be increasing. Continuation of these trends would delay the time when the dramatic effect of CFCs would occur." The article said that unless the oxides of nitrogen gases would increase faster than the chlorine from the CFCs, ozone depletion would increase dramatically. The same oxides of nitrogen which in 1971 were said to be "threatening ozone" in SST exhaust were now described as "defending" that same ozone against the new enemy CFCs.[2]

What's going on here? How can the same chemical compound be said to "threaten" the ozone layer when the environmentalists wanted to ban the SST and then "protect" that same ozone layer when the environmentalists wanted to ban freon? The answer, as Krug so well points out, is that the "ozone depletion scare" has little to do with science and everything to do with the politics of fear. The ozone scare with its images of people's skin being fried in UVB light and becoming leprous with cancer worked so well with the SST that the environmentalists—who make careers out of "protecting" us from dreaded monsters lurking in the unknown—simply could not give it up. They invented a politically self-serving thought formula that goes something like this: An incredibly thin and vulnerable ozone layer in the stratosphere is all that stands between us and dreaded radiation which threatens to turn the earth into burnt toast ('Ozone depletion is now so serious ...that it now amounts to a threat to the future of all life on earth' Greenpeace, 1991). This vulnerable membrane about which you know nothing is about to be destroyed by (fill in the blank with a human activity you want suppressed and which can plausibly demonize as ozone threatening)." In short, the alleged "threat to the ozone layer" was not discovered by objective research, it was invented and imposed by political forces seeking to profit by fear-mongering the idea. How else can you explain that the alleged "threat" to the ozone layer changed with such political expediency. The idea is a political unreality substituting for known scientific facts.

We are not exaggerating when we call CFC ozone depletion a scam and a racket. Krug has documented that the popular belief in CFC ozone depletion is a myth which has succeeded only by suppressing scientific information. Those of us who are about to lose our freon-based refrigerators and air conditioners should, at least, be informed about the most significant of these suppressed facts. No less an authority than the head of the French equivalent of the EPA, Haroun Tazieff, tried to tell us about it in 1991. Tazieff said, "The Rowland and Molina theory [of ozone depletion due to CFCs] is unscientific because it is based upon a model of chemical reaction sequence without having proved the existence of the intermediary products; *these reactions, which no one has ever reproduced in the laboratory, have never been observed anywhere.*" (italics ours) Did you get that? The way that CFCs are supposed to destroy the ozone has never been observed anywhere and indeed cannot even be reproduced in the laboratory. Freon is being banned at an estimated cost of well over a trillion dollars based upon a paper "theory" of a chemical reaction between ozone and freon which has never been observed and which environmentalists have been unable to produce in the laboratory. How much more politically unreal can you get?

The paper theory was first put forward by F. Sherwood Rowland in an article in *Science* magazine. Dr. Arthur Robinson, himself an organic chemist currently conducting environmental research with the private Oregon Institute of Science and Medicine, explained how the Rowland thesis may have short circuited normal scientific controls. In a private conversation, Dr. Robinson said that Rowland's original article established what scientists term a "hypothesis." This consisted of equations for a speculative complex chain of chemical reactions which were, in Robinson's opinion, most probably mathematically sound. That is, the Rowland equations were consistent with known energy transfers and requirements associated with chemical reactions.

Dr. Robinson cautions, however, that there are many hypothetical chemical reactions which are coherent with the mathematical laws of thermodynamics but which are reactions which don't actually occur. The fact that Rowland could provide mathematical feasibility for his reactions did not prove that they actually happened.

The problem, according to Robinson, was that a scientific hypothesis was elevated to the status of a "fact" without going through the rigors of scientific control. A chemical hypothesis is a speculation founded upon mathematical feasibility and guided by what Dr. Robinson called the "intuition" of a well-trained expert in the subject. It must be submitted to experimental validation before it is accepted. Rowland's hypothesis was elevated to the factual status without such validation, most likely, in Robinson's opinion, by the lay press which saw the hypothesis' advantage to environmentalism.

Dr. Edward Krug, whose newsletter *Environment Betrayed* is an attempt to snatch authentic science from these voodoo fires of environmentalist unreality, has a knack for unraveling the science-babble which the Greens use to mystify the common man. He points out that the amount of man-made freon which could possibly be "blamed" for "killing" the ozone is so minuscule in comparison to the volume of the atmosphere that a "super killer" mechanism had to be invented. For every part of chlorine, the alleged "killer," from the CFCs there are 100 billion parts of air (10^4 tons of Cl to 10^{15} tons of air). To make the scare work, environmentalists had to make every chlorine atom "kill" 100,000 molecules of ozone. They achieved this sleight-of-hand through Rowland's paper "model" by which every chlorine atom is alleged to combine with ozone, breakdown the ozone molecule, then separate and commence the process all over again. This is supposed to reoccur 100,000 times until the process is finally exhausted. Thus, one atom of chlorine could "kill" 100,000 molecules of ozone.

There is a slight problem with this paper theory. The destruction of ozone it postulates has not been produced in the lab, let alone been observed occurring naturally in the atmosphere. It could easily be proven true by an obvious common-sense test. Reproduce the conditions in which the alleged reaction is said to occur and see if it actually does. Create a stratospheric-like atmosphere with the proper amount of ozone in a sealed container, inject freon at the prescribed rate and photodecompose the freon. It would not "kill" the ozone.

Why? In answering this question, Krug is much harsher on the Rowland theory than Robinson has been. Krug argues that the paper theory is not only wrong, but that it is junk chemistry as well. The paper theory alleges that the "super-killer" chlorine molecule–what scientists call dimers of chlorine monoxide–must break apart at the point it is strongest. As Krug notes, "Of the many ways that this chain of atoms [dimers of chlorine monoxide] could break apart, ozone theorists say that the chain breaks at its strongest links–the chlorine-oxygen bond. They say that the weakest link–the oxygen-oxygen bond–does not break apart! Imagine that!"[3]

Dimers occur when two molecules of a compound weakly join together. They become something of a "duplex" molecule and do not form a new compound because they can relatively easily be separated again. They are like magnetized ball bearings joining together. The ozone-depletion theory asserts that when two ball bearings are thus joined, one of the ball bearings will break in half before the two can be forced apart. We are being asked to believe that, if you strike two magnetically connected ball bearings with a hammer, one of the ball bearings will crack before the magnetic attraction breaks.

It gets worse, folks. Forget the simple test of injecting an experimental atmosphere with freon—or even chlorine monoxide—and see if it "kills" the ozone. No, these practitioners of political unreality have spent time and money to see if they could force the molecule to break at its strongest bond. If they could force such a breakage once, under laboratory conditions, they then could assert that it "occurred" naturally hundreds of thousands of times per chlorine atom in nature. No need to "prove" that it actually was occurring. Bet you've already guessed it. They couldn't do it.

Krug points out, "No one has ever observed the chlorine monoxide dimer breaking at its strongest link and not at its weakest link." Unable to produce the reaction which the paper theory demanded, they did the thing that the self-deceived must do in such politically sensitive areas. They went for a substitute, another molecule which they pretended was "like" the molecule in question. Krug continues, "Indeed, the ideal that this chain of atoms would break at its strongest link had to be inferred from the behavior of a different chemical molecule—CLONO$_2$. And, of the numerous experiments run on this proxy molecule, only once was it demonstrably seen that this strongest link—the chlorine-oxygen (CL-O) bond—nearly always broke. *Problem*—This one favorable study cooked the sample with high energy lasers." After great numbers of studies on a "substitute" molecule, the defenders of the paper theory were only able to get the molecule to break apart at the predicted bond one time, and that with the infusion of massive amounts of energy.

Let us review then why your refrigerators and air conditioners are currently at risk. Freon is being banned because a paper theory was presented by a political advocate which predicted that each atom of chlorine in that freon would "kill" 100,000 molecules of ozone by a method which has never been observed in nature nor produced in the laboratory. It is asserted that we accept the politicized paper theory as established "truth" because on one occasion, and only one occasion, a substitute molecule was shown to break apart in the predicted way after being bombarded with massive amounts of energy.

How can this one experiment, obviously "cooked," as Krug calls it, stand in the stead of rigorous testing of the actual theory. Why would the breaking apart of a "proxy" molecule under high energy bombardment be given more "weight" than the simple observation that the actual chemical reaction predicted by the paper theory never occurs, either in nature or under laboratory conditions? Chlorine monoxide simply never acts as the theory's proponents claim, either in the presence or outside the presence of ozone. The test is simple enough. Even a layman can think of it. In a controlled environment reduce a known amount of ozone to simple oxygen by the introduction of minuscule amounts of chlorine monoxide. It is not done because it cannot be done. The advocates of the "ozone scare" know this. There is a reason that the "proxy" experiment replaces factual observation, but it has nothing to do with "science." The proxy experiment is used because it helps establish an artificial "reality." It is following the rules of political unreality.

In establishing belief in political unreality, one deals in plausibles, not facts. One must make an artificial reality seem plausible in the same way that an alibi must be made "plausible" while factual reality is ignored. The "proxy" experiment described above was designed to shore up the "ozone scare" theory's plausibility, not test its factuality. It is crucial to recognize the intentions of the advocates in these matters. The experiment, or at least its significance, is designed to overcome the psychology of disbelief. It is used to address a state of mind, not factual or external conditions.

Here again is the essence of political unreality. One observation of desired consequence is given more credibility than the sum total of all natural observations combined. The will to believe is given more authority than either the objective witness of the senses or the rationality of the mind.

Environmentalists have indicted themselves as deliberate practitioners of unreality by the fact that evidence which strongly and directly contradicts the "ozone depletion theory" has been suppressed. During the scare that SST aircraft would "deplete the ozone," the National Cancer Institute actually established a monitoring network to see if the allegedly thinning ozone would allow an increase in high-energy ultraviolet (UVB) to hit the earth's surface. Even though the environmentalists succeeded in

killing the SST program, the UVB monitoring system kept
gathering data from 1974 onward. By 1985, when greens began
arguing that "ozone-killing" freon leaking from refrigerators was
going to fry us all, the UVB monitoring system had collected 11
years of data. Unfortunately, the monitoring data didn't support
the "ozone depletion theory." Not only was there no increase in
UVB radiation reaching the surface, but there was an actual
decrease during the period the ozone was supposedly "thinning"
from CFC contamination. "Ozone depletion theorists," if they
were interested in factual reality, should have wanted data on
UVB hitting the earth's surface after 1985 since they had just
"discovered" the alleged "ozone hole" at the South Pole,
supposedly depleted through CFC contamination. Instead, the
National Cancer UVB monitoring network was summarily shut
down. Its data didn't help the "ozone depletion" unreality and had
to be suppressed. When the National Cancer Institute finally
published its UVB data in 1988, environmentalists attacked the
data, saying UVB rates were "masked" by alleged "air pollution."
Unfortunately, many of the sites, including the master site at
Muana Loa observatory in Hawaii, were not subjected to air
pollution.[4]

Least anyone is trusting enough to believe that the elimination
of the UVB monitoring system was not connected to a desire to
protect the "ozone depletion theory" from real-world data, consider
what happened when a high government scientist suggested
reestablishing UVB monitoring at the earth's surface to "test" the
depletion theory. According to the newsletter *Inside Energy*, Dr.
William Happer, the chief scientist at the U.S. Department of
Energy, approached the office of Vice President Albert Gore to
get aid in restoring the monitoring of UVB radiation. Gore, who
is known as an "environmental activist" and author of
environmental books, has been warning the nation of the "health

dangers" from alleged freon poisonings of the stratospheric ozone layer. Happer, who had apparently taken the Vice President's words seriously, had thought we should resume the UVB radiation monitoring canceled in 1985. Did the environmental vice president grab Happer's hand and shake it as a "concerned scientist?" Not exactly. The Green vice president— who had once warned the nation of an imminent danger from a "hole in the ozone" which he inaccurately predicted would open over the U.S.—fired Happer on the spot for making the suggestion. The ozone depletion theory and its voodoo chemistry must be accepted on faith and anyone suggesting that the idea be tested against real-world data was a friend of the damnable skeptics.

Obviously, environmentalism is not concerned with an actual threat from ozone depletion. They have not rejoiced at finding unthreatening surface radiation levels, but have cursed the researchers for contradicting their carefully crafted artificial reality. They have made sure those measurements won't be taken again. The "reality" of ozone thinning is what they say it is, not what if has been found to be. They believe their words create reality and are not committed to an objectively determined truth.

But why? How can the environmental movement so rigorously desert objective fact for favored belief? The answer, I'm afraid, is that that environmental movement is emotionally feeding the ideological appetites of its adherents and has little or nothing to do with objective conditions in the real world.

It has perhaps become a cliché to repeat that environmentalism is not conservationism. Environmentalists do not *conserve* natural resources to human use, they defend nature *against* human use. It is rooted in a form of prejudice, being *for* nature and *against* human activity. The movement began in unreality because the very words "nature" and "humanity" were given an artificial meaning of a very peculiar sort. One has to go back to the ancient pagan world to find an intellectual precedent. A kind of sanctity or sacredness was imposed upon the concept of "nature."

This is not a wild exaggeration. The Colorado Sacred Earth Institute invited the UN regional director for the Environment, Noel Brown, to speak at a 1994 conference. Brown told the audience that the only way to prevent population pressures, pollution and energy consumption from destroying the earth, was to embrace what he called a "new spirituality" which recognized the earth as sacred. The theme was also taken up by Al Gore in his book *Earth in the Balance*. In one place, Gore reinterprets the Biblical story of Cain slaying Abel, asserting that the sin was not the killing of a brother made in the image of God, but the "polluting" of the sacred earth with blood. In 1992, the U.S. Forest Service sponsored a Washington conference called the "Spirituality/Wildland Interface." Workshops included "Symbolism and Spiritual Values in Experiencing Nature," "Sacred Land, Sacred Sex," and "Gaian Buddhism." The "sacred earth" concept has recently been baptized with the name of the ancient earth goddess Gaia. The earth-as-goddess idea has even crept into "science" with the "Gaia hypothesis" which holds that the earth is a "living organism." This is treated as a "serious scientific theory" in environmental circles.

With the very concepts of the "earth" and "nature" being mystified, human activities which might impact the "earth" and "nature" also take on a novel artificial meaning. In the eyes of environmentalists, human objects and activities don't allegedly threaten scientific facts, they profane the temple. Pollution is not a practical problem, it is a violation of the religious sentiments. Unclean unbelievers have invaded the sanctuary and are trashing the Holy Order.

In carefully looking at environmentalism, one can see the methods and origins of the phenomenon we are calling political unreality. The eco-movement invests the natural order with presumed meanings, overlaying it with a religious sentiment. They have lost the capacity for objective thought because the world must fit into preconceived patterns and categories of their own making. Reality becomes what they have presumed it to be, not what it is discovered to be. They have overlaid the world with meanings of their own invention and call it "reality."

Reality becomes what we presume it to be, not what it is discovered to be. The "proof" for the presumed "truth" is social opinion, not fact. Consider the fate of two men of "science," one who sought to pursue fact and the other who lent his weight to the "popular" religiously-motivated opinion on ozone. The first was the Dr. William Happer mentioned earlier as the object of a vice-presidential purge because he suggested that the "danger" alleged by the ozone depletion theory actually be tested. The second is Dr. F. Sherwood Rowland, "father" of the currently fashionable theory that ozone is being "killed" by your refrigerator.

As we have noted, Happer was fired by the office of Vice President Albert Gore after the scientist had attempted to get Gore's aid in refunding an ultra violet monitoring program which had been canceled in 1985. On June 17, 1993, an article revealing the Happer firing and its implications appeared in the *Wall Street Journal* (Bad Climate in Ozone Debate). The revelation was "refuted" by Michael Elroy, Chairman of Harvard's Department of Earth and Planetary Sciences. Prior to his firing, Happer had testified before a congressional committee and revealed the actual data collected by the 1974-1985 monitoring of UVB radiation hitting the earth. This was considered "treason" by environmental enforcers since the actual data discounted the fashionable ozone depletion theory. In a letter to the *Wall Street Journal*, Elroy—with the full weight of Harvard "earth science" behind him—discounted the controversy by ridiculing Happer.

According to this spokesman for establishment orthodoxy, Happer was deserving of his treatment because of alleged impure motives in attacking the credibility of revealed ozone "science." To reveal data which could disprove accepted "truth" was considered a treasonable act. To ask for even more such data only emphasized the treason. Thus a scientist asking for data, the very object of the scientific method, was condemned as a heretic in one of the nation's leading forums by someone wrapping himself in the mantel of scientific "authority." Later, we will find out that much political unreality is sustained by "political appointees" to high positions in the sciences and the university, political appointees who confer legitimacy upon favored untruths with their alleged "authority."

Now contrast this treatment of Happer at the hands of "authoritative" science with that given F. Sherwood Rowland. Rowland is the author of the "super-killer" chlorine-atom theory, the dimers of chlorine monoxide which supposedly break apart in a way contrary to the laws of chemistry and have therefore never been observed to do so. As Edward Krug points out, "Rowland's hypothesis predicts neither location, chemistry, nor rate of ozone depletion and Rowland's hypothesized reactions have been observed in neither nature nor laboratory."[5]

Rowland was a chemist with the University of California at Irvine in 1973 when he invented the paper theory which was subsequently used to justify the draconian freon ban. His own attitude, as shown on a 1993 Discovery Channel television program, indicated that he, himself, recognized his unsupportable voodoo theory as a kind of career coup which would give environmentalists the pseudoscientific rationalization they needed to reignite the ozone-scare scam. He demonstrated that he trivialized the alleged "threat" to the ozone, but was enthusiastic about its impact upon his career. He said that when his wife asked him about his work, he replied, "It is really going very well. But it looks like we may see the end of the world." People who actually believe the world is about to "end" don't glow enthusiastically about the prospect. Someone who sees a bright career prospect in making others believe it might.

Needless to say, Rowland has been paid handsomely for providing a "theory" which can be sold the public as a "plausible" ozone depletion mechanism. Both he and his absurd science have been the recipients of "conferred legitimacy" by politicized "authorities." In August of 1994 it was announced that Rowland would be enshrined in the Smithsonian Science Hall of Fame. In 1995 Rowland was awarded the Nobel Prize in Chemistry.

The Nobel Prize citation says of Rowland that he "contributed to our salvation from a global environmental problem that could have catastrophic consequences." This is the same "environmental problem" which got William Happer fired for trying to measure it. A member of the Academy which gave the award said it went to Rowland to put pressure on a forthcoming international meeting of the "Montreal Protocol on Substances that Deplete the Ozone Layer." Significantly, this same member of the Swedish Academy admitted that the award's "prestige" was designed to overcome resistance from authentic science to Rowland's voodoo chemistry. Academy member Henning Rohde said, "The Nobel prize will put a rest to this debate on whether the ozone hole really is a result of CFCs."

You know, gentle reader, of what this "debate" consists. Rowland's "theory" has never been tested and cannot be tested because it violates the laws of chemistry. It is a debate between reality and political unreality and is to be resolved in Rowland's favor by the granting of a prestige award. Truth will now be determined by a politically-constructed committee which will vote upon which particular "truth" they prefer and confer an alleged honor upon it. As Krug states, politically-appointed scientific "authorities" like the Smithsonian and the Swedish Academy are "now passing off a disproved hypothesis as science fact."

The environmental movement has no need for truth and reality because they have THE FORMULA. The Formula is something akin to a fill-in-the-blanks complaint form, an easily recognizable model which tells them what to believe when someone fills in the blanks. The Formula goes something like this: Our precious environment, that most *holy nature,* is being *desanctified* by (fill in the blank) which is the *profane* man-produced substance or the result of the *profane* human activity (fill in the blank) which will inflict the punishment upon us of (fill in the blank). The "reality" is created when all the blanks are filled in properly. An attitudinal predisposition by which all things natural are "holy" and all things human "profane" gives power to The Formula and makes it easy to determine that the blanks have been filled in properly. It matters not one whit whether or if The Formula, as completed, makes a coherent and scientifically accurate statement. It is not evaluated scientifically. It is evaluated as fulfilling a religious prejudice, that of treating nature as sacred, and chastising man for violating that sanctity. The Formula, "Our precious environment, that most *holy nature,* is being desanctified by (ozone depletion), which is the profane man-produced substance or the result of the profane human activity of (the freon in our refrigerators), which will inflict the punishment upon us of (increasing skin cancer)," meets the criteria and is therefore "true," regardless of what the scientific evidence says.

The point is that environmentalism uses an artificial mental formula of religious origins which is being imposed upon and substituted for factual reality. It is a deliberate political unreality, in the sense that it is a system which is immune to factual correction. Least someone think we are making a politically-inspired unfair characterization of environmentalist thought on the basis of ozone depletion theory alone, we can offer other examples of The Formula which are and have been immune to factual correction.

Recently, the Club of Rome paid M.I.T. to "generate" a computer model showing that man-induced mercury into the environment was reaching poisonous levels. The model was designed to fit The Formula: "Our precious environment, that most *holy nature*, is being desanctified by (mercury), which is the profane man-produced substance or the result of the profane human activity of (using mercury in industrial production), which will inflict the punishment upon us of (exposing us to poisonous mercury levels)." Dr. Edward Krug, probably the most significant critic of environmentalist fraud in the nation today, again exposed this deception. He wrote, "By skillfully replacing reality with perception, the mercury (Hg) monster was revived. The new 'reality' sold by M.I.T./Club of Rome was that human inputs of Hg to the environment are enormous." [6] The computer "model" was made to predict "poisonous levels of man-induced mercury" by the simple expedient of using false numbers. The amount of mercury which nature puts into the atmosphere was reduced by a factor of 100, from 25,000 tons to 250 tons. One volcano in Hawaii puts more than 250 tons of Hg into the air every year. By this simple expedient, most of the measured mercury levels could then be called "man induced." But how did the "model" get those massive doses of "man-induced" mercury to build to poisonous levels in the future? The answer was simple. Lie again and use false figures. Leading experts in chemical recycling by the atmosphere say that mercury is removed in a 36 year period. The computer model simply upped this by a factor of 1000, saying it took 3,600 years to recycle mercury out. Now, all that phony "man-induced" mercury would not come out for a phony four millennia and, bingo, your kids have only got dropping dead from "mercury poisoning" to look forward to.

Obviously, the M.I.T. computer "model" was made to fit The Formula and was immune to correction by factual reality. In this case, factual reality was simply changed to fit The Formula. The actual "amount" of *profane* human-discharged mercury is irrelevant to the environmentalist religion. "*Holy*" nature is "*desanctified*" by any contact with mercury from "*profane*" human origins.

Nor are the ozone and mercury scares the only cases of environmentalist political unreality being imposed upon factual reality. Other examples of imposed unreality abound. The "endangered" Northern Spotted Owl was used to decimate the Northwest timber industry. Now information has revealed the Spotted Owl was neither "endangered" nor even a separate species from the numerous California Spotted Owl. The so-called Northern Spotted Owl is really a sub-species with minor differences between it and the California Spotted Owl. When the two "species" meet in the Northern Sierra Mountains, the differences between the two tend to disappear. They interbreed and blend into a single population. To "protect" the owl, environmentalists managed to reduce tree harvests in Washington's Olympic National Forest by 97% and by 90% in California forests. In 1991, a Medford, Oregon newspaper said that "more than 200 rural timber dependent communities stand on the brink of economic collapse" because of Owl protection. However, it has now been proved that the environmentalist studies used to justify the forest shutdown were false. New, objective studies have proven that the owl thrives in a wide variety of forest tracts, not just the "old growth" which environmentalists claimed. Further, objective owl surveys conducted after the forests were shut down, indicated that the owl was much more numerous that the environmentalists had claimed. The survey found that the number of owls actually sighted exceeded the numbers set by a committee as a "recovered population." Environmentalists distorted both the facts about owl habitat and the numbers in the existing population of the sub-species to justify a forest shut down. Another case of politically imposed unreality.

The Alar-on-apples scare of the last decade is another example of imposing The Formula on the facts. In the late '80's, a highly-publicized environmentalist news conference claimed that a growth regulator used on apples caused cancer. It was implied that the regulator, sold under the trade name of Alar, would result in thousands of deaths. Sales of apples dropped to nothing. Orchardists caught with their crop of "tainted" apples in the warehouse sustained a complete loss of that crop. This writer personally knows of an orchardist in Washington's Columbia Basin who was driven to bankruptcy and lost his farm due to the scare. The public was not told that it would require eating thousands of pounds a day of Alar-sprayed apples to gain any carcinogenic effect. This fact was simply ignored in favor of The Formula: pristine, "natural" apples tainted with profane, man-made Alar equals cancer.

Environmentalists have as much as admitted that establishing a pattern of sentimental prejudices, what we have here called The Formula, in the public mind is one of the highest priorities. They are turning to Hollywood filmmakers who specialize in provoking emotional reactions, not scientific institutions. Greenpeace is currently spending a good deal of money to hire a Hollywood horror-film director, Roger Gorman, to produce horror television spots which will establish The Formula in the public mind. One of Gorman's "successes" is an ad showing a mother beckoning her children who begin loving her, then begin violently scratching her to drag her dying to the ground.[7] It is The Formula in dramatic visual metaphor. Mother Earth (sacred nature) is attacked by her children (man's profanity has driven him mad) and sacred nature begins to die (dire consequences). As we have seen such patterns of religiously oriented sentiments are being imposed as an alternative reality which, because of their religious and prejudicial natures, are immune to factual correction.

Nor are environmentalists the only people to impose artificial, formula-thought patterns upon reality, patterns which are immune to factual correction because of their religio-emotional nature. They are not the only practitioners of the politics of unreality. Feminists, "anti-racists," homophiles and other practitioners of left-wing causes are similarly guilty.

A high profile rape case at Princeton created a fire storm of feminist outrage. The alleged rape became a rallying point against the "general abuse" women supposedly suffered from men. The furor began when a coed told a feminist "rape confession" rally alleged details which whipped the sisterhood into a frenzy. The woman alleged she had been forced into a male student's room, cruelly raped and then told that she was a "public-school bitch" and that his father "buys me cheap girls like you to use up and throw away." The story seemed tailored for a leftwing audience, demonstrating males using women as "objects." It also presented sexual abuse as a form of class oppression. Here was the rich and evil bourgeois abusing the poor and innocent "public school" girl. The story was so well crafted to leftist ideology that the campus newspaper published her "confession." The story generated a flood of sympathetic letters condemning "sexism" and "classism." The woman claimed she was living in dread because the university had only suspended her attacker for a year and he was back on campus putting her at risk again. The story began to unravel when it was discovered the Dean of Students had no record of a "rape" complaint. To shore up her crumbling credibility she named a male student. Finding himself under intense harassment, the student filed a charge of slander, and the woman was forced to publicly retract. She admitted she had never met nor even talked to the man she had charged and said she had fabricated the story.

The feminist leadership, which had used the story for a prolonged propaganda campaign, announced that the guilt or innocence of the accused, the truth or falsity of the woman's story, was "irrelevant" since it still illustrated "patriarchy" which subjected women to a continuous condition of rape. The feminist concept of "patriarchy" is also an artificial formula thought pattern imposed upon reality which is immune to factual correction. The charge had been made up in the first place because its author had been trained in this feminist "patriarchy" formula, that all men are everywhere guilty of rape. She also believed the actual deed to be "irrelevant" to the charge.

Similarly, biological "claims" by homosexual advocates in California in 1991 were scientific absurdities but were reported in the press as factual. An ad taken out by homosexuals during a local dispute over giving spousal economic rights to homosexual couples made the claim which was picked up by *Insight*, the magazine of the *Washington Times*, and reported as factual. The ad read, "Religious extremists oppose Domestic Partners because their interpretation of Scripture tells them homosexuality is 'unnatural.' Those Scriptures can't explain why scientists have found so much homosexuality in nature—including five species of lesbian lizards."

The ad goes on to claim that the Whiptail lizard egg reproduces without a male and only after the female carries on a lesbian dance with another female lizard. This claim is pure biological fantasy. The only form of asexual reproduction known in nature is cloning (i.e. the splitting of a cell or organism to create two) and this occurs much lower on the life scale than reptiles. Bearing offspring via an egg is a form of sexual reproduction. To claim otherwise is an act of politically inspired ideology, not science.

Nonetheless, it was reported by the establishment press, the *Washington Times* and others, with a straight face. Newsmen, who were trained in the emotional prejudices of the moment, were unable to detect a biological absurdity. The "finding" fit the left-wing formula that homosexuality is "natural," a formula to which adherents are strongly emotionally attached, and so this formula was imposed upon biological science, short-circuiting common knowledge and logic in the process. It was never modified to conform to known biological facts.

The politics of unreality, then, is the creation of "truth" which serves a political agenda and does not need to conform to objective, factual reality. Its nature was succinctly stated in a satirical novel about Bill and Hillary Clinton. In Daniel Graham, Jr.'s novel, "The Politics of Meaning," the Clinton stand-in character has a brilliant political consultant who creates slick, media images of the politician, images which seem immune to the scandals which the fictionalized Clinton's moral and political corruption should produce. The consultant takes a shyster politician up to his elbows in graft, who has the morals of an alley cat, and packages him so well that the public doesn't see the reality. He says his objective is to make this packaging job "the truth" in the minds of the public. The consultant, named Blisdale in the novel, says, "The...objective of politics is to define the truth in your image. In time, you become the truth. Thereafter, you never fear scandal because no one would ever believe you capable of anything but the truth....So Gentlemen, the art of politics is the art of definition: the language, your agenda, the truth..." There you have the politics of unreality in a nutshell. Create an image which is 180° away from reality, polish it so well and repeat it so often that it becomes "the truth" and no one will believe the objective facts which contradict it. It becomes immune to "scandal."

It is our contention that the politics popularly known as "left-wing," "liberalism," "socialism," or even "centerism" (as defined by the left-wing agenda) are not so much the pursuit of policies often thought to be characteristic of them (i.e. anti-racism, feminism, abortion advocacy). Rather, the "left" is better characterized as committed to a " methodology," something we have called an imposed reality. Surprisingly, the actual agenda is largely irrelevant. This statement may strike some as shockingly inaccurate because the left is generally believed to be passionately committed to their goals. They are thought, for example, to be "passionately committed to ending racism in this country." Actually, they are "passionately committed" to creating the public perception that racism exists. It is really quite self-serving. As those raising the "alarm" about the problem, they then become the brokers of the "solution" which translates into political and social power. The actual existence and/or extent of racism is irrelevant. In fact, it must be invented or, at least, exaggerated, and these "racist" claims will be largely immune to correction by factual reality. The left profits not by serving an actual condition, but by serving a perceived condition and have become masters of psycho-social propaganda techniques which impose those, to them, profitable perceptions. This is why we say the left is not defined by its alleged goals, but by its methodologies used to impose reality.

A current example well illustrates this characteristic. In mid-November of 1995, The FBI announced the results of its survey of "hate crime" in the United States. The Clinton FBI told the press that the largest category (58%) consisted of white crimes against blacks. This announcement represents an "imposed reality" by a highly politicized FBI made "sensitive" to leftist propaganda needs. That it is a case of political unreality is revealed by a comparison with the actual raw data from the Justice Department. Significantly, the real data has only been published in the foreign press. It has not been published in the United States because it shows a pattern which is exactly the opposite of that claimed by the FBI. Blacks attack whites at a much higher rate than do whites blacks. The real facts were revealed in a Sydney, Australia, *Morning Herald* article from May 20, 1995. The author of that article, Paul Sheehan, simply reports figures taken from several Justice Department sources, but concludes, "All these are facts, yet by simply writing this story, by assembling the facts in this way, I would be deemed a racist by the American news media."

The "racist" facts which cannot be printed in the United States are very interesting. The raw FBI data tells a completely different racial-crime story than that announced to the press. The period during which blacks were called the highest victim category for "hate crimes," blacks actually killed whites 18 times more often than whites killed blacks. When comparing rates for all violent interracial crimes, blacks are over 50 times more likely to attack whites than whites are blacks. Further, the data suggests that much of this black-on-white crime may be racially motivated. Quoting Sheehan again, "These breathtaking disparities [between black vs. white interracial crime rates] began to emerge in the mid-1960s, when there was a sharp increase in black crime against whites, an upsurge which, not coincidentally, corresponds exactly with the beginning of the modern civil rights movement." In other words, the explosion of black-on-white crime reflects politically generated hostilities of blacks towards whites and thus would constitute "hate crimes." The numbers are staggering.

Nearly 25 million whites have suffered violent assaults from blacks since 1964 and nearly 45,000 have been killed, a greater casualty figure than suffered during the Korean War. Sheehan characterizes this phenomenon as a hidden war on whites. All this is going on in the background as the FBI announces that blacks are the highest victim category of their new "hate crimes" designation.

On one hand, the designation of blacks as official victims by the FBI is expected. Such has been the leftist party line for years. It is amazing, however, that the designation was not done in ignorance. It was, after all, FBI and Justice Department statistics which have tracked the 30-year rise in black violence, much of it directed at whites. Why does a police agency, whose very purpose, indeed, whose very instinctive reflexes direct it to identify crime patterns and hot-spots, suddenly ignore real patterns in favor of illusionary ones? It is obvious how the distortion was created. Only white instances of racially-motivated crimes were considered. The objectively much larger pool of black-on-white instances were obviously mostly ignored. Someone in the FBI had to "count" each interracial crime either as an instance of "hate crime" or not. That "someone" probably knew that it was career-wise to count whites as "hate criminals" and dangerous to "count" the many more black-on-white crimes as "hate." Characterizing black-on-white violence as "hate" would probably risk a "racism" charge. The very category of "hate crime" became what we have previously called an "artificial formula" superimposed upon objective reality. FBI agents knew the formula called for identifying white-on-black crime as "hate," but never or seldom black-on-white assault as such. Using the formula, new "statistics" were constructed which created an image in direct contradiction to the objective facts, and the FBI went into the political unreality business.

2. Artificial Reality & the New Fascism

We have seen how politically-formulated thought can be imposed upon objective fact to create an artificial "reality." We have considered examples of this politicized unreality in environmentalists who ignore the laws of chemistry and suppress objective measurements of scientifically addressed phenomenon, in feminists who continue to treat a proven lie as factual evidence and in patrons of racial minorities who invent myths about racially motivated crime which are the exact opposite of objective reality as revealed by real-world crime data.

The reason these practitioners can so blithely desert the factually-based world in favor of a politicized perception is that reality for them has become nothing but a "viewpoint." They no longer believe that reality is singular, fixed and something external to the individual. They have no sense of reality as externally defined, as something to be discovered and as something to which one must conform his ideas. Reality for the ideologues is not objective and fact based. Rather, they have been convinced that "reality" is fluid, multiple (as in "your reality or mine") and

31

subjective in character. "Reality" is something to be "chosen," not discovered.

If reality is only a "viewpoint," then the question logically follows, "Whose viewpoint?" The political left is successfully imposing political unreality precisely because it has a systematic answer to that question. The left has converted certain sentimental attachments they hold for people and causes into an advocacy of a supportive viewpoint for those people and causes.

In essence, these people and causes have become "clients" of the left, whose alleged interests are advocated, often to the harm of non-client groups. The demands of racial minorities, especially blacks, are advocated against whites, feminist ambitions against males and Sodomite pretensions against those who hold a moral preference for sexual normality. This favoritism on the part of the left for some social groups over others has recently evolved into a unique form of fascism, something we will call "social fascism."

While these "clients" of social fascism are often groups, this is not always the case. With environmentalism, a pantheistic concept of nature is defined as the "client," the interest of which is urged against the economic practices of the dominant culture.

Social fascism may be defined as the use of state power in the interest of "clients" against the dominant ethnic nationality and culture. The fascistic character of this social favoritism has been made manifest by the increasing willingness of law and government to dictate conduct in private spheres to correct alleged "social inequalities." A federal judge dictated that the city of Yonkers, New York, must build a public housing project out of tax funds in order to bring more minorities into the city, thus imposing a tax burden on the citizens of Yonkers and suspending their representative form of government. Across the nation federal courts have ordered similar tax burdens upon school districts by forcing expensive bussing programs to "correct" supposed racial imbalance in schools socially composed by the private preferences of people in choice of neighborhoods.

Probably the most severe case of judicial social fascism was the suspension of all legal protection for a class of people in the interest of feminist sexual conduct. Local jurisdictions were forbidden the recognition of unborn children as persons needing protection of law in order to allow promiscuous women and the career-minded to slaughter their progeny with impunity. Those who rose to defend the rights of the unborn quickly found their own rights suspended by fascistic courts. Courts have ordered a pro-life radio program in Kansas City off the air; dictated that San Diego pro-life defendants not use words in court which personalize the unborn; ordered pro-lifers to remain silent who were attempting to convince abortion-bound women to change their minds; ordered signs at pro-life protests removed; ordered ministers not to speak on the subject of abortion, including sermons to their congregations; ordered pro-lifers to silence in front of aboritoriums while making no similar demands on noisy abortion advocates demonstrating in opposition to the pro-lifers; and ordered the complete banishment of one pro-lifer from the city of Brookline, Massachusetts, the site of that state's most notorious aboritorium.

These and numerous other examples demonstrate that social favoritism is now heavily influencing courts and law. Essentially, the courts are saying, "Tell me who your are, what social group you belong to, and I'll tell you what your rights are." While it is not within the scope of the present work to discuss the corruption of the American judicial system, suffice it to say that a rigorous commitment to equal protection before the law has fallen before a view of law which reflects sentimental social preferences. Sympathies are culturally generated for the "clients" of the left— for homosexuals, racial minorities and women who have deserted their biological function for independence and careers (feminists). More to our purposes is the fact that these same sympathies are being used to define an artificial "reality." In the notorious Rodney King case, racial favoritism was used to construct just such an unreality.

In March of 1991, King, a black felon, led Los Angeles police on a high-speed chase and could only be forcibly arrested by use of night sticks. Most people are aware that a home video was made of that arrest, since it was played *ad nauseam* by the establishment media. Most people are not aware, however, that they are familiar only with a very carefully edited portion of that video. They are completely ignorant of what the whole video reveals about that arrest.

The media believed they had evidence in that video for one of their more cherished, ideologically-patterned, thought formulas. According to the formula, blacks are perpetually victims and whites are perpetually their victimizers. White cops are archetypal villains, according to the formula, and have been since 1963 when Birmingham, Alabama, cops broke up an illegal black protest with night sticks for the benefit of national television. Rodney King was made into a "martyred hero" by the national media, made to fit the formula and portrayed as an innocent black man brutally beaten by "racist" cops. Information fed the public was carefully screened and the video edited to a few seconds, showing King receiving baton blows from police, to create this impression. A massive campaign was conducted by the media. The edited video clip was shown over and over by all three networks. The King arrest was kept "fresh" by network news programs for months. Every public comment on the case became a new occasion to reshow the edited video.

The massive media campaign came partially unglued when a Simi Valley jury acquitted the police officers of brutality charges in the spring of 1992. The jury had been presented information which had been systematically censored by the media, information which forced a different conclusion. The media began an attack upon the jury. Polls were released by the networks which showed that 89% of the public, using the limited information provided by the media, disagreed with the verdict of the better-informed jury. A San Francisco newspaper called it "the jury from hell."[8] Those who actually sat through the trial and had the information given the jury were not as "scandalized" by the verdict as the media claimed the general public was. According to one source, "The censorious nature of national media coverage was confirmed by an article in *Reason Magazine* titled 'You Had To Be There.' Los Angeles-based writer, Charles Oliver, said he and others who followed the trial locally were not as 'shocked' by the verdict as were those whose only source of information was the national media. Oliver said that local sources gave some information about King's actions prior to the alleged beating which made both the police actions and the verdict more comprehensible."[9]

Two of the policemen who arrested King were subsequently imprisoned by a second "double jeopardy" trial provoked by a black riot in Los Angeles following the Simi Valley acquittal. That riot, portrayed as "outrage" at the verdict, was the most expensive civil disturbance in American history. 7000 stores were torched, 10,000 looted, over 2,000 casualties were suffered and the riot cost nearly a billion dollars in damages.

And what was the information censored from general knowledge which Oliver of *Reason Magazine* said made the verdict "comprehensible?" Only the last 17 seconds of the video tape were ever shown the public, the portion showing the police striking King with their batons. Never were the first 3 1/2 minutes of the tape shown, which documented King's resistance and assault upon a police officer. Never was the public told of King's continuous resistance which nearly caused a frightened female highway patrol officer to pull her gun and introduce deadly force. The public was not shown that King threw off police officers like rag dolls who tried to tackle him before the beating, or told of his drugged resistance to attempts to electrically stun him into submission. The media carefully concealed the video of King's assaulting charge against officer Larry Powell. It did not reveal that King was a dangerous black felon with a long police record including violent crimes, or that two black companions with King meekly submitted to police orders and were arrested without incident or harm.[10]

The media surrounded the King arrest with political unreality, portraying him as an innocent "black motorist"—a term used like a litany by all television networks—supposedly being beaten by "white cops" who were implicitly "racists." The innocuous term "black motorist" was obviously deliberately chosen to hide the fact that King was a felon with a violent past who police thought was drugged at the time of his arrest. These facts were also carefully kept from the public. The media's false impression of King and the arrest was defended only by careful censorship of full information.[11]

For several months prior to the Simi Valley acquittal, the blacks who ultimately rioted had been fed a media diet of the "innocent" King being assaulted by brutal "racist" cops. The black community had not been prepared for even the possibility of the verdict. Elements of it rioted.

A second trial was hastily, and possibly illegally, constructed by the federal government. The feds used an 1866 Reconstruction law which made it a crime for local officials to deny citizens life, liberty or property. In doing so, the federal government violated its own guidelines for applying the law. For a second trial to proceed under the 1866 law, the federal government must determine that the first trial was "tainted" by illegal bias. "According to *Reason*, 'If the state prosecutor proceeded in good faith before an unbiased trial court that admitted the appropriate evidence, an acquittal may indicate that the jury honestly harbored reasonable doubts.' In such cases, the feds should not retry the defendants." [12] In any case, a second trial was convened which convicted two of the officers by the expedient of carefully selecting jurors and keeping the information given the first jury out of the court room.

The media demanded, and ultimately got, a court decision based upon "racial sensitivities," not the facts of the case. It did so by creating an artificial stereotype of the arrest—one constructed in the alleged interest of the client minority—an artificiality sold to the public by suppressing information which contradicted the desired political unreality.

CBS journalist Paula Zahn revealed her belief that this artificially-generated public opinion should have prevailed over fact during the first Simi Valley trial which acquitted the officers. During a hostile interview, Zahn asked a Simi Valley jury member why the jury had not considered the impact of their verdict upon "the public" in making their decision.[13]

Immediately following the verdict the rioting began, which was the most obvious "public" reaction to which Zahn was referring. She was essentially demanding that the jury distort their decision to conform with the public perceptions which the media had been able to generate by its highly censored and inflammatory coverage. Zahn was demanding the jury ignore the actual facts of the case and vote a "popular" verdict coherent with media-imposed political unreality. No clearer admission of the demand that judicial proceedings be distorted to favor a client group sponsored by the media could have been made than Zahn did during that interview.

Members of the media, of course, would claim that they were only "doing good" by opposing oppression. Such claims are neither morally binding nor objectively true. Hitler thought he was "doing good" to rid Germany of its Jews since he believed Jews were socially destructive for the German people. The media passed the boundary from authentic representation of the oppressed to "clientism," when it distorted reality to create the perception of oppression.

The advocacy, or representation, of client groups carries with it a commitment to the "client viewpoint." In the current example, the client viewpoint consists of the presumption that blacks are the victims of white racism. That presumption was applied to the King arrest, and the facts were either distorted or suppressed to fit the presumption. With environmentalism, the client viewpoint consists of the presumption that "holy" nature is perpetually harmed by "profane" human activity. With feminism it is the presumption that our social life is "patriarchal" and perpetually destructive of the independent ambitions of the feminists' non-biologically-founded "new woman." With sodomites and other practitioners of sexual perversion who are taken as clients, it is the presumption that all forms of sexual conduct are "normal" and blameless, and that any opinion or fact to the contrary is "hateful" prejudice.

In adopting the client viewpoint, the ideologue operates much like a lawyer who attempts to interpret circumstances and events in a way which is sympathetic to his client. Truth is irrelevant. Gaining public acceptance of interpretations and perceptions which favor the client is everything. The ideologically patterned thoughts we earlier discovered being imposed upon factual reality, are actually services being provided various client viewpoints.

3. A "Stealth Marx" of Political Unreality

Social fascism, however, could not successfully substitute the client viewpoint for factual reality without first being philosophically corrupted in the way that truth and reality are identified. Choosing the "client viewpoint" as "reality" means that one first has to believe that "reality" is only a viewpoint. Without such a general philosophical corruption, the proponents of political unreality would be seen as intellectual slap-stick comics stumbling in absurdity. Without a largely unrecognized corruption of the way we determine truth and reality, the phenomenon of political unreality simply could not exist. There is a largely unrecognized "first-root cause" of the phenomenon we have identified as political unreality. That hidden source is found in the field of philosophy. It is towards that "first root" to which we must now turn our attention.

In the late '60's, the historian Clarence Carson wrote a book titled *The Flight from Reality*. Even at this early date, Carson saw glimmerings on the horizon of what would become full-blown political unreality. The absurdities of the client viewpoint standing in place of chemical and biological knowledge, of replacing hard crime statistics with a reverse image of them, had not completely developed. Carson, however, detected the beginnings of what was to become a mature phenomenon 30 years later.

Carson found an air of unreality creeping into the arguments of those he designated the "reformers" of the period. For example, those advocating foreign aid used a humanitarian argument stating foreign aid would end the deep poverty of third-world countries. Carson points out, however, that the foreign aid was spent on "prestigious items such as steel mills (though it cost them much more to produce steel than they could have bought it for on the world market) and airlines."[14] While the aid was used to build the "prestige" of third-world governments it did little or nothing to end the endemic poverty among the people which its advocates claimed for it. In our terms, the arguments for foreign aid were incipient political unrealities, claims about the consequence of aid which were accepted despite contradictory facts which demonstrated otherwise.

While Carson's examples are certainly dated and almost trivial in comparison to contemporary political unrealities, his book does identify the philosophical corruption required to accept political ideology as "reality" over known fact. In essence, it required a complete rejection of what he calls "a great tradition of philosophy to which all those in Western civilization are heirs." He says, "The central insight of the Western tradition of philosophy is that there is an enduring, even an eternal, reality."[15]

He noted this tradition was shared by both ancient and modern philosophers, by "Thales, Pythagoras, Plato, Aristotle, Cicero, Augustine, Anselme, Aquinas, Duns Scotus ... Spinoza, Hobbes and Kant." For several millennia, the Western mind has held that reality consisted of several components. Among them is the idea that reality is objective. "To put it more deeply, there is a reality which exists independently of the human knowledge of it. Reality is something we come to know because it exists, not something which comes into existence when we take cognizance of it."[16] It is this concept of objective reality which founded thought from Plato to Kant and which the contemporary practitioners of political unreality are undermining.

Carson gives some insight into why they do so and anticipates how it has been so successfully accomplished. He writes, "The major obstacle of unlimited reformism [of the left] is *reality* itself. Historically, the major obstacle to the rise and triumph of a reformist bent has been the *conceptions* which men had of reality."[17] (Italics original).

The Western concept of reality, that "reality is objective — that is, exists outside the mind;...everything has a nature that is fixed and immutable;...[and that] men do not create [reality]; instead, they discover, represent, reproduce, copy and report [it]," must be undermined before the left can succeed. Why is this so? The left succeeds by portraying distinctions, social and otherwise, as unnecessary and "unjust." What happens if these distinctions which the left exploits for political power are founded in biological reality, for example?

What if the social roles traditionally appointed women were founded in biological differences between the genders? What if women were biologically designed to give emotional and physical nurturance? If objective reality revealed a female mental process inclined toward emotionally-laden thought rather than pure reason and an inclination to connect via feelings and to manage human relationships instead of control externals for economic purposes, such objective reality might damage the feminist viewpoint that traditional female roles which specialize in human relationships (mother, wife, nurse) are socially-appointed exploitation. Feminist demands for "gender equality" would be undermined by an appreciation of such objective reality.

Similarly, if biologically founded racial differences extended to the areas of human potential, differences in economic outcomes between the races might be "reality based." If, for example, it were discovered that the black genetic pool gave advantage in the areas of physical coordination and athletic ability, it might be discovered that blacks became over-represented in professional sports. And if it were discovered that the European-white genetic pool gave advantage in the area of mental ability, an advantage of, say, the 15-IQ-point difference routinely discovered between the races, it might be expected that whites would be over represented in occupations which require mental agility.

An appreciation of such an objective reality, however, could not be tolerated by the left. It would imply that differences in occupational outcomes are to be expected and not the result of unnecessary and "unfair" social distinctions. Objective reality itself becomes an enemy of the perceptions the left needs to achieve its political power. Objective reality becomes the enemy.

We might grant that the left has a motive for attacking objective reality as it was traditionally conceived in Western culture. But what method has it used to attack this 2000-year-old allegiance?

To successfully break such a strong foundation—one which produced all that is superior in Western art and science—is itself an amazing feat. It represents an intellectual revolution of major proportion, one akin to the Reformation, the Renaissance or the apparent victory of Darwinism.

That such a revolution could occur without the public being conscious of it strains our ability to believe. But that, gentle reader, is exactly what has occurred. For you see, the attack came not directly against our commitment to objective reality. It came by stealth. It came as an attack upon our language—as a subtle redefinition of what our language is. By accepting that redefinition of language, often without realizing that we had done so, our commitment to objective reality also fell. It fell silently and outside our consciousness. And that is a story worth telling.

Carson is aware of the relationship between language and reality. He writes, "A conception of reality is embedded in our language, informs our thought, is elaborated in our institutions, is implicit in our customs and can be found in books in our libraries. The fact that a new conception of reality has been developed in the last century or so does pose problems of validating the older conception."[18]

Carson is wrong in blaming 18th and 19th century philosophers for the mass desertion of objective reality in Western culture. That "honor" belongs to a 20th century "philosopher of language" whose name we will shortly reveal. But he is right in realizing that a concept of reality is embedded in our very language.

If our concept of the words we use is changed so that we no longer believe those words reflect an external reality, then our commitment to external reality itself is undermined.

The very distinctions we use to differentiate elements of the objective world in order to "appreciate reality" are linguistic in nature. For example, our recognition of the color "yellow" resides primarily as a word in our vocabulary used to describe objects in the world. We needed to differentiate the yellow leaf from the brown one. While scientists may consider "yellow" to be a frequency of light wave, for most of us it is a word we attach to a perception. It is very difficult to think of the color as disembodied and floating outside of the word we use for it.

This strong connection between words and our perceptions of external reality makes our ability to appreciate reality vulnerable to the manipulation of our language. For example, if I can make you doubt your definition of the word "yellow," I simultaneously make you doubt the accuracy of the perceptions to which you have attached that word. If I deceitfully desert the meaning of the word "yellow" and say, for example, that the brown and yellow leaf are both "yellow," I will make you question the validity of your own perceptions. I will leave you wondering if you are seeing things correctly. I have undermined your confidence in your ability to perceive reality accurately.

A desertion of objective definition, that is, making words shift in meaning, has become an essential tactic used to establish political unreality. We have already seen examples of this tactic. The FBI shifts the meaning of the phrase "racially motivated crime" depending upon the race of the victim. Massive numbers of black on white crimes are not counted as "racially motivated," while a much smaller number of white on black violence is so counted. By making the meaning of the phrase "racially motivated" shift in meaning depending upon which race is the victim and which race the perpetrator, the FBI was able to announce an invented "statistic" which was just the opposite of what real world data showed. Whites are assaulted 50 times more frequently by blacks than they assault blacks. Yet the FBI describes blacks as being the largest category of "hate crime victims." Replacing objective definition with private and changeable "meanings" to words has made such an absurdity possible.

George Boas, a university professor of leftist leanings, indicates why the political left might be hostile to words of fixed and permanent meaning. Since the left is committed to change, to "permanent revolution" or continuous social upheaval, fixed meanings to words are at enmity with the perpetually "new" perceptions they require. Boas writes, "If everything is in a state of change, the names which we give them become misleading, for as soon as we label something we seem to give it a 'nature' which is lasting. But nothing endures, all such labels are a vain and childish attempt to arrest the passage of time, to grasp at fleeting shadows...."[19]

For the political left, or more accurately, its latter-day practitioners of political unreality, truth itself is flexible and may be changed according to the political needs of the moment. Words, or more accurately, the meaning of words must change to reflect this shifting reality.

Perhaps nothing better illustrates this need to shift "meanings" than two books issued by American Jewish Committee operative K. S. Stern. In 1994, Stern released a book titled *Loud Hawk* which supported a reign of armed terror conducted by the Marxist Indian group, The American Indian Movement (AIM). Stern wrote sympathetically towards AIM and its terrorist campaign, which included the firebombing of the court house in Custer, South Dakota, the murder of Sioux tribal councilman Leo Wilcox, the bombings of Mount Rushmore and the South Dakota Bureau of Indian Affairs office, the killings of FBI agents and the beatings of Reverend Ray McHue in an extortion attempt of Des Moines churches.

In *Loud Hawk*, the lawyer Stern describes his legal defense of AIM members and his efforts in support of AIM leaders Leonard Peltier—later convicted of the execution killing of two FBI agents—and Dennis Banks. The two had been stopped in Oregon with a motorhome which contained "a cache of weapons from which the serial numbers had been removed, a set of bomb-making instructions, and enough dynamite to destroy a ten-story building."[20] Stern considers such weapons as needed for "self defense" against a government which had "genocidal" intentions towards AIM. Stern used as "proof" telegrams sent to Washington, D.C., by leftist supporters of Banks after the leader and other AIM militants had seized Wounded Knee, South Dakota by force of arms in 1973.

Stern writes, "These [telegrams] were my proof. It was not only the Indians who feared that the militarized FBI–the new

Seventh Cavalry –was actually capable of wiping them out." The "opinions" of the political left that AIM terrorists were "threatened" by the FBI established the "fact" that Banks' and Peltier's explosives and untraceable weapons were being held in "self defense."[21]

In 1996, however, this same Stern issued another book, *A Force Upon the Plain,* in which he argues that another armed group, the militias, which consist primarily of ethnically white Americans, should be suppressed regardless of any illegal acts they may have committed. In this case, guns in the hands of "angry whites" are made to "mean" something quite different than guns in the hands of American Indian terrorists. Both of these "meanings" are artificial and imposed.

Various armed groups calling themselves "militias"—named after the militias of the Revolutionary War—have emerged since 1992. These groups were organized in response to two notorious lethal assaults by federal agents. In the fall of 1992 the Randy Weaver family was surrounded and two family members killed in Northern Idaho. In April of 1993, the Branch Davidian religious community in Waco, Texas was essentially exterminated by a fire which broke out during a federal tank assault on the group's living quarters.

The government investigated itself in these cases and "officially" found itself innocent. Evidence widely circulated in an informal network of talk radio and underground newsletters, however, convinced many people otherwise. Such facts as the incendiary nature of the CS gas used in the Waco tank assault were unreported by the establishment media and led some to suspect that "disfavored" people and groups were being killed with indifference by the government. The Weaver family was alleged to be "racists" and the Branch Davidians a "cult."

In any case, Stern argued that these militias should be

suppressed because they held their arms in threat to the government. Such groups were dangerous because they incorporated in their ranks people whom Stern disfavored. They allegedly held pro-lifers and supposed "racists." The *New American* writes, "From [Stern's] perspective, the militia movement is part of a network consisting of everybody from the pro-life lobby to the Aryan Nations....Stern describes the right as a funnel passing through space. Activists enter through the wide aperture of mainstream concerns, such as taxation or environmental legislation, and are drawn down into narrower and more 'extremist' concerns. At the narrowest end of the funnel, [in the words of Stern] "you get someone like [Oklahoma bomb suspect] Tim McVeigh popping out."[22]

Stern described militias as dangerous because they were said to share guilt for the bomb which ripped the Oklahoma City federal building apart in April of 1995, killing nearly 200 people. Although militias had nothing to do with the bombing, Stern considered them guilty because they supposedly "shared ideas" with the alleged bombers. Stern could cite no examples of militias actually using their weapons in violence, so he had to indict them for their ideas and, in classic social fascist style, for being "people of disfavor." He writes that it was "the ideology of ... pro-violence, antigovernment private armies [that was] behind the carnage at the Murrah Building."[23]

Obviously, the "meaning" of guns in the hands of Indian militants, a group which Stern favors, is different than the "meaning" of guns in the hands of militias composed of people Stern disfavors. AIM members held their guns in "self defense," despite a long history of carnage and violence. Militia members held their guns in "threat," despite a clean record. The guns not only "mean" different things, they "mean" the exact opposite of what the objective circumstances would indicate. "Meaning" has been divorced or cut off from any factual foundation. Reality is what Stern wants it to be.

Stern establishes political unreality by making opinion stand for "fact." The "fact" that the cache of bomb-making devices and untraceable guns of two men who were caught while conducting a violent, aggressive campaign are "self defensive" weapons is established by the opinions of left-wing supporters. The "fact" that militia weapons are held in "threat," despite any real-world example of the weapons being so used, is also established by opinion. In the words of the New American, "[Stern] argues that the fears of possible militia violence expressed by federal workers and liberal activists are sufficient evidence to indict militias."[24]

Is Stern only pretending that aggressively violent AIM members held their guns "in self defense?" Or is he doing something else? Is he perhaps using language in a new way, one in which "meaning" is no longer connected to objective fact but is imposed by the human mind and by human desires.

Stern is not being deceitful. He can really believe that the AIM members hold their guns in "self defense" because, in the ideological culture in which he operates, there is no reality to words anyway. Words can be made to "mean" anything anyone wants them to "mean." "Realities" are verbally created rather than being tied to external facts. "Facts" themselves are established by opinion and not external evidence. AIM guns can be held "in self defense," or they can even be held "as pets." The "meaning" of AIM guns is anything your mind wants to make it to be.

This is the linguistic corruption which has formed Stern's arguments. Elsewhere, he gives strong evidence of his belief that words "create" reality. When the National Rifle Association called the Bureau of Alcohol Tobacco and Firearms "Jack booted thugs" for their murderous assault at Waco, Texas, and other examples of forceful entries into people's homes, Stern called the description "extreme rhetoric [which] depersonalized and demonized federal law enforcement."

In Stern's version of verbally created "reality," however, the actual killing of federal agents—if done by client minorities—is less offensive than the NRA's words. Of an AIM member who executed two FBI agents Stern writes, "He had spoken of the FBI agents like American soldiers in World War II talked about Nazis ... about killing them proudly. Agents Coler and Williams were not human beings to him, just dead enemy troops, faceless, nameless 'FBIs.' Their death generated pride and maybe, in a way, even hope." In the twisted "reality" of K. S. Stern, the words of the National Rifle Association "depersonalize" and "demonize" FBI agents, but the actual murder of the same creates "hope" when committed by a favored minority class.

In this, Stern and a myriad of other practitioners of political unreality are employing a form of linguistic corruption taught to them by a philosopher by the name of Ludwig Wittgenstein. Many, if not most of them, may not even know the name "Wittgenstein," but they are practitioners and disciples of his "method" of language. Wittgenstein is truly the "stealth Marx" of political unreality.

Wittgenstein is little known outside the universities, but his influence has vastly exceeded his reputation. Wittgenstein provided people with a new lens on reality, a new way to practice their language which was easily learned and adopted as a cultural phenomenon. It was spread by the simple expedient of talking or writing with a novel sense of one's words, a "Wittgensteinian sense." Technically, what he did was teach people to talk without any referent to external and objective conditions. He taught people that their word "meanings" were private and their own and did not belong to an objective external reality.

It was a delicious and flattering idea. One was the author of and held the power over "meaning." One did not have to learn correctly or discover what things meant. Further, one did not have to learn the philosophy behind this new sense of language. One merely had to practice it. It was rapidly spread by social communication and the name of Wittgenstein, its father, just as rapidly receded from the knowledge of the new practitioners. This is tragic because a rational examination of the philosophy behind the idea shows that it is poisonous, a poison millions have unwittingly taken.

Ludwig Wittgenstein was a Cambridge philosopher of language, a Viennese Jew, whose book *Philosophical Investigations* was published posthumously in 1953. Perhaps not insignificantly, he was also a homosexual.

Wittgenstein's book is essentially the repudiation of a Christian, reality-based view of language as described by the fifth-century Christian philosopher, Augustine. In a single paragraph in the *Confessions*, Augustine describes how the noun base of language is nothing more than the attaching of linguistic signs to objects in the real world. That is, the "meaning" of a word is defined by the object to which the word is attached.

Wittgenstein wrote a full book to refute this single paragraph, which Augustine wrote almost casually and in passing. The objective of *Philosophical Investigations* is to prove that "meaning" in language is not tied to external reality, but is subjectively imposed by the mind.[25]

There is no reality in the word "chair," Wittgenstein argued, because different "chairs" have so many accidental differences in feature—color, size, material of manufacture, etc. The inclusion of all the distinct and differing objects under the verbal category of "chair" is purely arbitrary, Wittgenstein says, because they really are not the same thing. Supposedly, there is no "chairness" in the real world; there is only "chairness" in the mind of the beholder.

The belief that the word "chair," or any other noun, describes reality is purely an illusion. These are, according to Wittgenstein, only verbal conventions, agreed-upon, arbitrary meanings we "impose" upon the world. These supposedly very different things are lumped together into a category of pure human invention. "Reality" becomes a mental operation, an "opinion," because our words are only mental categories of our own invention and identify no external, objectively real condition.

It is sometimes best to nip a sophistry in the bud. In his "chair" example, Wittgenstein either doesn't believe in abstract reality, or more likely, hides the existence of abstract reality to sell an absurdity. Color is also an abstract reality which takes many different concrete shapes and forms. Should we also say that the word "yellow" has no objective reality because "yellow" takes shapes and forms which have nothing in common with one another? The word "yellow" defines an abstract reality, now known to consist of a certain wave-length of light. Similarly, the word "chair" has an abstract reality defined not by size, shape color and material but by function and design. We don't call something a "chair" because of what it looks like. We call something a chair because it was designed for sitting and functions for that purpose. We have the ability to perceive that design and purpose abstractly, that is independently of any accidental feature differences between chairs. When we recognize that design and purpose we call the object, quite accurately, a chair.

On first impression, grown men arguing whether a "chair" exists or not strikes one as superficial, as a kind of academic silliness. Wittgenstein even writes to further that impression. He deliberately affects a "witty" style in *Philosophical Investigations*, making his points as if he were engaged in clever parlor *reparté*. He once said, "Don't for heaven's sake, be afraid of talking nonsense! But you must pay attention to your nonsense."[26] Don't be mistaken. Such witticisms are used in deadly earnest. They are seductions, used as verbal sleight of hand to seduce readers to accept his absurd premise and give language a synthetic, unreal quality. The style, by the way, is known as "camp" in homosexual jargon.

The synthetic quality to which Wittgenstein wants to convert the language is one in which people determine their own "meaning" to words. He wants to take language and convert it from its objective-reality base and make it the private reserve of the whims of the individual. To make the definition of words subjective rather than objective in this manner, corrupts the language in a way few recognize. The language loses its capacity to transmit factual information. In the Wittgensteinian view there are no "facts" left to transmit. All is whimsical. All is arbitrary. All is imposed by the mind. When words "mean" what we want them to "mean," "reality" becomes what we want it to be.

Probably the most underrated modern author is Lewis Carroll (Charles Dodgson). In his Alice series "children's" books, Carroll examined what kind of "reality" must exist when words become whimsical and slippery as Wittgenstein proposes. The difference between Alice's real world and the dream world into which she slips is primarily use of language. In the real world, Alice encounters things as they are called. In both *Wonderland* and *Through the Looking Glass* she encounters a topsy turvy world in which words take on private meanings, become nonsensical or are used in inappropriate contexts. As Humpty Dumpty tells Alice, "Words mean what I want them to mean." It produces a world of madness in which tears become oceans and in which "cabbages and kings," that is honor and commonness, are thrown into a random, nonsensical Wittgensteinian mix.

What Wittgenstein proposed, and what a generation has

bought, is an "Alice in Wonderland" view of language, a view sold by an artful manipulation of the emotions. Wittgenstein addressed a culture which unconsciously assumed its language was firmly fixed in reality. He invented slightly pejorative terms for this assumption, calling it "commonsensical" and "nativist," thus implying those who hold allegiance to reality-based language are naive and unsophisticated.

He offered what he portrayed as a "higher view." Of our language, he suggested that "important things" are "hidden because of their simplicity and familiarity." His views of language, on the other hand, were "remarks on the natural history of human beings ...which [previously] escaped remark because they are always before our eyes."[27] He offered to remove us from our low "commonsense" view that our language was defined by and referred to objective reality.

And what was this "higher view" of language, this alleged escape from the "commonsense" prison of our words? It was nothing less than the assertion that all words are given "meaning" by subjective psychology and there is no objective reality to which they refer. Wittgenstein called language a "game" in which meanings were only "moves," that is, meanings were only intentions of the user of language. Words only had meaning insofar as I intended them to have that meaning in my particular "language game." Meanings were not tied to the objective world as Augustine had asserted. They were only mental apparitions, ghosts of the mind.

Wittgenstein went so far as to assert that language was incapable of making descriptions which were objectively true outside the subjective state of those who made them. Statements are about the belief of the utterer, not about objective, verifiable conditions in the world. Thus Wittgenstein writes, "Every statement [may be written] in the form: 'It is asserted that such and such is the case—But 'that such and such is the case' is not a sentence in our language—so far it is not a move in our language game."[28] He goes on to assert that we must hear a statement of fact as an "assertion" or as a statement of the inner belief on the part of the utterer before that statement has meaning. Language ONLY identifies the inner state of the individual. It does not, *and cannot*, independently identify objective external conditions. All scientific statements, all statements about any fact are absurd, according to Wittgenstein. They are only statements about beliefs, about the inner mental states of the users of language.

He went to great lengths to attack the notion that language could identify objective reality. In the Wittgensteinian view, our very concept of "reality" is an arbitrary linguistic organization. There is no real difference even between sanity and insanity. The categories which our words name are only the random placing together of objects which really have nothing in common. Those objects could just as easily be rearranged in new categories and thus create new "realities." Louis Carroll's "Cabbages and Kings" could become a new "thing" a new category with as much reality as the current order imposed by our words. The ravings of a madman could become "sane" and "reality" if his imaginations were generally accepted.

Naming the world, according to Wittgenstein, is not the identification of abstract reality and the categorization of objects by that reality. Naming for him is an "occult baptism." Words are turned into fetishes. They become a snake pit of private meanings. By his novel redefinition of language, he makes words seem irrational and arbitrary. All names are mystical, he asserts. All objects are unique and singular, to which random word-tags are simply attached. Wittgenstein and, by projection, those who have followed him, are completely philosophical nominalists who believe there are no "real" categories of things, only conventional lumping of discretely unique objects into arbitrary groupings.

This occultish and nominalistic point of view is revealed in Wittgenstein's ideas of naming real-world objects. "Naming appears as a queer connexion of a word with an object. —And you really get such a queer connexion when the philosopher tries to bring out the relation between name and thing by staring at an object and repeating a name or even the word 'this' innumerable times. ... And here we may indeed fancy some remarkable act of mind, as if it were a baptism of the object." Wittgenstein goes on to call such naming "so to speak, an occult process."[29]

Wittgenstein's 1953 book taught that language is disconnected from reality, that the appearance of reality is only an artificial linguistic ordering by the mind and belief in that order is a low "commonsense" viewpoint. Language does not have the capacity to make objectively factual statements, that is, "true" statements, because such statements are really only assertions of belief, or reflect the mental state of the person making the assertion. No statement can be true or factual independent of the utterer because the statement only represents the utterer's personal "truth."

The "meaning" of our words is not given by objectively real characteristics which we accurately discern and to which we apply linguistic signs. "Meaning" is imposed by the mind and may be changed randomly and at will by the simple expedient of using the word in a different sense. "Meaning" is only a move in the "language game." By making language synthetic, that is, an artificial imposition of the mind which is disconnected from objective reality, Wittgenstein has rendered language useless for real-world, factual description.

The Wittgensteinian synthetic view of language has had a major impact, and the damage has been considerable. This is so because Wittgenstein's ideas are no mere academic esoteria, but provide a method, or "script," to use language in a novel and damaging way. He didn't teach people what language "is" as claimed. He actually taught people how to use words in an "Alice in Wonderland" way, as disconnected from real-world referents and with "meanings" of their own private choosing.

Subsequent to the publication of *Philosophical Investigations*, whole academic fields have been built upon the Wittgensteinian sensibility of language. Noam Chomsky credits Wittgenstein for the "intellectual breakthrough" which founded the field known as "psycholinguistics."[30] Psycholinguistics, according to Chomsky, studies the way "a system of knowledge and belief, that develops in early childhood and that interacts with many other factors to determine the kind of [language] behavior we observe."[31] In other words, the Wittgensteinian idea that language is imposed by inner mental processes is now used to "study" language as a sub-field of psychology.

Wittgensteinianism has also negatively impacted the philosophy of science. Thomas Kuhn and others are now seriously asserting that scientific descriptions do not and cannot describe external reality. Reality is considered to be unknowable by scientific language because that language is considered to be a completely subjective phenomenon.[32]

This has lead to the adoption of what Ed Krug calls the "cynical" scientific viewpoint which has replaced the traditional skeptical viewpoint. Scientists are not "discovering realities" by correcting their imperfect ideas with new objective data. They are now said to be imposing mental constructs which Kuhn calls "paradigms" and which are said to be either "useful" or "not useful," but never real. Scientists are becoming "cynical" because they no longer believe they can know reality, nor that "truth" even exists.

Wittgensteinianism applied to science no longer tests scientific theories for their factual basis, since language is incapable of describing objective, external fact, and all such descriptions are subjective impositions of personal "meanings." One "viewpoint" is as good as another. This corruption is the reason that the political unreality of Rowland's "ozone depletion" theory emerged triumphant. It didn't have to be tested by evidence to be determined "true." It was determined to be "true" because it was advantageous to be considered "true."

Wittegensteinianism was introduced into social science by a group initially calling themselves "ethnomethodologists." By deliberately violating "commonsense" social rules and noting the reaction, they allegedly demonstrated the way that societies and cultures imposed "meanings" upon the world. Supposedly, these rules were "taken for granted" and considered part of the natural order of reality by "commonsense actors" until they were exposed by the ethnomethodologist as arbitrarily imposed "meanings."[33]

This view that societies impose artificial "meanings" eventually established the generally accepted proposition in contemporary sociology that reality is "socially constructed;" that is, that "reality" is an artificially constructed social belief which changes from one society to another. No one "socially constructed reality" is truer than any other. Western medical science, for example, has no greater truth value than the superstitions of nature worshiping shaman in primitive cultures. Scholarly books have actually been written to prove the "authenticity" of primitive belief systems.[34] This, of course, was the foundation of modern "multi-culturalism" which teaches that no culture is superior to any other, and all are equally valid.

The influence of Wittgenstein spread to other academic subjects as well. The movement known as "deconstructionism" in literary criticism has its roots in the Wittgensteinian view of language. Critics "deconstruct" literary texts by demonstrating that the "meanings" intended by the great authors of literature are illusionary. There is another "meaning" hidden in the text which is revealed by the critic. This newly revealed "meaning" usually is, supposedly, a hidden class or gender agenda of the author. The deconstructionist tactic is Wittgensteinian in that language is considered to have no fixed meaning. The words are supposed to be disconnected from their real-world referent and to have private meanings; the deconstructionist can flatter himself as a "discoverer" of those private meanings.

Recently, the Wittgensteinian language corruption has even spread from the universities into the public school system. The language teaching method known as "whole language" is purely Wittgensteinian. Public school reading "expert" Constance Weaver says in her book *Reading Process and Practice* that Whole Language is "psycholinguistic in nature, emphasizing the fact that meaning is not 'in' the text itself but rather develops…during an active transaction between reader and text."[35] Weaver is arguing, a la Wittgenstein, that language has no fixed meaning to be extracted, but that meaning is "imposed" by the mind of the reader. She says that "reading involves bringing meaning to a text in order to get meaning from it." Now even six year olds are to be taught synthetic language and converted to Wittgenstein's dark faith that there is no truth in language.

More central to our purposes, however, is the spread of Wittgensteinianism into the general culture, for it is there that Wittgenstein has become the father of political unreality. We have defined political unreality as ideologically motivated assertions which are immune to contradictory fact.

How is it, however, that the practitioners of political unreality can so easily ignore contradictory fact? How can environmental scientists ignore the complete failure of experimental science to confirm alleged "ozone depletion" via CFCs and still assert that

CFC ozone depletion is a "fact?" How can the FBI ignore their own racial crime statistics and assert that the largest category of "hate crimes" are conducted against blacks by whites? How can the "anti-racist" writer J.S. Stern ignore a violent crime spree by Indian militants and describe their weapons as held in fear of attack against themselves?

We know that such distortions of reality are committed in support of what we call political "clients." Knowing the motive, however, does not explain why the practitioners of political unreality do not suffer psychological disturbance from their blithe desertion of the truth. It was Wittgenstein, or, more accurately, the way he taught people to use language synthetically, which has immunized political unrealists from seeing themselves as frauds.

Political unrealists are undisturbed by contradictory facts because they will not allow those facts to have "meaning" for them. They have accepted a view of language which equates the "truth" of an assertion with the will to believe in it. The synthetic use of language makes them believe themselves to be the "author of meaning." A synthetic language user holds an illusionary power; a belief that he can pick and choose from among the "facts" and determine which ones will be "allowed" to be significant.

Political unreality could not exist in a culture in which the language was still firmly tied to objective reality. A culture for which the meanings of words were firmly fixed—the words being objectively defined by the real-world object to which they refer—such a culture would quickly smash political unreality. When language is authentic, the facts have ultimate authority. Only when language becomes synthetic, that is, when meanings become fluid because such "meanings" are "authored" by the mind and are not tied to real-world referents, does the desire and the will have ultimate "authority" to determine what will be allowed as "reality." Taking "meaning" out of the world and placing it in the mind of the beholder, has made political unreality possible.

That the current practice of political unreality is Wittgensteinian in nature, that is, that it presumes the power to define the "meaning" of objective fact, is fairly easy to prove.

One of the more bizarre examples of a politically motivated unreal treatment of an abortion issue revolves around such a presumed ability to define "fact."

At issue was the partial-birth abortions which congress attempted to ban in the spring of 1996. The procedure is truly ghoulish. An often viable, late-term unborn child is forced into a breech delivery while the mother is left undilated so the head will be caught and left inside the womb. Scissors are then jammed into the base of the skull of the inutero head. Once the scissors have penetrated the skull, they are driven into the brain and forced open to create a large aperture in the skull and brain. This aperture allows a vacuum tube to be inserted by which the brains of the child are sucked out. Only then is the lifeless body fully delivered.

The procedure is not only brutal, but it is fraudulent as well. Extreme caution must be taken that the head does not slip out of the birth canal. Four inches further and the schizophrenic state would call the killing "murder." The vacuuming of the brain tissue is also suspicious. The wound to the brain should be sufficient to kill the child, but there is an economic value to the brain matter. It is used in the treatment of Parkinson's Disease.

The procedure is so vile that a pro-abortion nurse who assisted in one such killing quit in disgust and became an activist seeking to ban the method.

These are the raw facts which social fascists in service to client feminism sought to give a different "meaning." An alternative "reality" must be imposed which serves the client abortion seeker and eliminates the perception of the child as the victim of a rather brutal method of killing.

At first the reality managers tried to claim that the abortion was performed on an already dead child, that the stab to the skull was unnecessary to kill him or her. They attempted to render the stab "meaningless" by inventing a political unreality to the effect that the wound was irrelevant to the child's fate. He was supposedly already dead. The Associated Press sent out a dispatch which claimed, via a Planned Parenthood news release, that "Late second or third trimester abortions are performed to remove a severely deformed or *already dead fetus* that could cause the mother to die, become infertile or otherwise desperately ill." (italics ours)

The massive attempt of the media to create an artificial "reality" for this procedure is indicated by the absurd claim that an abortion is performed on an already dead child. The "source" of this claim is the invention by abortionists that anesthesia administered to the mother kills the unborn child. This claim was necessary to eliminate the image of the jamming of scissors into the skull of a baby and sucking out its brains by making it "meaningless" in the public's mind. The "baby killed by anesthesia" unreality was invented and disseminated by Planned Parenthood in the summer of 1995.

The chief publicist attempting to make the stab wound publicly "meaningless" (it was obviously already "meaningless" in her own mind) was columnist Ellen Goodman. Goodman wrote in the *Boston Globe*, "You wouldn't even know that anesthesia ends the life of such a fetus before it comes down the birth canal."

Goodman did not report the facts which contradicted the political unreality of "baby killed by anesthesia." Neither did most of the other media report them. The nation's anesthesiologists, many pro-abortion, were finding their pocketbooks affected by the false claim. Pregnant women scheduled for surgery, or other treatments which require anesthesia, were becoming frightened that the anesthesia would kill their unborn children.

Professional societies of anesthesiologists felt compelled to correct the record. Doctors Norig Ellison of the American Society of Anesthesia and David Birnbach of the Society for Obstetric Anesthesia told the House Judiciary Constitution Subcommittee on March 21, 1996 that the claim is absurd and not true. These and other medical authorities testified unanimously that the "anesthesia given to a pregnant woman does no harm to the baby."[36] The unanimous testimony of medical authorities, however, was completely suppressed by the Associated Press and the other social fascist media. As noted above, the "dead baby" myth had become a common element of AP "reports" upon the procedure.

The second assault by reality managers upon the brutal facts was an attempt to change the "meaning" of the procedure itself. An attempted redefinition of the procedure was made. They tried to repackage it from a gruesome assault upon the child, to an act of "mercy" protecting the mother. This was done in two ways. First, they redefined the child as the aggressor and the woman as the victim while ignoring the facts of the procedure as well as the testimony of experts. Second, they used Wittgensteinian categorization, making a selected part "mean," or stand for, the whole of the category of women who had their late-term unborn children executed in this manner.

It was claimed that forcing a woman into the breech delivery of a six to nine month unborn child while she is undilated, and maintaining her in a partial birth posture while the child is killed was done to protect her health from a "child monster." The cruelty might be ignored if it were done in "self defense." Of course it was never discussed why it might not be better to simply effect a premature, normal delivery of the "threatening" child. Would not a normal delivery be safer?

The source for this particular version of unreality is Planned Parenthood which issued the media a "news release" which was dutifully "reported" as fact. The news release of November 1, 1995, claimed that the procedure is "done only in cases when the woman's life is in danger or in cases of extreme fetal abnormality." The Associated Press added a novel touch to the political unreality. They created an image of a grotesque baby-monster threatening the life of the mother. These children were "severely deformed fetuses ... [that] could cause the mother to die, become infertile or otherwise desperately ill."

This attempt to put a new "meaning" to the procedure—the victim mother and killer child—has no basis in reality. Dr. Pamela Smith, director of medical education in the Department of Obstetrics and Gynecology at Mt. Sinai Hospital, Chicago, said, "There are absolutely no obstetrical situations encountered in this country which require a partially delivered human fetus to be destroyed to preserve the health of the mother."[37]

If the director of medical education at a major teaching hospital finds no cases where the "monster baby" must be executed in this manner to save the "victim" mother, where did Planned Parenthood get the idea? And why did the press repeat the political unreality when, according to Right to Life spokesman Douglas Johnson, the press had been given evidence that there were absolutely no authentic cases to build the "monster baby, victim mother" image?

Johnson said at an April 1, 1996 news conference, "Some reporters embraced the claim [that the procedure was done to protect the health of the mother and to eliminate deformed children] despite the abundant documentation to the contrary."[38] The created "meaning" for the procedure was sustained by establishing a theatrical "reality" which substituted for factual reality.

Wittgenstein gives us a clue as to how this theatrical "reality" was imposed. Wittgenstein had taught that "meaning" is established by usage. That is, if you act upon a belief, that action makes that belief linguistically "real" to other people. The "monster baby/victim mother" definition for the abortion procedure was made "real" by presenting carefully-selected people who posed as if they had acted upon that belief. A very small number of women who had been unrealistically convinced that their health was endangered by their "monster babies" were publicized, while the majority of women who used the procedure for convenience sake were ignored.

We know how the "monster child" imagery was created. There were two identified practitioners of the abortion procedure, one "Dr." Martin Haskell and one "Dr." James McMahon. McMahon had been scheduled to testify before a House subcommittee considering legislation on the subject. He refused to appear but supplied the subcommittee with a graph purportedly showing that half the babies he executed by the method were "flawed fetuses."

Planned Parenthood and the media took McMahon's "flawed fetuses" description and created the "monster baby" definition for the reason behind the procedure. McMahon's "flawed fetus" became Planned Parenthood's "extreme fetal abnormality" and the Associated Press' "severally deformed fetuses."

These descriptors were imposed meanings achieved by carefully selecting out a small number of cases from McMahon's "flawed fetus" category for their propaganda value. Facts were ignored to construct an artificial meaning for the category.

Information was suppressed about many of the conditions which McMahon considered as "flawing" the baby. A good number of these were compatible with long life, although the child might be handicapped. For example, he executed nine children because they had cleft palates.[39]

McMahon's "flawed fetuses," now converted by careful selection into "severely deformed" monsters which allegedly threatened the life and well-being of the mother, were not even the majority of late-term unborn executed by the thrust of scissors into their brains. Haskell told the *American Medical News* that 80% of his executions are "purely elective" abortions. McMahon's own graph shows that half of his late-term killings are performed electively on the likes of frightened young girls and older women who are depressed about the late stage of their pregnancies.

Facts, as we have seen, hold little bearing when "meanings" may be imposed and McMahon's minority category, his "flawed fetuses" now transformed into the "monster child," became the new "definition" for the whole of the procedure, the way to escape from gruesome images of stabbing scissors and sucking vacuum tubes.

Ellen Goodman, social fascist supreme and adept in the black art of creating artificial realities linguistically, has become so confirmed in the new "meaning" for the procedure that she "morally chastises" those who dare describe it factually. In her May 7, 1996 column she uses tones of moral outrage to make "victims" out of those who commit the atrocity, and "criminals" out of those who object. She thus stands reality upon its head.

What needs to be seen, however, is that the language Goodman uses to create this effect is composed of artificially constructed "meanings." The very words she chooses have taken artificial and private meanings imposed upon them by the pro-abortion movement. It is a practical application of the Wittgensteinian teaching that "meaning" is imposed by the mind, not contained in the real world. Her readers, not aware that her word meanings are privately constructed, may mistakenly believe they refer to the real world.

In that column Goodman writes, "Then in April, the president, surrounded by women who had needed such a procedure, vetoed the ban," and later she said, "to pretend that these are healthy babies and callous mothers, to project the most gruesome visuals and to lay the political debate onto the women who wanted babies, is a very special cruelty."[40]

Some evils are so profound it seems almost trivial to expose their method. That such a brutal crime is being defended in deceptive language while affecting a self-righteous moral tone indicates the seared conscience of a sociopath. Nonetheless, let us proceed, word by word, to show how those words have been invested with private "meanings," from feminist abortion advocacy, to create an artificial reality.

We were told that a pro-abortion president who was determined to continue the atrocities, surrounded himself with women "who had needed such a procedure." What is the "meaning" of the word "needed." Objectively defined, the word "need" means "required to sustain life." Was there a medical necessity? On examination we find that there was no medical necessity, but a group of fearful women, who were convinced by abortion advocates of such a "need," were paraded before cameras to tearfully plead for the urgency of the procedure. Ignorant belief was substituted for medical fact.

The women who were chosen to "represent" recipients of the procedure were not from Haskell's 80%-elective-abortions category. Haskell is the major provider of partial-birth killing. Of the two practitioners publicly identified, Haskell was the innovator of the procedure and the largest provider. Most of his "clients" were not chosen to represent the whole. Neither were the other half of the minority-provider McMahon's "clients" so chosen. Nowhere to be found in Goodman's description of "recipients" were the majority who wanted their six-to-nine-month-old unborn killed in this brutal fashion because the child inconvenienced them. Goodman and other pro-abortionists had eliminated the largest category from being considered "possible recipients," in order to give an artificial "meaning" to the procedure.

As we have already seen, abortion advocacy had earlier attempted a different artificial meaning for the procedure built upon McMahon's "flawed fetus" category. It was asserted that women's lives and health were being threatened by monster babies called "extremely deformed fetuses."

The propaganda used to establish this perception was a marvel of ruthless deceit. According to an article titled "The Dead Baby Society" in the *Wanderer* newspaper of June 27, 1996, Blythe-Clinton surrounding himself with five, carefully chosen women when announcing his veto of the partial-birth abortion ban. The five were made to stand for the thousands of women who had eliminated their children with the scissor thrust.

The five were chosen because they had been successfully frightened into the procedure by the "monster baby threatening the health of the mother" line. They had been convinced of an unreality and had acted upon it. The *Wanderer* states, "each woman was completely persuaded by her doctor that she had no medical option, that her own welfare was in critical jeopardy. They were told that if the baby died while it was within them, resultant toxins could cause hemorrhage and possibly a hysterectomy. They were told that natural labor would increase the risk of cervical and uterine rupture."

The *Wanderer*, however, consulted two gynecologists who revealed the abortion advocates had taken vulnerable women, in crisis pregnancies, and terrorized them with lies. The newspaper states that both experts agreed that "there are very minimal health risks to a mother who continues to carry an unhealthy child to term or to his natural death, if she is properly monitored." The doctors were not equivocal in their "minimal health risks" assessment and are supported in their opinions by Dr. Pamela Smith, director of medical education in the Department of Obstetrics and Gynecology at Mt. Sinai Hospital, Chicago.

Nonetheless, these women believed, not what authentic medical science knows, but what abortion advocates told them. They were paraded before the public after acting upon that false belief. They were good witnesses for the unreality, having become pathologically committed to the belief by their horrendous act. In reality, they are pathetic creatures; much like women in a primitive tribe who reluctantly give their children up for sacrifice to placate the local gods.

Since this "self defense" definition of the procedure is vulnerable to contradictory expert testimony, Goodman also provides an alternative, and different, "meaning" for the abortion of McMahon's "flawed fetuses." Recipients of McMahon's "flawed fetuses" services are now caring mothers who "wanted babies." One of the women chosen to stand with Blythe-Clinton because she had been effectively deceived, had once actually been pro-life. She had been told that it was "impossible" to carry her child to birth as she had wanted, and her own health was at risk. She "baptized" the baby before having it slaughtered.

It is clear that the moral reasoning of these five frightened women had been distorted by the abortion. Inaccurately convinced by pro-abortion medical professionals that their health was at risk, these women said they decided to kill their babies, since the child would die "anyway." Since all of humanity is going to die "anyway," that rationale would justify any murder. It completely ignores the distinction between life ending naturally, and being abruptly severed by human agency and will.

In any case, by believing the "monster baby/mother's health risk" formula, these women felt absolved of any responsibility for the killing. This is what allowed Goodwin to call them "caring." One woman even claimed she would have gladly traded places with her aborted daughter, a patent absurdity since she had sacrificed the child to what she believed to be her own health needs.

Isn't Wittgensteinianism marvelous! When words are disconnected from objective referents and become the preserve of subjectively imposed "meanings," new "meanings" can be traded for old without batting an eye. A handful of deluded women are made to represent the whole category of abortion recipients. We are informed that these "representatives" had ordered the scissor thrust for their babies to protect their own health. We are now led to believe they actually did so out of concern for the child. Of this minority category chosen to represent the whole, we are told they "wanted babies" and were not "callous" because they were foolish enough to believe and act upon an artificial thought formula.

We are told the babies are "not healthy," implying that the scissor thrust is a form of health care. The concept of death as a form of "health care" is one of the novel "meanings" of the left. In objective language, "health care" means providing treatment and comfort to a patient to aid him in overcoming and/or coping with his health problems. Killing him neither aids nor comforts, but might comfort someone who profits from the death.

In language which still refers to objective reality, these recipients were not women who "wanted babies." They were women who had abandoned all nurturance for and protection of the real children in favor of the diagnosis of a pro-abortion medical profession. Since the prognosis for the pregnancies had been so clearly distorted by abortion advocacy, why not the diagnosis for the children as well?

Objectively, the word "callous" means uncaring. If these women are "not callous" then they are "caring." Objectively, the word "caring" means to be inclined to provide nurturance and aid to someone. To describe someone as "caring" who orders her child slain, especially in this brutal manner, requires a novel meaning to the word.

In the world of social fascist death vendors, however, it is considered "caring" to eliminate relatives whose disabilities are psychologically or materially inconvenient. It is especially "caring" if the patient cannot express his own wishes, as in the case of a Kansas City auto accident victim, who was conscious but without speech, whose food was taken from her—and as in the case of Goodman's recipients. "Little Johnny wouldn't want to live with a cleft pallet speech impediment. Everyone would make fun of him."

The point is that the language of social fascism has increasingly become disconnected from objective referents, and words are given subjective and novel "meanings" which are used to create unrealities. In Goodman's case, those who insist upon objective, reality-based descriptions of the abortion procedure under discussion are almost criminal, are committing a "very special cruelty." This "cruelty" is committed against the artificial image of the aborted women, which she created with her novel meanings. The "caring mothers" who "wanted babies" become, not the executioners, but the victims of those who describe the procedure realistically with their "gruesome visuals."

Goodman can actually be quite instructive on the methods by which Wittgensteinian meaning shifts are used to construct artificial realities. The single most common characteristic of the use of synthetic word meanings is that they select out the events which confirm their novel meanings. Only women who believed in the "monster baby/mother health risk" thought formula were presented as examples of the abortion procedure. Ignored were the much greater number who had aborted as a matter of convenience.

The synthetic usage is *presumed* to stand for all concrete examples, while the whole of the phenomenon is deliberately obscured to prevent real details from discrediting the artificial meaning. The synthetic use of language consists of the replacement of such obscured details with a novel artificial meaning which becomes "reality."

K. S. Stern, the defender of the AIM terrorists we considered earlier, boldly admits that novel synthetic meanings require the obscuring of factual detail. In his legal defense of Peltier and Banks, the AIM members caught with explosives and arms, Stern says that he deliberately left vague and unanswered any questions about the purpose to which the two Indian terrorists intended to put the weapons. Stern writes, "No one asked about Indians with firearms, 350 pounds of explosives, and what they planned to do with them. Our case was best that way."[41] Too much factual detail would undermine the synthetic meaning, the *presumption* that the weapons were held "in self-defense."

This is the practical application of Wittgensteinian language. That philosopher created a description of language which made the ties of words to objective reality seem illegitimate, and replaced them with a concept of subjectively imposed meanings for those words. This description of language, fairly easily grasped, became a method for practicing language as Wittgenstein described it, and thus to apply it in a synthetic and artificial way. Goodman, Stern and other social fascists are practically applying that method to create artificial reality. Unfortunately, when words take on subjective meanings in the real world, the phenomenon does not produce the "Wonderland" humor of Lewis Carroll. Imposed subjective meanings are being used to further brutal social movements.

4. The Media as Enforcers of Unreality

The point we wish to make is that the contemporary American left deals not in facts, but in perceptions. Sometimes those perceptions stand at odds with known facts, yet are made to substitute for the truth. This is often done in support of a new ideology which emerged from the civil rights movement, and which we identified as social fascism. Social-fascist ideology treats certain social groups and political movements as "clientele," and will advocate the viewpoint of that clientele even against known facts. We have called this imposition of an ideologically desired reality over known facts "political unreality." We have noted that a chemical "formula," a formula which cannot produce real-world observations, and which would have been rejected as junk science if it hadn't fulfilled a propaganda need of the environmentalist movement, was given the Nobel prize. This piece of voodoo science was called "true" in the face of overwhelming contradictory evidence because it fit an ideologically patterned formula; pantheistically conceived "nature," treated as a "client," must be protected from the economic activities of human culture.

73

"Tell me it ain't so, Joe!" Surely authentic science would have risen up in righteous anger to strike down the pretender. That might be expected, unless the voice of "authentic" science has been suppressed, and a mechanism for that suppression does, in fact, exist. The contemporary media has sufficient control over the flow of information to make authentic science turn invisible and give public credibility to such mythical nonsense as Rowland's "ozone depletion" theory.

Since the late '60's, the national media has been increasingly centralized and taken on an ideological conformity reminiscent of single-party totalitarianism. The two newspaper town has become largely a thing of the past, and the dailies which have survived this pruning process are often owned by giant chains like Gannett. Newspapers no longer express local independence in editorial decisions but have begun to reflect the policies as set down by a far-away board of directors. Similarly, with the nearly total collapse of the United Press International, national wire service is now monopolized by the Associated Press. With the loss of independence in the local newsroom and dependence upon a single source for national news coverage, it is little wonder that newspapers have come to resemble one another. They all might as well be titled "*Son of U.S.A. Today.*"

This centralization of the control of information has been accompanied by a frightening level of ideological conformity in the newsroom. This centralized, and ideologically conformist, media has shown itself dedicated to ignoring facts which might embarrass its shared ideology. One of the beneficiaries of this tendency has been the environmentalist movement. This is the reason that the public knows next to nothing about the failure of experimental science to confirm the Rowland "ozone depletion" theory, and why that failure had to be revealed in an "underground" newsletter like *Environment Betrayed.*

What evidence do we have for this rather sweeping and, to some, shocking statement? Are we alleging that a monolithic media has the power and desire to knowingly suppress even scientific fact in the interest of ideology? Are we asserting that the media acts as a collective to defend a shared ideology against known reality? Are we actually claiming that thousands of people who staff these institutions have made such a pact with the Devil? In a word, yes, we are so claiming.

Around 80% of the media have admitted leftist sympathies to researchers and said they ideologically bias their reporting in favor of those sympathies. The *Intelligence Digest,* one of England's most respected journals identifying emerging military and political trends, did a survey of polls which had been conducted upon newsmen and media personnel around the world. The 1992 *Digest* article states, "Over 80% of today's most powerful journalists and broadcasters admit to tainting their news from a liberal or socialist perspective." This is quite a confession. Eighty percent were willing to admit in private interviews what they would never confess to their viewers and readers. They tailor the news to a leftist ideology.

The *Intelligence Digest* survey simply reinforces the study done by Robert Lichter and Stanley Rothman in the '80's. That study was compiled in the book, *The Media Elite.* The authors interviewed leading journalists and media personnel with outlets which the authors believed define the news agenda for the whole nation. These were the three most influential newspapers, the *Washington Post,* the *New York Times* and the *Wall Street Journal,* as well as the television networks and the national news magazines *Time* and *Newsweek.* The results of the Lichter/ Rothman interviews were also compared with media studies previously conducted by news outlets themselves.

The fairly extensive study shows that those who are selected for positions by these nationally important outlets are not representative of the American people. They were selected from a much narrower pool, both culturally and ethnically. Jewish representation in the media, for example, is ten times greater than Jews are represented in the general population.[42] Further, nearly 70% of those Lichter and Rothman characterize as the "media elite" are selected from the East Coast. The South, Mid-West and the West are vastly under-represented. In short, national media personnel are taken from a very restricted cultural pool which might be characterized as the Jewish/Cosmopolitan Eastern Culture.

The political attitudes of the "media elite" show that they are, statistically, a different population. These attitudinal differences between the media and the general population are most pronounced in those areas we have characterized as forming ideologically patterned thought, in exactly those areas which are currently producing political unrealities. As we have noted, political unrealities are being manufactured by ideologically-patterned feminist, "anti-racist" and environmentalist thought. In these areas, media allegiance to the "patterned thought" is nearly universal, an ideological conformity not shared by the general population.

Consider the near ideological conformity which Lichter and Rothman found among media leaders in these areas. Among the Lichter and Rothman's "media elite," 81% are sympathetic to environmental claims, 80% are prejudicially predisposed to favor blacks as evidenced by their support of government-enforced job quotas for that race.

The numbers are even higher for their predisposition toward feminist/sexual "liberation" claims. Ninety percent support abortion with nearly 80% strongly supportive of the practice. Ninety-seven percent want no restrictions upon sexual behavior, at least not by law. Seventy-five percent believe homosexuality is normal and right, with 85% believing homosexuals should not be restricted from having influence on children as teachers.[43]

The same patterns were found when the *Los Angeles Times* sent a questionnaire to 3000 newsmen and journalists in 1985. Support for feminism via support for abortion, racial preference for blacks as measured by support for government enforced quotas, as well as sympathy for homosexuality, were in the 80-90% range.

The *Times*, however, also sent the questionnaire to 3300 randomly sampled non-journalists. The differences were quite significant. While the chances that the general public would support the ideological goals of minorities, homosexuals and feminists were only 1 in 2, the chances approached near certainty with the journalists, that is 8 out of 10. Eighty-two percent of the journalists supported abortion while only 51% of the general public did so. Eighty-nine percent of the journalists supported "homosexual rights in hiring" while only 56% of the general public held the same view. Eighty-one percent of the journalists supported government dictated employment quotas for minorities, while only 57% of the national sample did so.[44]

It should be noted that these differences are so great they cannot be explained by random chance. If general attitudes in the above areas were a tub of mixed white and black balls representing different attitudes, it is statistically absurd to believe one could pull out a handful consisting of only black balls by pure chance. It is much more likely that the handful of black balls was achieved by carefully picking out only black balls from the mix, and something akin to this selection process is obviously how the current media was composed.

While Lichter and Rothman have clearly shown the existence of an ideological bias in the "media elite," they have not consciously addressed our current question. While the media may be nearly universally composed of leftists, do these leftist "brethren" use their ideology to construct artificial realities and engage in a kind of conspiracy to sell that artificial reality to the general public? Are they practitioners of political unreality who use their ideological consensus and considerable power over information flow to suppress facts which may contradict favored unrealities? This is a different and much more serious question, one which the Lichter and Rothman data can address, but one which the authors failed to do.

Lichter and Rothman, you see, share the journalist's belief about "reality," a belief which is the philosophical foundation of political unreality. They also believe reality is only a social/political opinion, something subjectively imposed, not something contained in objective fact external to the individual. They don't lament the *practice* of political unreality, only that the current versions are constructed by the left and not by the conservative ideology which the authors tend to favor.

The authors state, "We all reconstruct reality for ourselves, but journalists are especially important because they help depict reality for the rest of society." [45] Thus they believe that "reality" is in flux, as something chosen, or "constructed," by the individual. They do not believe that "reality" is something which is objectively external to the individual, and which must be mentally "extracted" from these objective, external facts.

In actuality, reality is something people "discover." It is not something they "construct."

Of their work they state, "We seek to know whether journalists' perspectives on social reality are guided by their backgrounds, their beliefs, and their inner needs."[46] Reality, for them, is only a "perspective," something which is "social" in nature and is "guided" by subjective psychological states. In taking this view,

Lichter and Rothman are only repeating a belief which is rampant in their own field of sociology.

The belief that reality is "socially constructed" is so firm in sociology that the idea is treated as if it were a well-established natural phenomenon and has been dignified as a field of study. It is called "the sociology of knowledge." As we have seen, that belief emerged from Wittgenstein's very influential book on philosophy which appeared in the 1950's. Lichter and Rothman were social-science professors at well-known colleges, Lichter at George Washington University and Rothman at Smith College, at the time of the writing of their book. As members of the university establishment, they repeat a belief which we will show is deeply implicated in imposing political unreality upon the culture.

Since Lichter and Rothman share the belief upon which political unreality is founded—specifically that reality is "socially constructed," that it is a kind of "group think" opinion, rather than contained in objective fact—they often fail to see the implications of their own study of the media. For example, their data shows that as many as 70% of the media leaders surveyed were willing to suppress factual information in the interest of supporting the viewpoint of ideologically favored social groups.

To gain this insight, we had to ask a different question of the author's data than that which they originally asked, to see if that data could give any new answers. In social science this is dignified with the two-bit title, "secondary analysis of the data."

Originally, the authors asked if their media subjects would "retell" a news story in a more "left-wing" way than would a group of businessmen. The authors were simply probing what might be termed "political bias."

We asked a more significant question of the same data. "How prone were the newsmen to impose ideologically synthetic "meanings" on the story, synthetic meanings which were defended by leaving out significant information from the original—information which might embarrass that political bias."

To be "politically biased" is one thing. To be a media-enforcer of political unreality is quite another, and we were interested in finding out how willing the media subjects were to perform that role.

The journalists were given two ideologically slanted stories on "black and/or feminist issues" which contained some information which could contradict the desired slant. The journalists were then asked to retell the story, and their retellings were graded blindly to see if they left out the contradictory information, included it or gave even more emphasis to it.

In the first story, the Bakke Supreme Court decision upon "affirmative action" was said to have provoked whites and males to aggressively protest preferential employment treatment given women and blacks. Several instances of worker anger in specific locations were mentioned. A victim of such preferential treatment was also quoted. These represented the "factual" basis of the story. These angry reactions to preferential treatment given members of favored social groups—preferential treatment which had cost others economic opportunities—were an authentic phenomenon. They were fully understandable, non-contrived, "natural" emotions. Collectively, they represented a legitimate event which deserved reportage. [47]

Yet fully 40% of the original story's space was dedicated to the "client viewpoint." Editorial space nearly equal that given to the *facts* of the story was given to the *opinions* of an advocate for minority preferences. He was allowed to comment upon the outrages of the victims of affirmative action and make their reactions seem wrong and dangerous because they were supposedly threatening minorities. Thus the victims were, journalistically, interpreted by the "client viewpoint." The angry reactions of those who had lost jobs and opportunity were said to be placing affirmative action programs in "severe jeopardy." Conservatives were blamed for "exploiting this reaction" and "throttling all efforts to bring women and racial minorities into the economic mainstream."

The journalists interviewed by Lichter and Rothman were asked to read the story and then retell it in their own words. This was done to see if they would further the interpretation contained in the client viewpoint in the retelling. Would they leave out contradictory factual information and shift the "meaning" of the story closer to that client viewpoint? The results of the study give us a microcosmic view of how the press manages political unreality.

The authors discovered a tendency on the part of the journalists to turn the reality of a natural, emotional reaction to one's own victimization into something else, into something dark and nearly evil by reinterpretations and shifted meanings. The anger of those who had suffered loss became an attack upon minority "rights." Those who felt such outrages were "wrong" in doing so. Thus, a politicized new meaning for the facts was used to replace the raw facts themselves. Legitimate grievances, anger at unfair economic losses, became "a wave of reverse discrimination cases that threaten the advances made in earlier equal opportunity decisions," or "a backlash effect that is jeopardizing affirmative action programs for women [and] minorities." These were the actual words of reporters for the *New York Times* and the *Washington Post* retelling the story to Lichter and Rothman. The voicing of grievance at unfair loss was redefined as "a backlash effect" and a "threat [to] the advances made in earlier equal opportunity decisions."

In these retellings, the faces of those wronged were obscured, the owners of those faces depersonalized. In reality-based language, they had suffered discriminatory hiring and promotion policies which were established to favor the racial and gender clients of social fascism. Either employment standards were lowered for members of client groups, or they were preferentially selected to achieve an alleged "equality" of outcomes, thus short-circuiting rational selections criteria such as merit and seniority.

The practice both cheapened occupational performance by making it irrelevant to ambition, and created social tensions as members of disfavored groups watched the less qualified or newcomers leap-frogging over them. The victims reacted to a deliberate ideological distortion of the work place which had abused them. They could not, however, be allowed that much "reality" by the defenders of the client viewpoint.

Their grievances were redefined by the client viewpoint as a negative, impersonal force threatening the client group. The victims became a "wave of reverse discrimination cases." Those who had suffered were redefined as being akin to a natural disaster, their emotions portrayed as something of an evil wind, as constituting a "backlash effect." A legitimate grievance was made to mean something else. It was made to mean a "dangerous force" which was threatening the only people allowed to have a human face—members of the client group. A false and artificial meaning was thus subtly imposed by dehumanizing the victims into an impersonal force. This required a suppression of any factual detail which identified them as real men with real lives.

In retelling the original story, nearly 25% of the journalists interviewed dropped any mention of the real life people who had been harmed by "affirmative action," and whose legitimate grievances had been the factual basis of the original story.[48] They left out the anger at factual harm and retold the story only from the client viewpoint. White firemen in Pittsburgh, passed over for less-qualified blacks, became part of a "wave of reverse discrimination;" and a college professor passed over in favor of an "affirmative action" female became part of "a backlash effect." Thus these real people became bodiless abstractions and their very real emotional discomforts an evil force.

The significance of Lichter and Rothman's near 25% should not be lost. Almost a quarter of the "media elite" were callous enough to censor-out details of the persons victimized by affirmative action. They emotionally slammed the door on these people because their stories discomforted the client viewpoint.

Twenty-five percent is probably sufficient to assure that these people's experiences with affirmative action would ultimately become "non-news." How many hands would this "story" have to go through, how many editors, rewrite men, wire service writers, before we are assured that reality would drop out of print or from the screen in such "sensitive" areas?

Lichter and Rothman found that, when the information which conflicted with the client viewpoint was not so personal, as many as 70% were willing to censor. When it did not require shutting off human sympathy, a much greater percentage were willing to support the client viewpoint by eliminating conflicting facts.

The authors presented their media respondents with a story about a claim made by a "major civil rights organization" that black income was "falling sharply" when compared to whites. The story noted, however, that "recent studies" challenged this claim by alleging that black economic achievements were "on an upswing." These studies claimed that differences in white and black income were due to "class differences" and were closing as blacks became more educated.

This view was called a "dangerous misconception" by the spokesman for the "civil rights" group who said it would increase "white resistance towards efforts to bring about racial equality." Thus the "client viewpoint," as expressed by a "civil rights spokesman," was given as comment upon the "undesirable" factual information. In objectively real terms, the contradiction between the claims of the client-group advocate and the findings of various academic studies could only be resolved by reviewing further facts.

The "media elite" apparently had another method of solving the contradiction. They simply discounted the academic studies in favor of the client viewpoint. By extrapolating from Lichter and Rothman's data, it appears that 60-70% of them tended to eliminate information about the contradictory studies in the retelling. The black advocate group's claim was left to stand alone as the "fact" of the story. "Reality" was chosen from among two claimants based simply upon the political esteem in which one the claimant was held.[49]

This technique of asking the surveyed "media elite" to retell stories was quite good because it duplicated what journalists actually do in the real world. The original story was a "set of facts" which contained both the self-interested interpretations which we call the "client viewpoint" and information which appears to contradict that viewpoint. The responding journalists were to "report" by retelling those stories. The willingness of journalists to eliminate contradiction to further the client viewpoint gives interesting insight into how reality becomes distorted by every-day reporting in the media.

In the first instance, only a hard-core 25% were willing to filter out factual information which discomforted the client viewpoint. In the second instance, between 60 and 70% were willing to employ such filters. What is the difference? The difference, quite obviously, is explained by a difference in the censored facts themselves. If the facts must be distorted to turn people—even "anti-clients"—into non persons, fewer of the media elite were willing to do so. If, however, the contradictory information is impersonal, of the economic statistical variety in this instance, significantly more are willing to do so.

There may be another factor, however. The media personnel may fear being caught in their distortions and thus lose credibility. Perhaps only 25% of the "media elite" were willing to dehumanize the grievances of those harmed by affirmative action because knowledge of those grievances is too wide spread. The grievances in this case are too well-known to easily characterize them as motivated by "racism."

For thirty years or more, and in thousands of communities, nearly everyone has seen women hired on road work crews and as policemen because they are women; blacks promoted to executive jobs because they are blacks. Those who have fallen victim to these preferential employment practices have complained, and the complaints are simply too well-known. The phenomenon cannot be ignored, so it must be "reinterpreted."

Even this is risky since few are willing to "see" Uncle Harry's anger over being bumped by Betty Feminist from the seniority list for a long-anticipated promotion, as a "backlash." The public has too much knowledge—that often of an intimate nature—to risk distorting the facts. That even 25% were willing to do so suggests a significant entrenchment of the ideologically-hardened in the current media.

Compare the level of public knowledge about the grievances of "affirmative action" victims with that same public's knowledge of the racially-compared economic statistics compiled by an obscure conservative think-tank or politically incorrect economics professor at some small university. The public has no general knowledge of these statistics and no independent access to them. It is relatively easy to filter out these facts, to make them "nonoperative," and 60 to 70% of the surveyed media elite opted to do so.

We are justified in drawing a conclusion from this information. The ideologically-conformist media can and will distort and/or disguise facts which discomfort the client viewpoint if the public has no independent knowledge of those facts and cannot easily obtain access to them. If, however, the public has an independent source of information about the distorted facts and/or media personnel must distort them to someone's personal harm, fewer will be inclined to fully support the client viewpoint.

What we have termed the "client viewpoint," that is, an attitude towards facts which reflects the presumed interest of client groups, effectively establishes a political unreality. Facts must be given artificial, subjectively imposed "meanings," *a la* Wittgenstein.

The black "client viewpoint," for example, demands that one presume all occupational performances to be racially neutral. No "truth value" may be given to the assertion that racial groups differ with respect to abilities. Observed facts which contradict this demand MUST be given artificial "meanings." The common observation that blacks are under-represented in highly skilled and professional jobs must be made to "mean" that hidden "white racism" is excluding them. Any explanation which identifies statistical differences in racial abilities as a "cause" is a forbidden explanation. The very idea, whether true or not, is called "racist" and vigorously proscribed. Several researchers who have reported IQ differences between blacks and whites have found themselves verbally abused and, in one case, researcher Hans Eysenck was physically assaulted by a mob.[50]

Lichter and Rothman's data revealed that the press was willing to suppress factual information in the interest of the black "client viewpoint." That willingness has produced a widespread suppression of information which threatens the presumption that black performance equals that of the whites. Information, which reveals that there are, statistically, biologically-determined differences in intellectual ability between races, is never mentioned.

For example, it was reported only in the column of the conservative columnist Joseph Sobran that elite Ivy League universities routinely give black applicants a 50 percentile advantage over white applicants in evaluating standard academic achievement scores for acceptance. Thus a black student, who has performed better than only 50% of the students taking a standard college entrance test, will be selected before a white student who has performed better than 95% of the students taking the test. Sobran was able to make this bit of information "shocking" to readers of the Catholic conservative publication, the *Wanderer,* simply because the fact had been buried, despite innumerable articles on race relations in the universities which had appeared in the establishment media. [51]

These facts were suppressed by the media so that an ideologically-patterned formula, an artificial "meaning," could be imposed upon well-known differences between the races in economic status. The formula "differences between whites and blacks in employment and wealth are due solely to white racism" cannot be allowed to be corrected by factual information which suggests that black limitations may be a major factor. The illusion of "racial equality" in performance must be maintained by lowering performance standards for blacks while simultaneously pretending that it is not being done.

Reality must be engaged in a "back room" way by men obligated to act upon practical racial matters. People such as university admissions officers trying to fill racial quotas are forced by necessity to recognize black limitations in academic skills and preparations. They lower the standards for blacks, but those lowered standards can never be admitted in public without threatening the imposed unreality that racial economic differences are caused by "white racism."

The media, as willing patrons of black clientism, have proven themselves willing to keep the "back-room secret" of university admissions policy. The Lichter and Rothman interviews suggested that the media was willing to suppress information in favor of the client viewpoint. Joseph Sobran revealed that media have actually suppressed such information by hiding the facts about university admissions policies which adjust for black limitations in academic skills.

It should be noted that the practice of reality distortion by journalists is not without its defenders in the universities. The university system is the second institution which has become ideologically conformist and is being used to enforce political unreality. It was in the universities that the philosophical rationalization for imposed "meaning" was manufactured by Wittgenstein. As we have seen, journalists now routinely apply Wittgensteinianism. They now make facts "mean" what the client viewpoint demands. University philosophy is being used to justify the reality distortion currently practiced by ideologically-controlled journalists.

Reality is now treated as if it were malleable, like clay, something formed by subjective opinion and human values. For the journalists, "reality" is no longer judged by how well it conforms to objective fact. Now what is asserted as "reality" is judged by how well it conforms to a value consensus, how well it services the client viewpoint.

The sociologist Herbert Gans has argued that "reality" chosen by journalists must serve "values." Gans wrote, "Values enter the news most pervasively in the form of reality judgments, the assumptions about external reality associated with the concepts which the journalists use to grasp it."[52] Here Gans admits that reality is "chosen" by the journalists, but he does not see this as a distortion process. To Gans, the selecting out of facts is called "news judgment" which expresses "the reform values of [the journalists'] profession...many [of these values] are shared by the rest of the audience. They are called motherhood values..."[53] These "reform values" represent the journalist's "long adherence to good-government Progressivism." In other words, the public wants the journalists to distort reality because they, too, share the "vision of the good society" which allegedly justifies such distortions. In this shared "vision" the races are equal in all essential abilities and anyone who reports facts to the contrary is a "racist."

It should be noted that the sociologist Gans made these remarks in the *Columbia Journalism Review*, one of the most prestigious publications read by the journalists' themselves. In other words, this outsider from the university made gratuitous and flattering remarks to the working journalists, obviously to make them feel justified, even noble, in their ideologically-directed distortion practices. The universities, especially the sociologists, have volunteered themselves as a "support group" for a media engaged in reality distortion because, as we shall see, the two are essentially in the same distortion business.

But is Gans' consensus in "news judgments" based solely upon "long adherence to good-government Progressivism?" Are these similar "news judgments" really only an oozy-sweet consensus, or is the apparent media conformity backed by a hidden iron hand? When reporters give facts which embarrass or discomfort the publicity images desired by favored groups, when a reporter violates the client viewpoint, does that reporter suffer sanctions? The case of reporter Paul Teetor, formerly with the

Burlington, Vermont, *Free Press,* suggests that revealing such facts may be career damaging.

The *Free Press* is a Gannett-chain newspaper which fired Teetor because he had included unwanted information in a story on a "race-relations forum." Teeter violated a formula unreality which is an important component of the black client viewpoint. It is a tenet of social fascism that "racism" is a "white disease," and blacks are seldom, if ever, guilty of it. According to the formula, blacks are allowed to act in the interest of their own race and to the exclusion, and even harm, of the national majority race, but they will never be publicly identified as being "racist" for so doing. The one exception to this, of course, is when blacks attack other client minorities, especially Jews. Thus, Nation of Islam leader Louis Farrakahn was identified in the press as an "anti-Semite" after he accused Jews of furthering the African slave trade, but his virulent anti-white statements largely go unreported.

The formula that "blacks cannot be racist" is established primarily by Wittgensteinian meaning shifts. A white acting exclusively for whites is defined as a "racist." A black acting exclusively for blacks is to be given a different "meaning." Black exclusivity is considered to "mean" he is "defending his race against oppression."

As with the "presumption of equal ability" for blacks, however, this imposed perception of "non-racist exclusivity" for blacks must be defended by careful control of information. In objective reality, blacks are capable of a virulent hatred for whites which can, and has, reached barbaric proportions.

In the late '70's in New York's Upper West Side, for example, a black woman who preferred white "boy friends" became pregnant by one of them. Late in the pregnancy she was kidnapped by two unknown street black men, taken to the roof of a building where the two tried to kick the partially-white child to death while still in his mother's womb. They accused the woman of being a "race traitor." The story was known by rumor—the current writer spoke to the woman personally to confirm it—but the information never appeared in print.

Further, as we have already noted, Paul Sheehan, writing in the Sydney *Morning Herald*, used largely suppressed Justice Department figures to show that a massive black-on-white crime wave rolled out the Civil Rights Movement and has now reached a proportion which Sheehan calls a "hidden war." That information has been suppressed in the United States because, as Sheehan stated, "By simply writing this story, by assembling the facts in this way, I would be deemed a racist by the American news media."[54]

Black exclusivity must always be presented as more or less harmless to the dominant group, and if not harmless, at least needed to rectify some long-standing "injustice." The political formula asserts that "racism is a white disease," so information about racially motivated black acts which are unjust or gratuitously brutal must be rigorously suppressed.

Reporter Paul Teetor for the Burlington *Free Press* contradicted the imposed unreality that racism is exclusively white by revealing a racially motivated black act which appeared violent and unjust. He was accused of being "insensitive," meaning he was insufficiently supportive of the required client viewpoint in his story.

Teetor accurately reported that a black mayoral aide had a white woman forcibly restrained and led away from a microphone being made available for public comment. The woman was physically restrained and dragged away from the microphone because she was white. The aide said that the microphone was to be reserved for blacks only. Teetor, who was angered by the manhandling of the woman, violated his obligation to make the violent suppression of speech a "non-event" in his coverage. Perhaps he was confused as to which "client group" his report should favor since the incident had brought a woman into conflict with a "minority." In any case, the black aide complained to the newspaper about the inclusion of the information in the published story. The aide didn't charge that Teetor was inaccurate in reporting the event. He admitted it occurred, but said that it should never have been made public. Teetor was fired for "insensitivity," meaning he included a fact which embarrassed the ideologically-imposed formula that "blacks may be exclusive, but they are never racist." The image of a black "leader" forcibly silencing a woman simply because she was white did not fit the formula.

Clearly, in Teetor's case the suppression of the discomforting fact was not left to voluntary "news judgment" but required a mandatory censorship from reporters, a censorship enforced by the ultimate employment sanction. Servicing the client viewpoint was expected of reporters as a condition of employment. Teetor was shocked by his firing and said that the decision had come directly from Gannett headquarters. He voiced bitterness since he recognized that his job was to represent leftist ideology, and felt that he had functioned well in that capacity in the past. He described himself as "very left of center."[55]

Nor is Teetor the only media person to discover that a conformist "news judgment" which suppresses unwanted information is mandatory. Another case illustrates what can and has happened to media personnel who incorporate ideologically-unwanted information in their programing. In 1993, an editor for the Fox Television station in Washington, D.C., was fired for attempting to bring what he called "ideological balance" to the reporting of news. The editor tried to make sure that his newsroom and news reporters were aware of the conservative viewpoints in their reports. He didn't want to make the reports exclusively conservative, only have that viewpoint represented along with the typical liberal spokesperson routinely approached for comment on news stories. He sought consultation with conservative groups to educate his news people to that viewpoint.[56] Again, attempts to incorporate information mandated for ideological suppression resulted in the elimination of an active journalist.

Finally, even media production personnel, whose jobs require them to make accurate, reality-based observations about racial minorities, may find their jobs in jeopardy if those observations escape the "back room" and find their way into public knowledge. Reality-based observations may not be consistent with the client viewpoint the media requires of all public pronouncements. CBS executive John Pike recently discovered his relationship with the network in jeopardy because of such an observation attributed to him in a magazine article.

Details magazine accused Pike of making "insensitive remarks about African Americans" while he considered the demographics of a late-night Halloween special he was programing. Pike was alleged to have said that blacks should be considered an important part of late-night viewer demographics because many have no jobs, no place to go in the morning, and can therefore stay up late. He also noted that the programing must be short since they have no attention span and find following hour-long dramatic programs difficult.

The truthfulness of Pike's analysis proved irrelevant. It mattered little that Pike's job required him to judge who the potential viewers were, and what type of programing best fit them. Once the magazine made an issue of the alleged analysis, Pike was threatened by the network. CBS Entertainment President Leslie Moonves said that, "If [Pike's remarks] prove to be true, the company will take appropriate action." She said, "CBS finds these alleged statements to be reprehensible."[57]

The media simply will not allow recognition of the fact that a significant proportion of the contemporary black population may be ill-trained public welfare recipients who find it difficult to follow a complex plot line. Not only must such facts be prevented from reaching the network's audience, but even back-office employees like Pike are expected to keep such realities penned in their "back office" and out of public consciousness. Once Pike's recognition of the reality had escaped into print, the executive had to be treated as a "racist" for daring to utter it.

Nor does the media limit itself to firing employees who "misuse" factual information which discomforts ideologically favored client groups. Some political unrealities the media is dedicated to helping establish are rather "fact sensitive," since contradictory information is well-known and easily accessible to the public. In such cases, the media has been known to turn their considerable power and influence to suppress any public expression of the contradictory reality, even by private individuals.

A case in point, of a belief-established unreality which is extremely vulnerable to "common knowledge," is the belief that sodomy or homosexuality is "normal." Anyone with even a minimal knowledge of the "facts of life" can be made to confront the fact that homosexuality is a perversion of a natural biological function. For this reason, the unreal belief in "normalcy" is extremely vulnerable to reality-based correction by almost anyone.

To combat this, the media has worked diligently to make private expressions of the biological facts surrounding sodomy to be socially and legally punished. For example, on the ABC television network program 20/20 of July 9, 1993, it was suggested that expressions of the sentiment that homosexuality is a perversion of the natural order should be suppressed by law. The alleged "news" program was covering a Topeka, Kansas, preacher who habitually held up signs declaring that homosexuality was an abomination and sin in the eyes of God. The ABC "news" personage Hugh Downs, declared the preacher "the most outrageous character we've come across," and one whose "message is hate."

The extreme reaction of Downs to the simple act of holding up a sign calling homosexuality an "abomination" shows how vulnerable the political unreality of "homosexual normalcy" is to commonsense correction. The act of holding a sign expressing that commonsense correction was the most "outrageous" conduct the alleged "news" program had ever encountered.

The other "news" personage on the show, Barbara Walters, suggested such expressions should be made illegal. According to Walters, this reminding of the public that homosexuality was unnatural constituted an attempt to "wipe out the homosexual community...using two powerful weapons—freedom of speech and freedom of religion." Walters then went on to suggest "there should be some kind of law...that protects people against this kind of harassment." She went on the say that "speech rights" should be modified to protect homosexuals from the preacher's signs declaring sodomy to be unnatural and an abomination, descriptions which have the power to factually correct the unreal belief in sodomite "normalcy" in about everyone who sees them. Walters was, of course, right. Reality is, in fact, a threat to homosexuals seeking favored status for themselves and their conduct.

Walters' suggestion, that public remembrances of homosexuality's "unnaturalness" are deserving of punishment as "harassment and hate," is instructive. It demonstrates that the establishment of political unreality is not dependent upon the media alone, but requires complicity with the legal system. Ideologically supportive elements of the judiciary are increasingly aiding the media in generating political unreality. For example, the issue of abortion requires that "realities" must be carefully managed to favor those who support the practice. Probably the most important reality-management goal is the complete suppression of any public acknowledgment of the victims of abortion. The child must cease to exist in the public mind. In the quarter century since legalization, there is not one recorded instance of a picture of a child-victim of abortion appearing in the establishment controlled media.

The Pro Life movement countered this media black-out of abortion victims by printing pictures, often large posters of the bloodied remains of abortion, and displaying them during public demonstrations. This tactic has enraged the press, especially when the pictures are shown to government school students, the ideological purity of whom the media is especially protective.[58]

When pro-lifers in Boise, Idaho, began leafleting the city's public high schools with pictures of aborted children in 1988, the city's Gannett newspaper, the *Idaho Statesman*, conducted a highly "incensed" counter campaign against the pro-lifers. In both editorials and news items the newspaper suggested the pictures were fraudulent. They announced them as "suspect" without once checking with the pro-life group for the source of the photos. It was an "after the fact" reality-management attempt.

Eight years later, the same issue reoccurred in that city, but with an ironic twist which demonstrates how the media uses Wittgensteinian meaning shifts to control information which it cannot suppress. In June of 1996, the pro-life group Operation Rescue again presented posters of the bodies of aborted children to a large rally covered by the city's media. The NBC affiliate showed out-of-focus and unrecognizable pictures of the posters, while allowing a representative for the nation's largest abortion provider, Planned Parenthood of American, to define the "meaning" of the posters and their use. The audience was told that the posters, which included the picture of a decapitated and bloodied head easily recognizable as that of a baby, were probably not real or factual. Further, it was implied by the abortion advocate that the use of such graphic pictures was vulgar and uncivil.

The media allowed those who profit from abortion to impose a "meaning" of their own invention upon the event. They were allowed to cast doubt upon the authenticity of the pictures without demonstrating any concern for documenting either authenticity or inauthenticity. Reality simply didn't matter. They were allowed to shift focus from the victim to those who revealed the victim. The pictures were defined to mean an "offensive exposure of gore," and the public was invited to "take offense," not at those who committed the atrocities, but at those who exposed the atrocities.

Ironically, NBC covered another political event that same evening which also used pictures of "gore," and the difference in "meanings" allowed the two events is instructive. Unlike pro-lifers, the second group possesses a "client relationship" with the media. The second set of "gory pictures" was presented to the media by an "animal rights" rally in Washington, D.C.

A cause favored by the left was presenting pictures of the bodies of animals which had been used in medical experiments. Unlike the pro-lifers, whose posters had been video-taped at a distance and blurred to unrecognizability, these were presented in pristine clarity. Not only were the pictures presented close up and in fine focus, but NBC actually added pictures of "atrocities upon animals" from their own files. Included among the pictures was that of the flayed body of a dog, obviously being dissected. Dissection is a discovery procedure in medical science which literally must destroy the body piece by piece. Of necessity, it is gruesome in appearance.

In the case of the "animal rights" coverage, however, a spokesman for the rally was allowed to provide the "meaning" for the pictures being shown, specifically, that the public had to be made aware of the "atrocities" being committed upon animals by experimental science. The very "meaning" disallowed the pro-lifers was granted the animal rights activists. A spokesman for the group explained to the camera that they had to bring the photos to the public's attention; otherwise, people would not know the "reality" of experimentation upon animals which took place behind the closed doors of labs.

The irony of this back-to-back media coverage should not be lost. The actual grotesque killing of human beings leaving half skulls with still recognizable faces and pulled-apart body pieces is obscured with shifted meanings while the killing of animals in medical experiments, experiments which help prolong human life, is made to seem "grotesque." In the world of media-enforced political unreality, animals are given greater credibility than people.

In California, in 1992, an ideologically aligned judge provided a surer reality suppression technique than the meaning shifts designed to obscure the pictures of abortion victims. Feminist judge Julie Congers, of Albany, California, simply ordered pro-lifer Bob Powers into jail for 30 days, and to cease handing out pro-life literature for three years, because Powers was "convicted" of showing pictures of abortion cadavers to students. Thus the judge determined that students allegedly old enough to "choose" an abortion, would be "emotionally damaged" if they were shown that there are victims to the procedure. The judge suspended Powers' speech rights for three years, to prevent him from breaking the "managed reality" that abortion is victimless, by exposing contradictory evidence.[59]

It may be instructive to digress a bit from our consideration of the media and consider how an ideologically-controlled judiciary system can impose an artificially-constructed "political unreality" upon known facts. Such a case occurred in San Diego, California, where a feminist coalition in the Department of Child Protection and the prosecutor's office subjected an eight-year-old victim of serial rapist Albert Carder, to 13 months of torture to "prove" the child had been raped by her father. Pinning the rape upon the father fit the feminist-desired profile of an "abusive male in relationship." All men are "rapist in patriarch society," according to the line. The father was, by definition, a "patriarch" and thus should be made into the prime suspect. This was no innocent mistake, made in ignorance, but required a continuous effort to ignore and suppress known facts and to "manufacture" new "facts" in order to paint the desired portrait of the father, to wrap him in an artificial reality as "guilty."

Carder was identified from the first as the culprit. Not only did the victim, Alicia, give a detailed description which fit Carder, but the man's footprints were found in the mud outside Alicia's window through which she was abducted for the rape. When feminist social workers accused the "patriarch" James Wade of raping his daughter, Alicia vehemently denied it. In order to create a new "reality," feminist case workers took Alicia from her father and put her under a feminist "therapist" named Kathleen Goodfriend, who spent 13 months in prolonged grilling sessions, attempting to coerce the girl to "confess" that the "patriarch," her father, had raped her.

During this period, a rape-traumatized eight-year-old was taken from her parents and put totally under the control of feminists trying to coerce the desired "confession." During the early part of the torture sessions, Alicia managed to convince a foster mother that the "patriarch" James Wade, her father, had not raped her. This one ally in her now dark feminist-controlled adult social world was soon taken from her. She was removed from the foster-mother after the foster-parent tried to intervene in behalf of the truth. Alicia was placed in a second home managed by a woman who had made a previous agreement to help Goodfriend obtain the "confession."

After thirteen months in a controlled environment which resembled a Soviet-style brainwashing apparatus, Alicia broke and "confessed" that her father had raped her. In later court testimony, however, Alica said she had only "confessed" to end the intense pressure she had been put under. In the meantime, the feminist coalition had looked to manufacture other "evidence" to convict the "patriarch." Wade was forced to pay $250,000 for "therapy" which included being shown pornographic pictures so that observers could record his "arousal state," and thus prove his "perverted" nature. After Wade was charged as a result of the coerced "confession," police determined that DNA in the semen left by the rapist exactly matched that of Carder, the serial rapist, the prime suspect at the time of the crime. Feminist District Attorney, Jane Via, still refused to indict Carder. Despite "a true finding of innocence" by the court, the feminist Via pushed to have Wade's parental rights revoked and to have Alicia permanently adopted. Only then did a San Diego County Grand Jury intervene and prevent the adoption.[60]

Clearly, this is a case of a cadre of ideologues in the judiciary using that system to create an artificial reality coherent with their belief system. They did so in a way which fits the pattern of political unreality. They ignored known contradictory facts, the initial identification of the rapist Carder, and proceeded to construct alternative "facts" to fit the desired "reality." They placed a traumatized eight-year-old child under the absolute social control of those desiring to manufacture the alternative "reality." They then subjected her to intense, unpleasant daily grillings which would only end if she "confessed" to the artificial reality they were seeking to impose. When the girl sought escape from the attempt to impose unreality upon her by appealing to a neutral adult authority figure, they removed that neutral figure from her circle of influence. Even after incontestable physical evidence was brought forward discounting the artificial reality, they still proceeded to act upon the artificial reality. They sought to have the court rule as if it were "real."

One shudders to think what might have happened had the coalition had more power in the police-judiciary, if they had the power, for example, simply to suppress the DNA test which finally broke the conspiracy. A symbolic "patriarch" would have been convicted of a heinous rape, proving that males in authoritative relationships are worse than untrustworthy. Sadly, the feminist conspiracy actually believed in the father's guilt even in the face of the incontrovertible DNA evidence because reality to them is opinion, not fact. This is the Wittgensteinian underpinning of political unreality.

5. The Power of the Media to Impose Artificial Social Images

The historian Otto Scott has observed that the media's ability to impose an "official reality"—that which we have called a political unreality—has created a tension in the general public between their private opinions and public utterances. He alleges that the power of the ideologically-conformist media is now so massive that people are afraid to express any view publicly, other than that imposed by the media.

In an article titled "Conversations" Scott states:

"The fact is that the United States today is a land of closely guarded—not to say fearful—speech. Open expressions of private opinions are aired only within small circles of close and well-known friends. Opinions expressed in groups are considered semiofficial, even when the groups are composed of persons gathered in the name of mutual opinion. Even then, expressions of opinions or observations are oddly similar: Everyone seems (or says) that they think completely alike. Middle and upper class Americans voice their opinions only when they believe they are safe, for there is danger in speaking too freely, if our views are not officially sanctioned. This unpleasant situation prevails even in sectors officially dedicated to free speech. The American majority has lost the pleasures of free and open conversation in a society not only totally permeated by government authority, but obsessed with race, ethnicity, class and politics."[61]

Scott has observed that people have lost their freedom of conversation in exactly one of those areas we have identified as coming under the "reality control" of the socio-fascist ideology. "After all, the term 'political correctness' may be called a joke, but it is, in fact, no joke in our universities, high schools, courts, social, religious and political life. Challengers to this 'correctness' have, through the years, suffered deeply from charges of racism and anti-minority prejudice that have achieved such hurtful power that they soar beyond the need for evidence—or any court protection against libel or slander."

This picture of people being afraid to publicly express an "unapproved" opinion is not new to the twentieth century. It was all too familiar under both Nazi and Communist totalitarianism. Scott is alleging that in areas of "race and ethnicity" the contemporary United States is mimicking one of these totalitarian societies. Apparently the only difference between contemporary socio-fascism and Nazism and Communism is that the former is a "stealth totalitarianism" while the last two "wore their colors" as visible political parties.

If Scott is right, and people are now afraid to express anything but "approved" opinion in the areas of racial differences, or, presumably also in the area of gender differences, or the biological foundations of sexuality, or upon environmental conditions, what brought this about?

Scott's answer is intriguing. He alleges that the media has simply constructed what might be termed an artificial community-life "reality" with false images, an artificial community life which is given more credibility than the factual reality of everyone's actual daily existence. He attributes it to "a huge media fantasy of an America that does not exist, a fantasy in which our social lives are happily [racially] integrated, where Christianity is the front of all bigotry, where the pioneers who founded the West were either murderous rapists, monsters, or craven idiots—and where everyone meekly agrees with political correctness or is a hate-filled racist. *The media has usurped and distorted the voice of America, and become, through the decades, our conversation.* Its echoes are heard when the [socio-fascist] liberals speak; no others are respected." (Italics ours)

Scott argues that this ability to impose an artificial image of American life was achieved by the complete suppression of media outlets which still reflected America as it was. A deliberate destruction of the media giving a semi-realistic image of American life left only those outlets which continuously gave "descriptions of our culture that fit neither everyday observation or experience," which he described as "false descriptions...repetitive,...constant, ...insistent."

Scott traces the demise of "reality oriented" media outlets to the conscious decision of large ad agencies—taken over by leftists in the '50's—to boycott publications which mirrored authentic American life.

He writes:

"Until the 1950's Madison Avenue continued to direct its client's advertising funds into such traditional publications as *The Saturday Evening Post*, *Colliers*, et. al. TV buoyed Ozzie & Harriet....Inside the major New York agencies, the [sentiment that the *Saturday Evening Post* didn't reflect urban, university-trained America] surfaced in a silent boycott of *The Saturday Evening Post*. Although it had one of the largest circulations in the land, its editors were appalled when firms whose advertisements had appeared in its pages for decades were no longer being placed. The huge ad agencies, who had achieved an almost mesmeric control over the direction of the flow of multimillions in ad budgets from major firms, convinced their clients that the *Post's* image of 'small town,' apple-cheeked America no longer existed....The *Post* was doomed. That stunning agency triumph, which wiped out the most popular publication in the land, proved to the coteries of Madison Avenue, that they held unprecedented power in their hands. Working silently behind the scenes, free of intellectual control by the same business sector that trusted them with millions, the agencies could break any established medium, *or create a new one*. That realization in Madison Avenue led to the changes in advertising and publications, and in the tone of the nation's media with which we are now familiar....*Colliers* fell, and in time even *Life*....New publications appeared, fattened with ads: *Mother Jones, New York*...and many others."

Thus we see another facet of the media's power to manipulate politically defined unreality. Not only do they have the power to censor out fact which would embarrass and contradict favored political unrealities, but since they also have the power over the visual image, they can provide artificial "models" for our social life. As Scott so clearly points out, our social "conversations" then become theatrical "dialogues" provided by the media. It is as if we have learned to imagine ourselves on the screens of our televisions or in the pictures in the magazines, and our real-life dialogue is made to mimic that which we have seen there. Those who resist adopting such an artificial public persona, to speak the words of political unreality as if they were our own, are soon intimidated into silence. Their private opinions become divorced from public conversation. In this manner, unreal men are manufactured to inhabit an unreal world.

Scientific Journals and Political Unreality

So far we have demonstrated that an ideologically conformist media services political unreality primarily by suppressing facts which could discount artificial mental formulae and that this service is performed primarily in the interest of favored client social groups. That media also has the power to encourage repetition of those artificial formulae among the public by offering flattering and positive images of those who express them. Further, we have shown that providing such factual-suppression and image-making service to client groups of social fascism is often a condition of employment in the contemporary media. Now we turn to a very specialized part of the media which has become extremely instrumental in establishing unreality in an area supposedly more prone to correcting false ideas with known fact, mainly science.

False science being fed the public in the interest of the environmental movement is, perhaps, one of the primary examples of political unreality. In the first chapter, we examined several examples of false science supplanting observed fact.

But how is this even possible since science may be defined as the falsification or confirmation of ideas through factual tests of those ideas? The testing of ideas through controlled reproducible observation is called the scientific method. Recently, however, this scientific method has been increasingly replaced by another "validator" of the falsity or truthfulness of scientific ideas.

The new "validator" of falsity or truthfulness is becoming the scientific journals of a certain sort. These journals give "prestige" to some ideas, thus tending to validate them, while withholding "credibility" from other ideas, which sinks them into a black memory hole. The ideas given credibility by being chosen for publication, and thus validated, are not so chosen because they ran a gamut of rigorous experimental testing. They are chosen by a vote of a panel, chosen often because the ideas fit a shared ideological agenda. This voting process is called "peer review" and these publications are called "juried publications." They are considered the "most prestigious" place to be published, and appearing in them gives instant credibility.

They are actually something else. They are the method by

which science has lost its experimental validation to become a cheap political process. Voting is a method by which a body politic determines policy, not the way a scientific discipline determines truth.

Dr. Arthur B. Robinson operates the Oregon Institute of Science and Medicine, a research facility which has been set up outside the "scientific establishment" of government-funded universities. He points out the way "peer review"—that is, determining scientific "reality" by means of a vote—and politically-funded science via government grants have worked hand-in-glove to debase science itself. He writes, "There is an unwritten but very strong rule among scientists today to suppress public discussions of most instances of favoritism and outright scientific dishonesty. Tax-based appropriations of private earnings are used to pay a large proportion of scientists. Public discussion of scientific fraud might threaten to close this money spigot...."[62] He suggests that the "peer review" boards are staffed by "scientists" who are, themselves, dependent upon government grants and thus economically committed to furthering the "scientific viewpoint" which keeps those funds flowing. Robinson continues, "Dishonesty in grant applications is virtually a way of life in science today. Those who are entirely honest about their work are at such a competitive disadvantage that they are often not funded....Is it any wonder that the scientific literature is swarming with politically correct, intellectually dishonest articles while most good scientists, afraid of endangering their own grants, look the other way?"

This politicizing of science has been accomplished by a major perversion of the way scientific facts have been historically validated. Science could not simply be "made up" to support politically defined ideas; it had to be perverted first. Scientific "facts" are now less established by the experimental method than by what might be termed "authoritative pronouncement." We have already encountered this phenomenon in the case of F. Sherwood Rowland's "theory" of ozone depletion. We noted that the "theory" has never been validated by scientific experiment because it violates the known laws of chemistry. It was "validated," most recently, by the Swedish Academy, one of whose members said they had given Rowland the Nobel Prize in order to "lay to rest" scientific criticism of the theory. Voodoo chemistry was "validated," not by the experimental method, but by a vote of a supposed "authoritative" committee.

The validation of science by authoritative pronouncement rather than by the experimental method is not unique to Rowland's theory. It is becoming a general principle. Responses by scientists on the Internet to scientific challenges to environmental claims show clearly that authoritative pronouncements now weigh more heavily with them than experimental results. An Internet discussion by scientists, about the facts challenging ozone depletion, shows clearly that they can ignore facts not "approved" by scientific authority.

The occasion of this discussion was the posting of the newsletter *Environment Betrayed*, edited and published by Dr. Edward Krug. Krug was the environmental scientist who proved that the acid rain eco-scare of the mid '80's was a fraud by demonstrating that acid rain was soil-climate related and that the eastern lakes supposedly acidified by the rain had in fact been acidic for centuries before the rise of the alleged pollution said to be causing acid rain. Krug's facts discomforted the politically-imposed "reality" at the time which claimed that acid rain caused by industrial pollution was threatening to deforest the east coast and kill all life in the lakes. His discomforting facts reached the public when he was interviewed on *60 Minutes*, and he is largely credited with unraveling the "death from the skies" political unreality being imposed upon acid rain. It proved personally costly. He has not worked in "official" science since, though he has put out more than 1000 resumés.

He began publishing *Environment Betrayed* which included scientific facts which punctured the environmental mythologies being pushed by establishment science, facts which did not receive attention in the "peer reviewed" official journals. It was Krug who revealed that Rowland's "Nobel Prize" winning "theory" did not and could not meet the scientific empirical test. It was Krug who revealed that the alleged levels of chlorine monoxide in the stratosphere used to support the Rowland "theory" were, in fact, not there, that the instruments that measured them could not measure the compound, and that more precise instruments which could prove those alleged levels simply did not exist. It was Krug who showed that solidly founded atmospheric science from the '50's, science "forgotten" by contemporary politicized "science," showed unequivocally that atmospheric chlorine levels alleged to be "threatening" the ozone and alleged to be "man caused" were, in fact, natural in origin coming from such sources as sea salt and volcanoes.

It was facts like these contained within the pages of *Environment Betrayed* which were posted on the Internet, facts which were largely missing in the "peer reviewed" journals. Responses of establishment scientists to the discovery of such "discomforting" facts is instructive.

Item: "On 9/21...S. Fred Singer...testified before Congress that CFC's were not damaging the ozone layer. I started to look into Mr. Singer's publication list and found the fact that 90% of his work is in non-refereed publications...." Translation: Singer's facts can be ignored since only facts voted by a committee, or "jury," as to validity will be acknowledged. Item: "By references, I mean publications in refereed journals, where the material has been reviewed by those knowledgeable in the field. Examples would be *Nature* or the *Journal of Geophysical Research*. [*Environment Betrayed* where the facts contradicting ozone depletion theory appeared] is, as far as I can tell, a totally unreviewed publication." Translation: Experimental results not presented in "authoritative" publications whose pages are protected by a committee vote can be ignored. "You must admit that a newsletter entitled '*Environment Betrayed*' does not induce in the reader a feeling of objectivity. I hope you won't mind, but I won't check your references unless I come up with them in another context which I consider reliable." Translation: Even references to scientific articles should not be followed unless approved by authoritative pronouncement. Not experimental method, but "approval," determine validity of the articles.[63]

These notes spontaneously posted on the Internet show the working mentality of those currently employed in alleged scientific enterprises. They also demonstrate why voodoo chemistry should be accepted as "true" in the absence of all experimental verification. Contradictory facts are simply not acknowledged unless they have been "validated" by authoritative vote, that is, "juried." Experimental results which are completely reproducible are not acknowledged as "true" unless they have first been "validated" by a "jury" and published in an "authoritative" journal. Even references to past scientific studies will not be read unless they are currently approved by the jury system.

The attack on the formal scientific method by ideologically controlled "science" has reached levels of previously unknown absurdity. One "environmental scientist" whose claims were "authoritatively validated" considered the rigorous application of the scientific method to his "data" to be the occasion for a law suit. Dr. Herbert Needleman of the University of Pittsburgh did studies of "poisonous levels of lead" alleged to be in the water.

His studies were accepted by the Environmental Protection Agency and became the primary source of an EPA campaign against alleged lead pollution. Needleman's research methods, however, came under attack for systematically exaggerating the lead levels. Needleman responded by suing those who critiqued his methodology. He sued both the National Institute of Health and the University of Pittsburgh to prevent them from further inquiring into his methodology. Once validated by the authorities at the EPA, the application of scientific rigor was considered abusive and, incidentally, unnecessary. [64]

6. The Universities and the "Client Viewpoint"

The contribution made by so-called "higher education" to political unreality is even more extensive than that provided by the media. Contemporary universities have manufactured whole fields of bogus "knowledge" in support of ideological clientele. False history has been imposed to flatter blacks, artificial psychology to please feminists and pseudo biology to justify homosexuals. This bogus knowledge follows the rules of political unreality and is immunized from contradictory facts.

The intellectual perversion of the universities is occurring because the university system has increasingly adopted a very peculiar view of how "truth" is determined. The notion that truth is discovered in objective fact, that reality is external to the mind and truth must conform to what that external reality dictates, is now passé. More and more, truth is considered to be *subjective* phenomena in the sense that a human viewpoint creates or makes something "true." Truth is considered an artifact of the mind, not as something essential to a reality which exists independent of the mind. This view became pervasive after Ludwig Wittgenstein taught the universities to use language subjectively rather than objectively.

"Truth" is being determined more by *who* says it, than by *what* is being said. To our contemporary crop of post-civilized intellectuals, all reality has been reduced to subjective mental states. They believe that an objective-based reality either is unknowable, or more likely, doesn't exist. To the post-civilized mind there are as many "realities" as there are possible opinions.

The only way to select from among a barrage of competing "realities" is to consider the source. "Reality" must be determined by sympathy and sentiment. The "reality" of supposed "oppressed" groups is preferred to the "reality" of their supposed oppressor. In this manner, what we call the "client viewpoint" of those groups sponsored by the ideology of social fascism have come to define "truth" for much of the university community, and this "truth" is immune to factual correction. It is the method by which the bogus fields of knowledge have been built.

To digress for just a moment, it must be said that the rise of artificial knowledge and bogus fields in the universities have not occurred because of political ideology alone. Social-fascist ideology merely took advantage of a much quieter revolution, one in the philosophy of knowledge. The universities first learned to disbelieve in objective truth. Only then could client viewpoints, as dictated by social fascism, replace objective standards. The existence of client viewpoints creating artificial realities in the universities can be well documented. The success of such a revolution in knowledge, however, cannot be fully understood without addressing the earlier philosophical revolution in the use of language led by Wittgenstein.

Artificial "facts" generated by client viewpoints, specifically those of racial minorities, feminists, homosexuals and pantheistic nature worshipers are rapidly replacing authentic knowledge painfully gathered by rigorous academic research. A mindless conformity to this process has been enforced by the establishment of "star chamber" type tribunals on university campuses which punish objectors as "oppressors" of the client group the viewpoint is allegedly supporting. This process has become known as "political correctness."

A few books, however, have appeared exposing the corrupting influence of the undeserved authority given an artificial "viewpoint." Such "viewpoints" are created to support social fascism's client groups. Some are written by university outsiders. Others are penned by courageous university professors whose commitment to objective fact is stronger than any impulse towards self-servicing careerism. Lynne Cheney is one of the outsiders.

Cheney was the head of the National Endowment for the Humanities under the Reagan presidency. She holds a Ph.D. in English and has taught at several small colleges. At the time of her appointment, however, she was the wife of former Secretary of Defense Richard Cheney, and was a Washington-based "outsider" to the contemporary universities. When she became NEH head, she brought 10-year-old academic standards to the job, standards which provoked intense conflict with contemporary college faculties. That conflict led to a book about current philosophical mind-set on the university campuses.

In her book, *Telling the Truth*, Cheney writes:

"What I gradually came to understand was that in the view of a growing number of academics, the truth was not merely irrelevant, it no longer existed. They had moved far beyond the ideas that have shaped modern scholarship—that we should think of the truth we hold today as tentative and partial, recognizing that it may require rethinking tomorrow in light of new information and insight to the view that there is no truth....As these academics saw it, all those things that we think are true are really the constructs of dominant groups, the creations of the powerful."[65]

The Cheney book documents the politics of unreality as practiced on contemporary university campuses. She reveals how client viewpoints are supplanting authentic subject matter. The well-known client groups are given academic departments, and the "fields of knowledge" which they put forth from these departments are really only artificial client-group viewpoints, viewpoints which are held to no rigorous academic standards and which are often excused from any requirement to present authentic knowledge in support of them. The client viewpoint itself becomes defacto "knowledge" and is presented as such. The departments which have been gratuitously added to universities are, of course, "black studies," "women's studies," and most recently "gay [*sic.*] and lesbian studies."

Cheney reveals how the client viewpoint—or what might be termed the mind set of minorityism—is presented as a synthetic knowledge in "women's studies." Peggy McIntosh, for example, is associate director of Wellesley College's Center for Research on Women. She teaches that the different thought processes characteristic of men and women are really virtues and vices, the female thought process being virtuous and the male being something of a vice. She alleges that "white males" exhibit what she calls "vertical thinking" while the client groups of women and minorities use "lateral thinking." Vertical thinking is bad. Lateral thinking is good.

According to McIntosh, vertical thinking is what "makes white males dangerous to themselves and the rest of us— especially in a nuclear age." Vertical thinking is allegedly "bad" because it is directed towards excellence in performance. It is supposedly designed for "winning" and "advancement." "Vertical thinking" is pragmatically objective, that is, it is an attempt to accurately identify the elements of reality so they can be successfully manipulated towards a goal. It is objective, closely tied to the real world, and this disturbs McIntosh and her feminist cohorts.

She much prefers an emotive, subjective type of thought which she calls "lateral thinking. " Lateral thinking is allegedly virtuous because it puts women and minorities "in a decent relationship with the universe."[66] It is emotional thought which redefines the world to satisfy the feelings. It is the kind of thought which calls a cripple "physically challenged" or the death of an unborn child via abortion "reproductive health care." The world is mentally formulated not by the discovery of objective external conditions, but by the "need" to feel a certain way about those conditions.

Actually, McIntosh's "lateral thinking" is simply applied Wittgensteinianism. The world is made to "be" what someone wants to "feel" about it. Subjective emotions shape and define reality, not objective fact.

McIntosh's distinction between "vertical vs. lateral thinking" actually juxtaposes reality-based thought with non-reality-based thought. In so doing, she gives us insight into the driving force behind much of political unreality. Her belief that emotions should determine the outcome of thought is absurd on the surface. To confuse "feelings" with "thinking" is an absurdity made possible by Ludwig Wittgenstein.

Thinking is a process of mentally manipulating concepts, that is words, to perceive new relationships, primarily in the objective world. We may have an emotional reaction to our thoughts, but that emotional reaction is not, per se, "thinking." Emotions can only be confused with "thinking" when they have the power to control the outcome of thought, that is when "meanings" can be imposed upon the world according to our feelings. This is, of course, exactly what Wittgenstein taught. All "meanings" are supposedly subjectively imposed, therefore directly under the control of feelings.

McIntosh becomes an advocate for feelings as a form of thought because the emotional/sentimental realm is supposedly a strength of a "client group," in this case women. She gratuitously adds that "minorities" are also strong in the area of emotional/sentiment-driven thought and are also practitioners of the "virtue" of "lateral thinking." Minorities are granted that high status because they are also clients and MUST share the thinking "virtue" denied the "anti-client" group of white males. The supposed female virtue of emotional sympathy is alleged to drive a more refined form of thought than the objective, goal-oriented and success-driven thoughts of men.

Actually this confusion of emotional sympathy with thought, denies the reality of both mental processes and creates a hostility between the two that does not exist. The doctor who objectively treats the wound does not take away from the mother who comforts her crying child. Objective, rational thought is directed toward a successful operation upon the external world. To give it a new name with a pejorative component is not creating "new knowledge." It is merely masquerading anti-male ideology as "knowledge."

We have, however, already encountered numerous examples of McIntosh's "lateral thinking" establishing political unreality. An emotional reaction to nature, a sympathy for "holy mother earth," is the driving force behind environmentalism and we have seen how thought formulated by that sympathy has corrupted objective science. Similarly, sympathies for minorities—the emotional desire to treat them as "equals" in all areas of human endeavor—has led to an inability to factually appreciate minority-group limitations and has created false standards and expectations for them as a whole. In several instances, minorities promoted by such "sympathies" to positions beyond their capacity to perform have reacted violently. In New Orleans, a failed black pilot went berserk and was violently constrained from crashing a plane into an airline office building. In several universities, administrators have been shot by blacks admitted under "affirmative action" policies but who could not perform the work.

McIntosh is joined by other university feminists in the gender-advocacy viewpoint which characterizes objective thought as an undesirable masculine mental process. Harvard psychologist Carol Gilligan wrote a book in collaboration with other feminists called *Women's Ways of Knowing*. In that book objectivity is called a "male construct." It is "a male sphere where abstract principles, intellect, rationality and logical thinking are valued."[67] Gilligan and the sisterhood advocate that the "male construct" of objectivity should be suppressed in education. It should be replaced by female "ways of knowing." Allegedly the woman's ways of gaining knowledge are "feelings, emotions and intuition." If it "feels" right or is "intuitively" believable, then it must be true.

Feminist hatred for the objective rationality which appeals to external facts—the foundation of all Western science and all authentic scholarship—is so strong that Sandra Harding suggests that Newton's *Principia* should be called a "rape manual."[68] They want objective rationality, now redefined as a "white male" thought process, to be suppressed in educational contexts. These women are urging that the client viewpoint must reign supreme in academia, that even rational science itself should be suppressed if its thought processes make women uncomfortable and at a competitive disadvantage.

It is obvious that "women's studies" are making a direct assault upon reality-based scholarship. Such scholarship is irrelevant to their purposes. Feminists are demanding that what is now passed off as "knowledge" in the university should consist of the advocacy of their viewpoint. Objective facts are largely irrelevant to this lawyer-like advocacy. Women's Studies departments are quite blunt in asserting that they want client advocacy and not objective scholarship in their curriculum. The Women's Studies department at Pennsylvania State University has made this clear—in writing.

At Penn State, the Women's Studies department informed other academic departments that courses would only be cross-listed with Women's Studies if they met the following conditions: They had to "recognize the existence of patriarchal structures in defining values and social roles;" and "empower women students to seek their own paths and define themselves as entities separate and apart from roles that patriarchal societies dictate."[69]

The Women's Studies department at Penn State was demanding that other departments desert data-dictated research conclusions in favor of the ideologically patterned thought which we have identified as the feminist "client viewpoint." No body of independent research has either discovered or confirmed these "patriarchal structures" which henceforth must be recognized as having "existence."

In reality, "patriarchal structures" are simply ideological reinterpretations being imposed upon such well-known institutions as marriage, the church and family. They are being described as "patriarchal" because of the historical/cultural/biological roles assigned men. Feminists demand a complete separation from such historical/cultural/biological masculinity. We have already seen how far they are willing to go in this, since they reject objective thought itself as a "male construct" and "patriarchal." This is advocacy, not discovery and they demand that "reality" must be defined to support the advocacy.

No authentic research which opposes the dictated "reality" would be tolerated. For example, no objective study of the rarity of matriarchy, its basic social instability and poverty would be allowed by the Penn State criteria. No study of the modern "matriarchy" in contemporary black society would be acceptable, since it is being imposed by a massive illegitimacy rate and the breakdown of the black-male economic role in the family. It is imposing a grinding poverty and a dangerous criminal environment upon black females and their children. Such a study would not be tolerated since it wouldn't "empower women" to define themselves as separate from "patriarchal society." The truth would lead to an unacceptable conclusion. The fall of such a "patriarchy" has led to disaster for American blacks.

The feminist complaint that objective thought is a damnable "male construct" has actually been successful in suppressing rigorous and demanding teaching in authentic academic areas. In 1993, statistician David Goldberg was punished by his department at Michigan State University when feminist-led students agitated against Goldberg's teaching methods. A difficult examination Goldberg had given led to a confrontation during which students demanded to know what "right" Goldberg had to administer a test which "presumed a variance of ability among his students." Goldberg was also accused of being demanding and confrontational in urging his students toward excellence. This was called "an academic form of social exclusion" when applied to women and minorities who "operate from a position of powerlessness."

Goldberg, you see, was imposing a "male construct" when he demanded objective performances from his students, when he gave intellectually difficult questions and demanded accurate answers. As punishment for the violation, Goldberg was removed from teaching any required courses by his department chairman. He was not serving the client viewpoint being demanded even of mathematicians these days.

None of these "fields of study" defined by the client viewpoint resemble traditional fields of study in anything but name. Traditional fields of study represent decades, if not centuries, of contributions to the understanding of objectively defined phenomena. One need only mention a few concrete examples to authenticate this statement: History and its sub-fields; Chemistry and its sub-fields; Mathematics and its sub-specialties. All of these represent an authentic corpus of knowledge founded upon multiple contributions over long periods of time, answering questions which were previously raised by earlier knowledge in the field. No one demanded that the findings establish a comfort zone for privileged social groups being held in clientage. No one has until now. These are authentic fields of study and bear only superficial, if any, resemblance to the pseudo "fields" recently established by the socio-fascist left.

The pretender fields were established by raw political power to serve a clientele and contain no authentic corpus of knowledge. They only serve an ideological predisposition. They use the now familiar process of client advocacy to "fill in" a body of "knowledge" where none existed. This invention process is what seems to so offend Lynne Cheney.

She mentions, for example, Leonard Jeffries, chairman of the "Black Studies" department at City College of New York. Jeffries invented a politically-inspired "history" which was not only immune to contradictory fact—our definition of political unreality—but Jeffries insisted his invented "history" be taught in government schools. Jeffries' "history" has no need to be tied to authentic documentation. Such "history" does not need to have actually happened. It need only be written to support the "client status" of American blacks. The purpose of history is to establish the client viewpoint, to establish the perception of blacks as perpetual victims and whites as perpetual victimizers. Fact and accuracy are irrelevant to ideologically patterned thought which immunizes itself from correction by contradictory data. Jeffries offers the following ideologically patterned formula for the "history" of white Europeans: the "Crusades and the corruption of the Roman Catholic Church" has produced "negative values" in Europeans, which consist of "greed, racism, and national egoism" and has moved them to "discover, invade and conquer."

Authentic history, of course, knows none of this demonization of white Europeans as the bearers of all evil in the human race. Even a casual acquaintance with the crusades reveals them as a little more complex than Jeffries' simplistic characterization of them as some kind of ultimate dark force in the human experience. In reality, the crusades were a curious mixture of greed and piety. The crusades ran the gamut from the tragic "Children's crusade" which sought to influence Islam by the simple piety of thousands of children marching unarmed into oblivion, to the sacking and looting of Christian Constantinople by fellow Christians. And nowhere in the doctrines and practices of the Roman Church can be found proscriptions for armed conquest. Jeffries must be confusing Christianity with Islam which does have a doctrine of armed conversion, a doctrine which swept Christianity from its strongholds in Palestine and North Africa and which ultimately provoked the Crusades.

If Roman Catholicism explains the "negative values" of Europeans, then what explains them for the African Zulus who swept down from the north to drive the native, non-Negroid Bushmen from their homes, or the armed aggressions of the Mongols, the Babylonians, the Egyptians, the Aztecs and the Incas? What about the conquests of Asian barbarians like Genghis Khan whose armies exterminated whole cities, reminiscences of which we recently viewed in the modern African state of Rwanda.

Christian European conquests were mild in comparison. The populations of Spanish speaking America are still largely Indian in ethnic composition and in English speaking America there are as many, if not more, native Indians today than at the time the Europeans arrived on the American continent. The European conquest eliminated many savage customs which victimized the native populations themselves. The brutal cannibalism of the Caribs was ended in the Caribbean, as were the massive slaughters on Aztec pyramids. Christianity ended the ritual child sacrifice among Indians in early Virginia, as described in John Smith's writings, as well as the custom of ritualized torture common to many tribes in North America.

The point is that the rich mosaic of authentic historical facts cannot support the simplistic political formula served up as "history" by an "academic" department which was established for the sole purpose of ideologizing blacks as "perpetual victims" and whites as "perpetual victimizers." Jeffries' "history" of white Europeans is just another political unreality which he wants forced upon school children by government edict.

Nor is Jeffries' political unreality the only absurdity invented to give artificial substance to a make-believe "academic" field serving the client viewpoint. Something called "African-American curricula" are produced by university "Black Studies" departments for government schools, and these curricula routinely maintain, against known historical facts, that ancient Egypt was a "black culture," and that this "black civilization" was stolen by white Europeans. A black classics professor at Howard University, Frank Snowden, has proven this to be nonsense.[70] To claim that a black Nubian province above Upper Egypt made the nation "black" is equivalent to saying that a Latin presence in U.S. held Puerto Rico makes this country Spanish American. It is simply another political unreality which is immune to correction by known factual data.

The known and well-established facts of Egyptian history are being suppressed and ignored in the interest of this client viewpoint. Nubia was indeed a province inhabited by blacks and located above the second cataracts of the Nile. Nubia was never a part of Egypt proper, but it was the policy of most ancient Pharaohs to control Nubia for security reasons, as they likewise fought to control Libya to the west. It was true that in the twilight of ancient Egypt a Nubian dynasty did rule Egypt. They followed a Libyan dynasty. The occupation occurred after the Chaldeans crushed the might of Egypt and formerly conquered peoples found the opportunity to subjugate the center of the stricken empire. It was similar to the period of the dying Roman empire when formerly subjugated German tribes were able to attack and sack a toothless and aged Rome.

The idea that ancient Egypt was ethnically "black" or Negroid at any time in its history is an absurdity which requires suppression of scholarly knowledge and a kind of willful ignorance even to assert. The ethnic composition of the ancient Egyptians was definitely known by the turn of this century. Authentic scholars are surer of the ethnicity of ancient Egypt than they are of the history of the kingdom. Not only did the Egyptians leave massive amounts of art depicting themselves and their appearance, but a study of the bones in thousands of graves and tombs enabled scientists to trace the ethnic origins and even physical changes the people had undergone.

An early Encyclopedia Britanica identifies this clearly. "The early civilization of Egypt shows remarkable coincidences with that of Babylonia, the language is of a Semitic type .... According to the evidence of the mummies, the Egyptians were of slender build, with dark hair and of Caucasian type. Dr. Elliott Smith, who has examined thousands of skeletons and mummies of all periods, finds that the prehistoric population of Upper Egypt, a branch of the North African-Mediterranean-Arabian race, changed

with the advent of the dynasties to a stronger type, better developed
than before in skull and muscle. This was apparently due to
admixture with the Lower Egyptians, who themselves had been
affected by Syrian immigration. Thereafter little further change
is observable....The Egyptian artists of the New Empire assigned
distinctive types of features as well as of dress to the different
races with which they came into contact, Hittites, Syrians,
Libyans, Bedouins, Negroes, etc."[71]

By 1910 it was known that the ancient Egyptians were Middle
Eastern Caucasians, whose last ethnic change occurred just
before the rise of the first Pharaoh, and who remained ethnically
constant through the full period of the ancient kingdom. In their
art, the Egyptians differentiated themselves from Negroes whom
they portrayed as being of a different and alien race. These facts
are no longer allowed in the Universities, as the client viewpoint
requires the Egyptians be considered black Africans. One now
has to consult 1910 Encyclopedias to even find the data reported.

"Black Studies" departments abound in such political
unrealities made up to provide a pseudo "corpus of knowledge"
for the pseudo "academic discipline." It is asserted, without
evidence, that the Ptolemaic queen Cleopatra from the period the
Greeks ruled Egypt was black. It is also asserted that Socrates was
black and that Aristotle "stole" his philosophy from the "black"
library in Alexandria Egypt. It is also asserted that blacks first
discovered America.

Never mind that there is no supporting evidence for these
claims. Like all political unrealities they are true by ideology and
are immune to contradictory fact. It is irrelevant that the library
in Alexandria, Egypt, was not built before Aristotle's time. It is
irrelevant that the Ptolemies who ruled Egypt kept strict racial
allegiance to their Greek lineage in marriage. It matters not at all
that no record identifies Socrates as black and many treat him as

an Athenian Greek. The practitioners of political unreality are immune to such factual correction. All of these absurdities are currently taught in the District of Columbia government schools and the largely black Prince George County school system in neighboring Maryland.[72]

A professor of Greek classics at Wellesley College has explained how the political unrealities used to create a bogus corpus of knowledge in "Black Studies" are effectively undermining the authentic discipline of history. Mary Lefkowitz writes in her book *Not Out of Africa,* "Afrocentrism [the foundational philosophy of black studies] not only teaches what is untrue; it encourages students to ignore chronology, to forget about looking for material evidence, to select only those facts that are convenient, and *to invent facts whenever useful or necessary.*" (Italics, ours)

Lefkowitz goes on, however, and correctly identifies the emergence of this political unreality as being made possible by a changing outlook of the whole of the academic community. She writes, "There is a current tendency, at least among academics, to regard history as a form of fiction that can and should be written differently by each nation or each ethnic group. The assumption seems to be that *somehow all versions will simultaneously be true,* even if they conflict in particular details." (Italics, ours)

In short, Lefkowitz is charging that the emergence of these pseudo disciplines with their bogus corpus of knowledge was made possible by a general desertion of all notions of "objective truth" upon the university campuses. Academics in general now see invented "history" which conflicts with known facts as legitimate. Truth is no longer determined by objective data, but is a "viewpoint" or an "opinion." Sympathy for the group which is alleged to hold that "opinion" now makes something "true." The black Egypt myth is accepted as "true" because a minority group held in clientage wants to believe it is true. As we have seen, there is reason behind this university-wide acceptance of "truth" as established by "viewpoint" and it consists of the Wittgensteinian philosophical shift which began occurring thirty years earlier.

It may be instructive to find out what happens to academics like Lefkowitz who still insist upon an objective factual history and try to correct favored political unrealities with contradictory data. She tells what happened when she tried to correct a "Black Studies" instructor who was telling students that the Greek philosopher Aristotle "stole" his ideas from the "black" library at Alexandria, Egypt. She writes, "So far as I knew, and I had studied the subject, Aristotle never went to Egypt, and while the date of the library of Alexandria is not known precisely; it was certainly built some years after the city was founded, which was after both Aristotle's and Alexander's deaths." When she asked "Black Studies" expert Yosef A.A. ben-Jochannan how Aristotle "stole" ideas from a library not yet in existence, the "black studies" expert said he "resented the tone of the inquiry." She was later charged with "racism" by several students for asking the question and accused of being "brainwashed by white historians." Lefkowitz told the *Washington Times* that since publishing her book which challenges "Black Studies" political unrealities with established historical facts, the charges of "racism" have intensified.[73]

What happened when Lefkowitz took her concerns to fellow historians, when she complained that the viewpoint of a racial clientele was replacing fact in the reconstruction of history? She was pressured to accept the verdict of the client viewpoint. She writes, "So it seemed to me that being called a racist was not my principal problem, false and unpleasant as the charges were. Such attacks could easily be repelled, as long as my colleagues were prepared to reconstruct what happened in the past on the basis of historical evidence. The trouble was that some of my colleagues seemed to doubt that there was such a thing as historical evidence, or that even if evidence existed, it did not matter much one way or the other, at least in comparison with what they judged to be the pressing cultural issues and social goals of our own time. When I went to the then dean of the college to explain that there was no factual evidence behind some Afrocentric claims about ancient history, she replied that each of us had a different but equally valid view of history. When I stated at a faculty meeting that Aristotle could not have stolen his philosophy from the library of Alexandria in Egypt, because that library had not been built until after his death, another colleague responded, 'I don't care who stole what from whom.' How could I persuade these colleagues, and many others like them, that evidence does matter, that not every interpretation of the past is equally probable, and that I was not trying to teach about the history of the ancient world in order to preserve or transmit [white] racist values?"[74]

In other words, the concept of history as "viewpoint" had been given ultimate authority. History is only considered a representation of such viewpoints, and the historian's job is to decide which "viewpoint" should rule. For every client viewpoint there must be, of necessity, an anti-client viewpoint, since social clientship is established to protect from alleged hostility against the client group on the part of the dominant culture. Citing facts which contradict the client viewpoint is merely the anti-client viewpoint. Reality is irrelevant.

Lefkowitz has proven that the invention of facts to support "history" from a client viewpoint is directly connected to perceived psychological needs of the client group. She uses by way of example the Afrocentric artificial assertion that the Ptolemaic Queen Cleopatra was black. Lefkowitz doesn't contest the absurd historical unreality that the Egyptians were a "black" race, she merely argues that the Ptolemaic rulers of conquered Egypt were Greek. Cleopatra was a Greek, not ethnically Egyptian. Yet the major high school resource for "Black Studies," The African American Baseline Essays put out by the Portland, Oregon school systems says, "Cleopatra VII ... was of mixed African and Greek parentage." This assertion, now a standard line in the black "client viewpoint" of Egyptian history, is founded upon no evidence save a single reference in the fictionalized play, *Anthony and Cleopatra,* by Shakespeare. The sixteenth century English playwright called Cleopatra "swarthy." This is in keeping with the way evidence is generally used to establish the "black Egypt" artificial history. A few ambiguous references in ancient texts are substituted for the massive evidence of the Egyptian tombs and their art treasures. In place of the study of thousands of Egyptian skeletons by Smith which we discussed earlier, we are offered a few lines of Herodotus to establish the ethnic "identity" of Egyptians. The ancient Greek Herodotus identified a group of people living on the Black Sea as Egyptians because they were dark and curly headed, terms which could as easily be applied to Semitic types as to Negroes. Yet we are assured this means the Egyptians were "black Africans."

In any case, evidence is irrelevant to the belief in Cleopatra's "blackness." That belief comes from other motives. The black classics professor Shelley Haley of Hamilton College has identified that motive. Haley has rejected her training in the classics which indicated that Cleopatra was Greek in favor of a new client viewpoint, the "black Cleopatra" myth. The new "knowledge" was not forced upon her by the data. She writes that the new understanding required a struggle between "my yearning to fit in among classicists and my identity politics."[75] By her own admission, "identity politics"—that is, affiliation with and allegiance towards the racial social group by supporting its need for group pride, required that Haley accept the "black Cleopatra" myth. This was done in the face of the evidence provided by her classical training. New "knowledge" for old. Identity politics and client viewpointism for objective fact and documented data.

There is an irony in all of this. Black's are being fed artificial histories in order to increase racial pride and to intensify hostility against whites with invented offenses. Yet authentic black history with contemporary significance is being ignored in the process. Few blacks recognize that "Afrocentrism" and "black studies" are themselves products of a hidden white manipulation of their fortunes. These phenomenon are clearly tied to the "blacks as perpetual victims" ideology put forth by the National Association for the Advancement of Colored People (NAACP). It is never revealed in most "black studies" departments that the NAACP was organized by whites to crush an indigenous black leader and his movement.

Shadowy white liberals built the NAACP and its "victimology" near the turn of the century. They used the black communist W.E.B. du Bois as a figurehead. They built the organization to oppose Booker Washington who argued that blacks would not really be free from slavery until they freed themselves economically. Washington established the self-help movement, named the "Tuskegee Movement" after the university he headed. He urged blacks to worry less about white attitudes and more about gaining real economically-based skills and assets. The hidden white leadership of the NAACP used their contacts in the white press to bury Washington and his self-help philosophy, while pushing the "black victim, white guilt" ideology of the NAACP and giving prominence to du Bois.

Tony Brown, the black social commentator on PBS, said in his book, *Black Lies, White Lies*, "The liberal whites who controlled the early NAACP and their handpicked black leaders shunned free-market competition with other ethnic and racial groups and, instead, advocated dependence on the largess of government and white people. This socialistic and assimilationist philosophy has influenced everything from legislation to literature, and it has been corrupt from its earliest days." [76] Du Bois is called "the protégé of those whites who were the dominant organizers of the black protest movement."

Many of the gains blacks had made under Washington's influence, especially in the skilled trades, were lost. Today blacks suffer an illegitimacy rate of nearly 70%—the legacy of state welfare—and masses of fatherless young men, with little or no economically tradable skills, seethe hatred against whites and invest their own lives in deadly criminal gangs. Telling them that Western Civilization was invented by blacks and stolen by whites may increase this hatred, but it will do nothing to change their circumstances, circumstances which might have been otherwise if Washington had not been suppressed.

The inclination to "invent knowledge" is not limited to the pseudo disciplines and the bogus departments—feminist or black "studies"—which have been established under the political sponsorship of the socio-fascist ideology. That corruption is also being manifested in traditional departments. Increasingly, universities are no longer places where knowledge is accumulated and the wisdom of the ages is reposited. They have become a refuge for knaves who impose their versions of invented unrealities upon captive and ignorant students.

Under the tenure system the practice of inventing pseudo fields of knowledge has extended to the individual classroom. This has been made possible by a perversion of the tenure system. Universities are the only employers who guarantee a privileged portion of their work force immunity from discharge. Granting "tenure" to a university faculty member means he can't be fired, period. In turn, this means the professor cannot be held to any standard of performance, objective or otherwise.

Professor of Economics Thomas Sowell is also a syndicated newspaper columnist and has explained in one such column how tenure is currently being practiced. "Tenure turns ordinary professors into little tin gods....Many turn their classrooms into propaganda centers for their pet ideologies, instead of teaching the subject listed in the catalog. ...Some teach about what they happen to be writing about, rather than what is fundamental to the fields. Thus a history department may have a course on the history of movies, but no course on the history of France or Germany, and a philosophy department may have no course on logic but several courses on feminist philosophy."

According to Dr. Roger Schultz, a history professor from Virginia, the whole of academic history is currently being defined by social fascism. Writing about the 1996 meeting of the American Historical Association Shultz states, "There is a prevailing attitude that American history is driven by racism, sexism and classism, and that history is the story of how exploited minorities struggle against dominant power structures."[77] That is, the alleged grievances of the client groups of socio-fascism have supplanted the factual history of the nation.

Even on the broadest level, such "history" is made artificially since the authentic purpose of the study of history is to explain current national conditions by past events. When the National Standards for United States History emphasized the "underground railroad figure," Harriet Tubman, and completely ignored Robert E. Lee in the period of the War of Southern Succession, that selection of material represents ideological sentiment, not valid historical perception.[78] The influence of Tubman on the events of that period was minimal, even if the contemporary left finds her aid to runaway slaves admirable. Lee, on the other hand, made a major impact upon the events of the period, and one is hard pressed to understand how any student could understand that war with Lee excluded.

U.S. history is being made to mimic Soviet history as it was formerly dictated by the Communist Party. As with Soviet history, "heroes of the ideology" are made to parade through vaguely understood historical periods while authentic figures of the period are either trashed or forgotten altogether. The purpose is to make "history" justify and legitimate the current ideology, and thus create an artificial but ideologically utilitarian "knowledge" of the past. Incidentally, it also completely cuts a people off from their roots.

A look at the details of the American Historical Association convention shows how far the "scholars" have gone in trashing authentic history in the interest of an artificial substitute. Subjects included such things as the emergence of a special "identity" among Latin American lesbians in American cities and the alleged need of those lesbians to hide that identity. Also included was a paper exposing the hidden prejudice against lesbians in debates over Federal child-care programs from 1917-1929. Another paper examined Southern homosexuals and their alleged suffering at the hands of "red neck" culture. In all these cases, the "focus" of history became alleged "oppression" of a client group favored by social fascism. History is reduced to a cheap melodrama of "good guys" and "bad guys" as defined by the prevalent ideology.

The theme was introduced in the opening plenary session when the black "historian" and former politician, Julian Bond, transfigured a significant event in recent American history into an ideologically-patterned formula. Bond told the historians that the bomb which took out a federal office building in Oklahoma City in April of 1995 was caused by "entrenched white supremacy."

Bond's charge is a classic case of political unreality ignoring contradictory facts. In the Oklahoma City bomb case, the federal government has charged that alleged bomber Timothy McVeigh acted to gain vengeance for the deadly federal attack upon the Branch Davidian church in Waco, Texas in 1993. The bomb exploded on the second anniversary of the Waco assault. Federal propaganda after the bombing has been directed at the militia and Constitutional movements. These movements had been pointing to Waco to claim that the federal government has usurped dictatorial and unconstitutional authority. After the bombing, they brought forth evidence and witnesses to suggest the federal government itself may have been implicated in the explosion by having an agent within the McVeigh group. Patriotic groups charged that the government used McVeigh as a "fall guy" to implicate them in an atrocity. Race is not the issue. Federal power is.

For University of Virginia "historian" Bond, however, the reality behind the bombing is irrelevant. The bombing was a traumatic event for the public, one which was emotionally stirred by intense media coverage. Bond simply wanted to attach the massive negative reaction against the bombing to the ideological "bogy man" used to establish the victimization status of blacks. Factual reality provided no significant inhibition to this purpose. For Bond, "reality" is what he can direct people to believe about the bombing, not what actually occurred. Such belief provides him with power and influence. Facts do not.

For a significant portion of contemporary universities, reality is malleable, something which can be manipulated and changed to meet political ends. We have seen this in the hard sciences where absurd theories, even data, are made up to provide support for the "disaster scenarios" which environmentalists parlay into power and influence. We have seen it in history departments where facts are invented; where false interpretations which are easily contradicted by real facts are accepted; and where any commitment to authentic bodies of knowledge is deserted in favor of bogus substitutes dictated by political ideology.

Given that these conditions exist, some obvious questions are raised. Primary among them is the simple "why?" Are we dealing with a massive collection of rogues who desert the truth to gain some personal advantage? Are we confronting a plague of mental aberrations akin to mass insanity? Are the practitioners a society of cynical con men who know better? Or are they simply deceived and, if so, why do they act so systematically to suppress those who offer factual correction? Why is Dr. Edward Krug, the environmental gad-fly, an unemployed pariah in academia; and why is Dr. Mary Lefkowitz, the corrector of Afro-centric pseudo-history, systematically assaulted as a "racist?"

The answer, I am afraid, is both ugly and instructive. These practitioners of political unreality are also true believers. They are passionately committed to their unrealities and vigorously attack anyone who tries to correct them by appealing to objective truth. It is clear that they do not share a commitment to objective fact as the determiner of reality, a commitment which heretofore has been the foundation of Western science and culture. They consider those who hold such a commitment to possess just another "political viewpoint," and one hostile to their own.

Practitioners of what we have described as pseudo-knowledge in the universities have been quite candid about identifying belief in objective truth to be a hostile political opinion. In an article in the *Campus Report, Washington Times* reporter Stephen Goode writes, "Inspired by Harvard professor Carol Gilligan's book, *In a Different Voice,* and other feminist texts, many influential feminists at American universities have declared that such concepts as objectivity and excellence are 'male constructs,' and therefore things to be avoided at all costs." [79] Those who appeal to objective facts to correct political unrealities are merely allied with the "patriarchy" and may be ignored or attacked as enemies of feminism.

George Roche is President of Hillsdale College, a school which has sustained a vigorous defense of the knowledge and methods of classic Western culture. Roche's book, *The Fall of the Ivory Tower*, identifies the trends which he believes have ruined American universities. It was named the Book of the Year by *Insight* magazine in 1994 and has received positive reviews in such publications as *Forbes*, the *Wall Street Journal* and *Reader's Digest*. As a college president, a professor of history and a member of the National Council on Educational Research, Roche has been intimately acquainted with the corrupting changes which have swept academia in the last three decades.

He writes, "[Political correctness] advocates also tell us that truth really isn't objective at all; it depends on our point of view. One person's truth is supposed to be just as good (or, more to the point, just as unreliable) as another's. What has passed off as 'truth' are merely the collective prejudices of the dominant ruling class and culture. We must be shown how to 'deconstruct' what we think is true." [80]

As Roche notes, the leftist takeover of American campuses was achieved by imposing a radical shift in epistemology. First, the targeted, would-be convert must be convinced that his belief in "objectivity," that is in a factual reality which is externally determined, is in error. He is then introduced to the notion that "truth" is multiple, that one "truth" is as good as another competing "truth." Once "truth" has been defined as a subjective belief with multiple possibilities, those things which the proselyte has known to be true in the past are "defined" as an illegitimate "opinion,"— the "opinion" of a ruling class which "oppresses." He is then prepared to accept a "non-oppressive" alternative "truth."

We have already encountered this treatment of objective reality as the "detested opinion" of a group defined as the enemy by social fascism. When professor Lefkowitz pointed out that Aristotle couldn't have stolen his ideas from the Alexandrian library in "black Egypt" because the library wasn't built before Aristotle died, she wrote, "Several students came up to me after the lecture and accused me of racism, suggesting that I had been brain-washed by white historians."[81]   The facts surrounding Aristotle and the library in Alexandria are removed from the category of "facts." Ignorant students, who knew nothing about the authentic history of the Alexandrian library, had never considered the data, had been trained to mentally convert undesired factual reality into an "opinion." A fact recognized as contradictory to their desired ideology was simply treated as the "brainwashing of white historians." This was done, apparently, instantaneously and without any intervening evidence.

Even in the so-called "hard sciences," factual reality which contradicts ideological assertions is converted to the category of "detested opinion." In the first chapter we noted that Dr. William Happer, then the chief scientist at the U.S. Department of Energy, had testified before a congressional committee that ultra-violet data collected before 1985 did not support the "ozone depletion" theory. A government monitoring program had revealed a decline in supposed cancer-causing UV energy hitting the earth, which was just the reverse of that predicted by "ozone depletion." When Happer suggested that the canceled UV monitoring program be resumed, he was summarily fired by the "environmentalist" Vice President Al Gore. The firing was justified and Happer attacked in the pages of the *Wall Street Journal* by Michael Elroy, Chairman of Harvard's Department of Earth and Planetary Sciences. Elroy characterized Happer's revelations of anti-ozone-depletion data as a version of treason. Factual reality was rejected as supporting the "detested opinion" of enemies of environmentalism.

As Dr. Roche identified, however, such cavalier treatment of facts first requires the acceptance of a belief, a belief that "truth really isn't objective at all; it depends on our point of view." The very existence of political unreality requires a radical departure— a revolution if you will—in the way truth is determined. In philosophy, the way that truth is determined, that is, the way that we "know" something is true is called our epistemology.

The absurdities of political unreality could not have emerged on the campuses—probably not even in the culture in general— without a prior epistemological revolution. Unseen by the public, such an epistemological revolution swept academia 20 to 30 years before political unreality in the guise of "political correctness" moved into the general consciousness. The attack didn't come as a direct assault upon our belief in absolute truth, but deceptively, by undermining our faith in language to reflect absolute truth. By undermining our language Wittgenstein succeeded in also undermining our objectivist epistemology.

We have already touched upon the substance of this revolution. In the simplest version, Wittgenstein redefined language so that it was disconnected from external, objective reality. What we called "reality" was allegedly just a linguistic convention, a set of "meanings" imposed by the mind. Language was supposedly about the inner workings of the mind, about constructing "meanings." It was asserted that our words did not really have the ability to identify objective truth or reality. We only "believed" that our words had this capacity and this belief was called the "commonsense" or "nativist" view of language. We supposedly made the world "seem real" by using our words as if they subscribed an external reality. Alas, Wittgenstein says, that is only an illusion. "Reality" is, after all, only a linguistic viewpoint, a subjectively imposed set of "meanings" upon a largely unknowable world.

By describing language as incapable of identifying truth and reality, Wittgenstein made the very concepts of truth and reality seem to be nothing more than personal belief. Since the number of beliefs is limited only by the imagination, multiple "realities" can be artificially created by a multiplicity of beliefs. These beliefs, often contradictory, may be laid out much like a smorgasbord and one picks and chooses from among them as if they were food items and with about the same standard. These beliefs, *cum* "reality," are "evaluated," meaning they are chosen by private emotions, that is, by how "comfortable" they make one feel. "Values" determine reality, and these "values" often are social/political "values." An emotionally shared commitment to what "should be" comes to define what "is."

One should recognize that the appeal of Wittgensteinianism is not intellectual, but emotional. This concept of language is most productively thought of as a kind of intellectual "vice," as being a mental version of moral depravity. People do not adopt linguistic subjectivism because they are honestly convinced of its merit. They choose it because it appears to remove their conduct from the constraint of realistic description. It is the type of language chosen by those who prefer to be defined as "sexually oriented" rather than sexually perverted, or as "pro choice" rather than favoring the slaughter of unborn children in the interest of promiscuity and self-serving careerism.

Before we become bogged down in the Wittgensteinian sophistries which "support" this curious modern epistemology, we should realize how radical a departure it is from the classical view of reality and knowledge. If it is not a belief, what then is "reality?" Reality is the manifestation of objects in the world as they move through space and time. These objects often impact one another with consequence, meaning new states or manifestations are created. These occur in orderly fashion, regulated by immutable laws governing mass and energy through time. The creation of these new states are events. These manifestations and events occur independent of, and external to, any mental ability to identify them. The human mind, however, has the capacity to accurately recognize events, objects and their manifestations, including abstract elements which otherwise dissimilar objects and events may share in common. Knowledge is acquired when these objects, their manifestations and events are accurately recognized.

The greatest intellectual problem with the Wittgensteinian view of language, as well as the practice of political unreality which it has produced, is that it forbids us the objective world by which we can reform and correct our thoughts and perceptions. We lose the distinction between the "true" and the "false." We are forbidden the capacity to misperceive or perceive accurately and are told that both are equally valid. We thus become disconnected from the very world of which we are part. It is, perhaps, the ultimate form of alienation, that being a deliberately-chosen form of madness.

This human capacity to distinguish between accurate perceptions of the world and inaccurate ones, between truth and falsity, however, requires something very similar to a moral commitment. We will recognize ourselves mistaken in our thoughts and images only if we are morally committed to make those thoughts and images conform to external objects, their manifestations and events. We must allow the external to have authority over our images of the external. We must allow evidence from the external to correct our mental images of it. This commitment has been the epistemological foundation of experimental science. It is a commitment which political unrealists refuse.

For this reason, if no other, we assert that practitioners of this revolutionary epistemology are not innocently deceived. The moment they refuse to allow the external to correct their understandings, they have conscientiously crossed the line to illicit mental conduct. Once again we confront the vice-like quality of Wittgensteinianism. Hidden beneath the slick rationales is a deliberate and willful corruption of the mental processes, a continuous refusal to have their images corrected by contradicting facts.

Having identified this revolution in epistemology as implicitly dishonest, we may examine its impact upon university culture without giving it undue legitimacy. The attempt to cut images of the world lose from external constraints is actually ancient. For example, the fifth-century B.C. Greek philosopher Xenophenes also believed "reality" was subjectively imposed.

What differentiates modern Wittgensteinian revolutionaries from Xenopenes and other ancient advocates of subjectively defined reality is the novel linguistic foundation for the philosophy. By making subjective "reality" an artifact of language, contemporaries have created an artificial "social validator" for subjective "truths." According to Wittgenstein, language does have the capacity to "communicate meanings," even if it doesn't have the capacity to identify objective reality. For the moment we will leave this absurdity uncontested in the interest of pointing out its significance. Language for Wittgenstein has a social component because people share meanings. One can identify "intended meanings" and thus many can learn to use those meanings collectively. Ultimately, language's only purpose is allegedly social, as people learn to share artificially imposed subjective meanings. Once these meanings have been disconnected from objective reality, the only way to validate one over another is the degree that they are collectively accepted. Language becomes a kind of vote on "truth" as one meaning becomes generally used. The use of social validators converts "subjective realism" from a philosophically-induced mental disturbance to a collective menace.

We have already considered a few examples of social validators substituting for an objective test of reality. F. Sherwood Rowland's "ozone depletion" mechanism could not be experimentally validated because chemical reactions do not occur as his "theory" required. His theory was then "validated" socially, by the Nobel Prize committee, with one of the members of the committee publicly announcing the prize was intended to silence critics. In other words, the social mechanism of "prestige"—the conferring of honors to influence public perceptions—was used to confer "truth" on a theory which failed the objective test of science. The Wittgensteinian principle of "meaning," in this case the "meaning" of CFCs being released into the atmosphere, was thus socially established by a general agreement of establishment science upon that view and to the exclusion of any appeal to objective fact. CFCs do not "mean" what reality dictates. CFCs "mean" what a social community has agreed they "mean."

Similarly, establishment scientists have told other critics of environmental claims that they will not consider contradictory facts unless those facts have first been published in pro-environmentalist, "juried" publications. The vote of the publication's "jury," that is the vote of representatives of a scientific social community, becomes the determiner of "truth" not objective test. Again the Wittgensteinian principle of social validation over objective validation has been applied.

Fifteen years after *Philosophical Investigations* argued that language cannot describe reality and consists of subjectively imposed meanings which are validated by consensus, that view became dogma in sociology. Wittgensteinian linguistics were brought to general acceptance in the book, *The Social Construction of Reality,* by Peter Berger and Thomas Luckmann. That book was published in 1966, at the height of the New Left rage, by a division of Doubleday whose address, 666 5th Ave., sends superstitious chills through Christians familiar with the book of Revelation.

In the book, Berger and Luckmann reiterate Wittgenstein's new "validator" for shifting and non-objective "reality." That "validator" is the opinions of a group or, as the authors call it, "the process by which *any* body of 'knowledge' comes to be socially established *as* 'reality.'" (Ital. original)[82] The authors claim they are writing within a sociological tradition and mention such names as Marx, Durkheim, Weber, Mannheim and Robert Merton, but in reality they are making a brazen thrust away from the "old" sociology which tended to be Marxist and positivist in epistemology. Without mentioning his name, Berger and Luckmann became Wittgenstein's stalking horse in the social sciences.

Their departure point was a rather insignificant field of sociology called the "sociology of knowledge" which essentially grew out of Marx's belief that ideas reflected economic class interest. While Marxists believed that accepted ideas in the Capitalist world were inventions of the ruling class, reflected their interests and were generally false—they called belief in them "false consciousness"—those Marxists also believed there was an objective reality to which they, and they alone, had privy. This belief on the part of the Marxists that they were "objectivists" was simple self-delusion. This is proven fairly conclusively by the pseudo-science imposed ideologically by Stalin (belief that learning is biologically inherited by the next generation), and by the failure of Soviet society to invent new technologies. The strongest proof, however, that Marxists are not really "objectivists" is the ease with which Wittgensteinian subjectivism, as voiced by Berger-Luckmann, overwhelmed the Marxists.

These authors asserted that the "sociology of knowledge" was not about ruling class imposed "false consciousness" vs. "objective" understandings of social conditions but "that the sociology of knowledge is concerned with the social construction of reality." In short, all reality was "socially constructed" or, in the terms we are using here, "validated" by social opinion. There is no room left for the Marxist's "objective" reality since even Marxist "reality" is "socially constructed." A revolution had been started in the snake pit.

Berger and Luckmann start with a deceptive definition of "reality," one which appears to be objectively anchored but is actually subjective in character. They define "reality" as "a quality appertaining to phenomena that we recognize as having a being independent of our own volition (we cannot 'wish them away')."[83] Right out of the chute, the authors appear to be attacking what we have characterized as subjectively-imposed reality. By the phrase "independent of our own volition" they obviously don't mean that we can't act upon "reality" and change it, to make real bricks out of what was once real straw and mud, for example. They seem to mean that the concept "mud" cannot be changed into the concept "brick" by some mental aberration, or, more to our point, the actual chemical performance of the chlorine monoxide of ozone-depletion-theory fame into some desired or hoped-for performance.

They seem to mean this but, alas, they do not. What they actually mean is that "reality" is established by a belief that people hold about it. They are restating Wittgenstein's view of the "commonsense" use of language—that people believe their imposed meanings are real. Indeed the authors even apply Wittgenstein's term "commonsense" to the unwarranted belief that one's particular "social reality" is fixed in nature. According to the authors something is "real" when people *believe* they cannot change their minds about what it "is." Reality is not defined by some external, unchangeable essence of the thing itself, it is made "real" by the belief in that unchangeability. It is essential to understand the difference between "reality" as defined by externals and "reality" as defined by the mind. Berger and Luckmann came down in favor of the latter.

Within a few pages, they have proven that "reality," by their definition, is, indeed, subjective, changeable and capricious. They state, "Sociological interest in the questions of 'reality' and 'knowledge' is thus initially justified by the fact of their *social relativity*." (Italics ours) The assertion that "reality" is "socially relative" means that it changes from one group to another and is not solidly anchored in objective externals. Berger and Luchmann quickly prove that this is indeed what they mean. "What is 'real' to a Tibetan monk may not be 'real' to an American businessman....It follows that the specific agglomerations of 'reality' and 'knowledge' pertain to specific social contexts."

One may note the curious language they choose to discuss "reality." Reality can be an "agglomeration," meaning a collection of unlike items into a single mass. You cannot "agglomerate" reality in the singular, as a state or condition. You can only "agglomerate" "realities" in the plural, as multiplicities in the sense that "my reality is different from your reality."

According to the authors this "multiplicity of realities" not only occurs between societies and cultures, between the "Tibetan monk" and the "American businessman," but for the individual as well. "Different objects present themselves to consciousness as constituents of *different spheres of reality*. I recognize the fellow men I must deal with in the course of everyday life as pertaining to a reality quite different from the disembodied figures that appear in my dreams....My consciousness, then, is capable of moving through *different spheres of reality*. Put differently, I am conscious of the world as *consisting of multiple realities*. As I move from *one reality to another*, I experience the transition as a kind of shock." (Italics ours)

All of this, of course, is patent absurdity and sophistry. Men and dreams are not different "realities;" they are different things in the same reality. To speak of "men in dreams" and "men in everyday life" as "different realities" which incorporate "men" is a pure artifice of language. These mental images are not "men in dreams." They are "dreams of men." The "men" still exist in the real world external to my mental processes. But what reason would someone have in wanting me to think of my dreams as a "reality?"

The real purpose of the artifice is to sell the idea that mental images, like dreams, are validators of "reality" and to weaken the mind's allegiance to external evidence as the sole validator of reality.

Sure enough, the authors began a systematic attack against objectivity as the validator of reality. Objective reality is given a new name, and called "the reality of everyday life." Objective reality thus becomes one "version" among many and is spoken of in problematic language, that is, language which opens objectivity to question.

Objective reality is said to exist "in prearranged patterns that *seem* to be independent of my apprehension of them." That is, the independence of external facts which validate reality is only a "seeming" independence. That independence is only an appearance. It is alleged that this artifice called "the reality of everyday life," a new euphemism for the objective reality which validates truth, this objective reality now called "the reality of everyday life" only "appears" to be objective. As the authors put it, "The reality of everyday *appears already objectified....*"

There is subtlety in this language, the subtlety of the Serpent in the Garden. First, reality is not objective; it is "objectified," meaning it has been acted upon by the mind to make it so. Second, that mental activity which gave reality the "appearance" of objectivity has already occurred in the past, but we are not cognizant of it. Our belief in "objectivity" depends upon a thought projection upon the world which occurred in our past and of which we are no longer aware. After Wittgenstein, the authors call this the "commonsense" world view which has been mentally "constructed" by a process of which we are unaware. Since we are allegedly ignorant of the mental process which "constructed" our "commonsense" viewpoint, we behave as if that "commonsense" viewpoint is the reality.

Now comes the sting, the little prick with venom powerful enough to kill Western culture and Western science. In fairness, it does not belong to Berger and Luckmann. It was invented by Ludwig Wittgenstein, but Berger and Luckmann use it, as do many other corrupters of the truth in the universities.

The unrecognized mental process which allegedly makes our world "appear already objectified," which supposedly gives us a false impression that we live in a world of objective facts, is contained in the language. "Truth doesn't exist, but you are a prisoner of your language and this makes you think it does," is the claim here. Following Wittgenstein, whom they never credit, Berger and Luckmann state, "The language used in everyday life continuously provides me with the necessary *objectifications* and posits the order within which these make sense and within which everyday life has meaning for me." [84] Translation: Language creates a false perception of the world as containing objective facts; these appearances of "objective facts" are really only the mental process of "objectification" contained in the words used to describe them. (All italics in above quoted material are ours except where noted otherwise)

The authors use that little word here which we have seen has had profound significance for the establishment of political unreality. That word is "meaning" which is being used in Wittgenstein's sense as a way to undermine our trust in objective facts as the validator of reality. Berger and Luckmann are using the word in this way when they say that our language provides "objectifications," that is, mental/social constructs which give us the *appearance* that "facts" are objective. These apparent but actually socially imposed "objective facts" allegedly give our "everyday life" "meaning."

Following Wittgenstein, they use the word "meaning" as meeting a novel mental necessity—as providing sense or mental order, an order which requires no basis in factual reality. The "meanings" of the madman may make "sense" to him so they fulfill the Wittgensteinian obligations of language.

An acquaintance of this writer was prone to hypothyroid-induced schizophrenic episodes. During one such episode, she became convinced that the color of packages which her spouse chose at the supermarket was some type of code. If the package were red it meant "danger," and was a signal being sent to some unseen conspirator. According to the Wittgensteinian framework, her "meanings" for the packages/choices were as valid as any other, since they made the world "sensible" to her. There is no requirement that her "meanings" factually appreciate reality. However, if she could convince the rest of "society" that the color of her husband's choices were code, that perception would become "objectified" and thus made "factual" since what constitutes "facts" are socially appointed, according to Berger and Luckmann. Who knows, the husband might even then be convicted in a feminist court for conducting a plot against his wife based upon the accidental color of the packages he picked up at the supermarket.

The car which is sliding into the side of my house is factual only so far as my mind or, collectively, "society" has made it so for me. First the mind, and now "society" are the arbiters of "reality." Things are" real" only because society or the mind consider them to be such. It was Ludwig Wittgenstein who, more than any recent intellectual, has poisoned that former fountain of truth.

7. "Civil Rights," Political Unreality and the Origins of Social Fascism

For several reasons, the "civil rights" movement of the early '60's was an unprecedented revolution in this nation's experience. It represented the ultimate victory of Civil War abolitionism, allowing it to reconstruct the whole nation, not just the South. In the process it birthed social fascism and made a politicized definition of reality a potent weapon against the nation's traditional culture. The "civil rights" movement thrived upon its ability to define reality. Indeed, the very title it chose for itself represents a Wittgensteinian meaning shift for the phrase "civil rights."

The "civil rights" movement added unconstitutional powers to the federal government by making a radical alteration in the definition of individual "rights." In the Constitution, "rights" are held by individuals as inviolate or "unalienable" and they are guaranteed by restricting the power of government. The Bill of Rights is replete with the phrases "congress shall make no law" and "the rights of the people shall not be infringed." "Rights" are thus considered freedoms possessed by individuals outside of government, and restrictions are placed upon government itself to prevent it from interfering.

The "civil rights" movement, however, redefined the term, "rights." They became social in character. Rights were no longer individual freedoms, but desired social treatments. This new concept of "rights" was no longer vested in individuals, but was primarily possessed by social categories or groups. Blacks as a group were said to be subjected to social discrimination and, therefore, as a group were suffering "rights violations." The alleged violators of the new concept of "rights" were no longer governmental agencies, but other social groups. Whites and their alleged "racist" attitudes were said to be responsible for these violations. Thus the principle of state power being used to establish "group rights" for a minority against the social attitudes and practices of the dominant group was introduced.

This idea—that state power should be used to further the interest of a social group, an idea born of a redefinition of "rights" as belonging to groups—is fascistic. Rarely, however, has its fascistic character been recognized. The idea is a mirror or reverse image of the national fascism of the '20's and '30's. It is a type of anti-national fascism. In nationalistic fascism, unlimited authority is given the state to establish the dominant nationality, often at the expense of minorities. In social fascism, unlimited authority is given the state to establish socially defined minorities, often at the expense of the dominant nationality. Both harness the power of state to ethnic particularism. Hitler's Nuremburg laws gave preferential status to ethnic nationals in German courts. American "civil rights" laws give preferential status to ethnic minorities in American courts.

"Civil rights" laws, which were enacted to further social equality for favored or "client" social groups, gave the government new jurisdiction in social settings formerly outside its authority.

The private actions and attitudes of members of the dominant nationality—actions and attitudes conducted in private spheres— were now said to violate newly defined "rights." The client groups were not receiving the desired social treatments in those private spheres. The freedom of association was severely curtailed. Dominant nationals were restricted as to whom they could hire, rent, enroll, subscribe and/or advertise. An unprecedented expansion of governmental power into these formerly private spheres was justified to establish and enforce these new "rights." Thus, massive usurpation of governmental powers was portrayed as establishing the new "civil rights." We had come full circle. Massive governmental power was no longer the enemy of "rights." It was the "friend and patron" of "rights." This social perception of the government as the "benevolent establisher of rights" was created by the new meaning given the word.

Governmental restrictions in the economic, political, cultural and social spheres were not seen as tyrannical, but as some new form of "liberation." Yet, behind the scenes, the fascistic face of the new ideology began to emerge. In their zeal as "social equality" enforcers, the federal government composed politicized units of the FBI which conducted a secret war against those holding proscribed social attitudes. Former FBI agent William Stringer has sworn in an affidavit given a Mississippi judge that an FBI "civil rights" unit in the late sixties and early seventies conducted a secret criminal campaign against segregationists. Stringer says the FBI unit ambushed and killed one segregationist, planted evidence to gain conviction of another and sent threatening letters to force a third to flee.[85]

These politicized units of federal police agencies continued to conduct a private war against those defined as "enemies" by a new "constitutional authority" which was rapidly becoming the social-fascist ideology. In the mid '80's they brought a group of "racists" up on "conspiracy" charges and the "conspiracy" consisted of the now proscribed "racist" beliefs. An Arkansas jury threw the case out. In Los Angeles, in the early '90's, an elaborate FBI plot to assault blacks and Jews was concocted, and "skinheads" were recruited and entrapped in the FBI scheme so they could be arrested and "exposed" at a well-attended press conference. In the summer of 1992, the family of Randy Weaver was assaulted by an FBI execution squad under orders from Washington to kill adult members of the family. Weaver and his friend were shot and his wife killed from a hidden sniper position. The Weavers were subjected to the non-judicial killing because they were allegedly "racists." The previous day, marshals had shot and killed Weaver's thirteen-year-old "racist" boy in the back as he ran home to his mother. He had been shot multiple times. A marshal had been killed as he fired upon the boy, possibly by adult members of the family trying to defend the fleeing child. Weaver was under federal siege because government agents had entrapped him on a minor gun infraction and were holding the charge over Weaver to force him to become a spy for them against a nearby "racist" collective. Weaver had refused.

The most frightening aspect of the "civil rights" movement and the social fascism which it spawned is its pathological nature. What other political movement has as its most explicit goal the suicide of its own culture and traditions? By definition, the movement represents the interests of ethnic minorities against the dominant nationality. The history, the religion, the forms of government and the values of the dominant nationality are only considered as sources of pain for the sponsored client minorities and are incessantly attacked.

From its very inception, this movement towards government-enforced "rights" in formerly-private spheres has had to practice propagandistic stereotyping. The management of the perception of reality was critical to their success. The movement has succeeded by creating emotional reactions to social groups and social institutions: sympathy for the minority client and hostility to the dominant culture. Actual conditions were often distorted to create propaganda imagery and events were often stage-managed for the benefit of the media. As we shall see, the tendency to "invent reality" was present with the civil rights movement from its beginnings.

A study by Michael Hoffman of the *Independent History and Research* newsletter examined 285 films and television shows released in the last twenty years which presented American whites and their culture as brutalizers of "client" minorities. The study found that whites suffered from propagandistic stereotyping. Southern whites are continuously portrayed as gratuitously victimizing blacks and other minorities. They are shown to be brutal, evil and stupid, while their minority victims are portrayed as sensitive and innocent.

Hoffman found that a major theme of these films was the ugliness and brutality of the indigenous American culture vs. the virtuous and sensitive culture of cosmopolitan cities. The city is characterized as anti-national, as accepting of multiculturalism, while the country is characterized as nationalistically American, ethnically homogeneous and brutal. Rural accents and grammar patterns are associated with malevolent and inexplicable violence against blacks, minorities and cosmopolitan liberals.

A typical stereotype is what Hoffman calls the "cretin from the country." In this theme, folk-influenced whites are presented as dumb to the point of deserving any evil that befalls them. They are presented as being "beneath identification." For example, the *New York Times* had this to say about the film "Out on a Limb" which mocks white working people in a logging town. "The film has several amusing moments, all involving the fraternal backwoods idiots ... with I.Q.'s well under 50." The reviewer was affirming the film's point of view, the viewpoint which identifies deficient minds as characteristic of the ethnic group, not of individuals who just happen to possess sub-human I.Q.'s.[86]

Hoffman has correctly identified cosmopolitanism as the idea which is allowing advocates of social fascism to trash indigenous American culture with apparent impunity. *Cosmopolitanism* is the idea that a tolerance for all forms of social conduct can replace the need for group belongingness. The cosmopolitan believes that if he accepts everyone and permits everything, there is no longer any need for the shared moralities and biological loyalties which define families and ethnic groups.

The cosmopolitan needs no one because he tolerates everyone. Everyone, that is, except those who still hold loyalty to their own national culture. In his mind, that culture must be destroyed because it still has power over and attraction for the people and is the one force which can still thwart the absolute domination of cosmopolitanism.

Cosmopolitans, called "liberals" in the American vocabulary, are tolerant for everyone except Christians and American patriots. That is why these groups are propagandistically treated as "hypocrites" and "bumpkins" in the film propaganda of social fascism.

The twenty-year's worth of formula films directed against American whites and their culture, were modeled after the actual television coverage of the civil rights movement. There was a direct and largely unrecognized connection between the relatively new medium of television and the success of this anti-nationalist revolution in America.

It must be remembered that the strong men of the 1930's used the then-new medium of radio to create a "cult of personality" around themselves which they used to radically alter the national forms of government. It was true of Hitler, of Mussolini, and it was true of Roosevelt.

While the strong men used the radio to directly sell their personalities to the people, the power of television and its ability to "tell stories" through images was politically realized in the civil rights movement. Without television and its ability to portray news in melodramatic imagery, the civil rights movement could never have succeeded and, most probably, would never have existed. The media was midwife at the very birth of the revolution of social fascism.

A brief review of the history of the civil rights movement reveals that it was the creature of television and not the "spontaneous outpouring of indigenous black anger at injustice" which the revolutionary historians must, of necessity, portray it. This is not to say that the civil rights movement didn't include "black anger," but only to note that such "black anger" was largely provoked and not "indigenous" at all. The movement largely consisted of programmed-for-television confrontations designed to provoke anger. It was staged soap opera being sold as news.

Television had become a "mass media" during the first half of the decade of the '50's as a majority of American homes purchased sets and American towns of any size were licensed to broadcast. Programing was provided primarily by the national networks.

Not quite coincidentally, the civil rights movement is said to have begun in 1955 with the Brown vs. Board of Education Supreme Court decision which overturned "separate but equal" educational facilities for blacks and whites. Incidentally, that decision destroyed a number of elite black high schools which had trained several generations of black leaders in rigorous scholarship in preparation for college.[87] Actually, the modern civil rights movement began one year later, when a political activist with strong Communist affiliations discovered that tweaking the beard of the Southerner made for good Northern television.

Martin Luther King, "hero of the revolution," whose birthday has now replaced that of George Washington in official government calendars, surrounded himself with known Communists, was photographed attending at least one Communist strategy session and was identified as a party member by an FBI informant. He claimed to be a "Baptist minister," but his taste for bizarre, multi-partner sexuality was so shocking that his FBI dossier documenting these appetites has been officially suppressed until well into the next century. It was King who discovered that television gave new possibilities to revolution. Events could be staged in one place by provoking local sentiments, but be viewed quite differently on television screens in another part of the country. The trick was to act locally but with a national audience in mind.

King realized, perhaps better than anyone else in his generation, that the new medium had a power to "define reality" which was much greater than either print or radio. Television imagery, brought people's senses, not just their minds, into contact with events. It intimately involved the viewer and had greater power to provoke his emotions. Television also had an advantage over actual physical witness of the event. It could be edited to evoke desired emotions. We have already considered how television-network sympathizers used such editing to provoke emotional reactions favorable to another black King, Mr. Rodney King.

To understand how King's simple but effective television script worked, one must be somewhat familiar with the history of the South at the time. In the nearly 80 years since reconstruction had ended, the South had created a social arrangement by which the two races could share the same geographical space while maintaining separate destinies. In part, this social separation was maintained *de juries,* but in a greater part it was a matter of convention. Separation by force of law was being vigorously undone by federal courts, as in the case of Brown noted above. The areas controlled by social convention were a little more difficult. Rigorous social separation of the races was sustained in public settings which were privately owned. Thus separate eating facilities, separate toilets and separate spaces on public transportation facilities were provided in some areas of the South.

While this "segregation" of public facilities was largely unknown in the north, there are great historical differences between the regions. Less than two generations previously, the South had undergone "reconstruction" during which Northern abolitionist Republicans imposed "black rule" upon the whites by illiterate, newly-freed slaves. Brawling, all-black "legislatures," hardly indistinguishable from public saloons, passed confiscatory taxes upon whites, and black "courts" protected black crime against whites *a la* O.J. Simpson.

Black rule thus continued the ruin of white Southern culture which had begun by invading Northern armies during the War Between the States. The Southern whites were "saved" by the early Ku Klux Klan led by former Confederate officers.[88]

The period of time between the end of Reconstruction and the beginning of the civil rights movement was about the same as the period of time between the Communist revolution/WWI and the present. Europe still has cultural memories of the horrendous slaughter of its young manhood during WWI, and the massive dislocations and deaths brought by Communism are not forgotten. At the time of the beginning of the civil rights movement, there were still Southern whites alive who remembered Reconstruction, and separation of the races was held collectively as necessary to survival.

Further, opposition to racial separation was not universal among Southern blacks. Blacks had established and built all-black towns in several Southern states. They were proud of their racial homogeneity and wanted to keep their separate status. City fathers in these communities were as opposed to the "outside agitators" of Martin Luther King and their integrationist ideas as were Alabama sheriffs.[89] The black writer Zora Neale Huston wrote of the Brown school integration decision, "How much satisfaction can I get from a court order for somebody to associate with me who does not wish me near them? I regard the [Brown] ruling of the United States Supreme Court as insulting, rather than honoring my race."[90] Echoes of this anti-integrationist sentiment among some blacks at the time of the civil rights movement is now being heard from contemporary black leaders. Clarence Thomas recently lauded all-black schools as "the center and symbol of black communities [which provide] examples of independent black leadership, success, and achievement." One of the flagships of the social fascist revolution, *Time* magazine, recently devoted a cover story to the lamentation that blacks now want segregated schools.

In 1955, the year after the school-desegregation court decision, Martin Luther King discovered the key which would propel the civil rights movement to the pinnacles of a social fascistic revolution. The discovery came somewhat by accident. A black woman by the name of Rosa Parks refused to acknowledge the racially separated facilities offered on buses in Montgomery, Alabama. She sat in the white section and refused to move.

This defiance of the customs of social separation created a mini-firestorm in the city. To defend the principle of separation, authorities arrested Parks. One of the key "roles" for the script, which was to be played over and over again to the media, was in place. Southern-white visceral reactions to the violations of the social separation conventions could be counted upon to appear extreme in the north.

King had attended Boston University and knew that a national audience would never understand why a woman should be arrested for refusing to give up a bus seat. He began the game of playing on a local Southern stage for a national audience by organizing a "boycott," allegedly to end racially separate facilities on Montgomery buses. Actually, King may not have been beyond "salting" the play for a better audience. King's house was bombed during the "boycott" while he and his family were conveniently away. No suspects were ever found, but the level of national media attention to King's Montgomery campaign increased significantly.

The boycott had absolutely no impact upon Montgomery bus segregation. That was later ended by federal court order. King's actions, however, were never intended to reform Southern culture internally. His strategy was to provoke the Southern white into the "heavy" role for the benefit of Northern television viewers, and this he did admirably. His national reputation soared even as racial tension increased significantly.

Historian Clarence Carson identifies what became the standard King *modus operandi*:

> "In the early years, he usually went into action by violating some custom or law, usually some law requiring segregation or requiring permits, which his group did not have. This brought him and his followers into confrontation with the authorities, and sometimes with onlookers or mobs. If arrested, he usually refused to pay fines, and he generally ignored the orders of all state and local authorities. In short, he operated in defiance of state and local authorities, as if they had no authority over him and his followers. In effect, King staged these confrontations, left violence to those whom he had provoked and sought to arouse national indignation against Southern (in the early years) local and state authorities. Quite often, he succeeded. The confrontations were staged mainly for the benefit of

national audiences by way of the reporters assembled for the occasion and for television cameras. The confrontations and conflicts were often real enough, of course, people did sometimes get beaten or otherwise beset by authorities and jailed. King undoubtedly hoped for and often managed to get Federal intervention either of the courts or the national executive to get him out of jail or change the local laws and practices."[91]

There you have the standard King operation in the South. He acted as if he were representative of a foreign power, which of course he was. He always staged his "confrontations" with a bevy of loyal reporters and, especially, television crews close at hand. He always refused categorically to follow orders from local authority, thus provoking them to "violence" which the cameras dutifully recorded. When arrested, he was contemptuous of his jailers, believing, correctly, that a higher authority in the form of the national government would suppress local powers. He was often right in this assumption. Clearly, his confrontations were meant for the national audience.

In this King melodrama continuously produced for national television, there are two parts. The evil Southern white and the innocent abused black. The Great White Evil had been cast admirably by the Rosa Parks incident. He also needed the followers whom he led to these televised "confrontations" to dutifully accept the role of innocent victim. It was not yet time for a media portrayal of black "justified violence," of a brain-numbed white America watching a video of a black hoodlum lifting a concrete block above his head to smash the skull of a prone white truck driver and consider the black to be the victim. The media had not yet stamped that level of ideological unreality upon the minds of the American public in King's day.

King's famous "nonviolence" was really a pragmatic strategy used to discipline his followers in the needed "victim" role for the benefit of the television cameras. One need only contrast the private Martin Luther King with the "pious" Martin telling his public, "I had come to see early that the Christian doctrine of love operating through the Gandhian method of nonviolence was one of the most potent weapons available to the Negro in his struggle for freedom."[92] One has a hard time visualizing this absolute commitment to "Christian love" when the hard-drinking "Baptist preacher" was taking prostitutes to his bed, two at a time. It is also hard to reconcile with the beatings he allegedly committed upon some of these women.

In any case, King's Southern campaign wrote the script which became the standard fare for network portrayal of "civil rights." It was always the same scenario: brutal white Southerner victimizes innocent black victim. Southern governors, driven by political expediency to defend Southern separationist sentiments if nothing else, became especially good media "heavies." This variation on the King script had the added advantage of allowing the federal government to play "white knight" and justify additional unconstitutional usurpations of power.

In 1957, Arkansas Governor Orval Faubus tried to prevent integration of Little Rock's Central High School. Federal courts ordered him to cease and when black children approached the school, a riot broke out. Eisenhower sent in paratroopers and the school was integrated at the point of federal bayonets. Faubus and rioting white Arkansas were the "heavies." It never occurred to anyone, taken by the "drama" of television, that American troops were being used against American citizens, not in the interest of "black education" or any other real benefit, but in the interest of forced association of two unlike peoples. The same thing occurred in 1960 when James Meredith "integrated" the University of Mississippi. Kennedy sent 3,000 troops to force the gates against "rioting whites." It was Alabama Governor George Wallace's turn in 1963 when he stood in the door of the University of Alabama to prevent its integration and was ordered aside by his own National Guard commander who had been federalized by Kennedy.

In all fairness, the question must be asked, "Is it right to turn tax funded institutions into private associations?" The power of state was being used to force blacks to pay taxes which were used to fund state universities functioning as "white only" private associations. Clearly this is wrong. What can be said, then? Did nascent social fascism rise up to defend a great principle of republican government?

Not quite. Recently, mature social fascism has found nothing wrong with using forced taxes to pay for schools functioning as black private associations. The issue is racial sponsorship, not principle. As clients of social fascism, black private associations may be funded at taxpayer expense. The dominant white nationality, however, must be absolutely forbidden the same privilege least they unify themselves again. Later events on the "civil rights" front would reveal that the attack was against white private associations themselves, not illegitimate government funding of all such associations.

The power to manage and/or define "reality" is also the power to desert principle. When whites try to operate government schools as private associations, the principle is evoked. When blacks do the same thing, the event is given a different "meaning." This becomes a celebration and expression of "black culture." If Wittgensteinian thought was as prevalent in the '50's as today, we might have had "separate but equal black cultural schools" while all white schools were simultaneously forcibly integrated.

A recent issue of *Time* made strong propaganda for government schools as black private associations. On the same two-page spread in a story about the black-desired segregation in education, the publication contrasted pictures of snarling whites, rioting against forced busing, with a picture of well-dressed, well-scrubbed black children dancing in a line. The picture of the ugly, rioting whites was incongruous, since it had nothing to do with the topic. It was included simply to reinforce the formula, "violent whites confront innocent blacks." That formula is now so firmly entrenched in the social-fascist thought process that it must be included in any story on the "races," even if it must be artificially created by page layout.

The attractive young black children were the real subject being discussed. They were students at an "Afro-centric" government school in Kansas City.[93] The J.S. Chick Elementary School offers a curriculum which emphasizes "African queens and kings," and students are taught to recite the geography of African nations. The pictured line of students was said to be rehearsing "for an African-culture performance." Of this government school turned into a black private association, *Time* gushes, "Something must be working: Chick's students out score some of the magnet schools' pupils on standardized tests."[94] Imagine justifying the University of Mississippi as a white private association on the basis of the academic performance of an all-white student body.

There is no need to come as far forward as the present to discover that social fascism is opposed, not to all racially-based private associations, but only to white private associations. The early civil rights movement made this apparent. The Supreme Court moved rapidly from nullifying state laws which established racial separation in schools to attacking the social patterns outside of law which created a culturally-based separation. The courts seized the power to break up white association in schools, even if that separation was caused by neighborhood ethnic patterns. They ordered schools to bus students to other districts in order to breakup white-only schools located in white neighborhoods. An historian writing at the height of the civil rights movement commented that the courts were issuing "judicial orders [which] required a basic revision of social structure and a root change in human relationships."[95]

The Constitution gives no power to the court to order a "change in human relationships," nor even the power to dictate the policy of local school districts. While many commentators have objected to this as a "usurpation" of powers, most have failed to recognize its root cause. A new "supreme authority" had supplanted the Constitution.

The goal which held a power greater than the letter of the Constitution was nothing less than the impulse to breakup the ethnic/cultural associations which defined the national identity. America was no longer to be thought of as a "white" nation or a "Christian" nation or allowed any other national cultural and ethnic homogeneity. It was to become a "cosmopolitan" nation, meaning a nation without ethnic or cultural principle. It was to be a nation with no constraints upon association and no constraints upon conduct. No one would be allowed to say, "I want nothing to do with you," and all would be brought into a great camaraderie of tolerance.

The high enemy of cosmopolitanism is the dominant national identity because it creates strong loyalties and those loyalties also exclude. To the cosmopolitan, the wife is like every other woman, and every other woman is like the wife. He dislikes private loyalties because they deny him access. He wants "tolerance of difference" to replace such human loyalty. It is he who invented social fascism, and it is he who invented the civil rights movement. Cosmopolitanism was the "authority" to which the Supreme Court deferred when it ordered children to be bused to break the social patterns created by their parents' choice of neighborhood.

There are several lines of evidence indicating that the civil rights movement was a cosmopolitan device which cynically used blacks as a weapon against the dominant ethnic nationality, and not a "liberation" movement for blacks, as claimed. First, the areas which the civil rights movement contested were trivial as far as black interests are concerned. The movement itself admitted as much as they deserted alleged abuse after alleged abuse when the conflict they had stirred had been milked for the maximum publicity.

Sometimes it is more profitable to judge by actions, rather than words, especially if those people whom one is reviewing are inclined to create "reality" by definition. At the height of the civil rights movement, its adherents expressed great outrage at various forms of petty segregation. In not one instance, however, did the movement pursue one of these "offenses" until it was ended. They moved with the cameras. Their very actions reveal that the real purpose behind these confrontations was influencing public perceptions not ending public practices. They acted primarily to create imagery, imagery designed to evoke emotional reactions to racial separatism by equating it with abuse. The civil rights movement was more concerned with redefining long accepted cultural practices than about liberating blacks.

King himself had dropped the celebrated segregated-bus issue in Montgomery after it had propelled him to national prominence. The issues chosen by the movement for the next few years were patterned after King's.

The next Southern civil rights target, after the King Montgomery bus boycott, was conducted by the Congress of Racial Equality (CORE) using materials they had compiled and published upon the King tactics. In 1960-1961, CORE conducted lunch room sit-ins throughout the South. Black CORE volunteers sat in lunch-room sections designated for whites. As with the bus boycott, the lunchroom campaign was dropped before it changed segregated counters, but after it had generated much sympathetic publicity, especially television publicity. It was dropped after the news value began to fade in favor of a newer civil rights story for the media. The lunchrooms were later desegregated by federal public facility laws.

CORE, however, moved on to a fresher story for the media with its "freedom ride" campaign. The "freedom-ride" campaign dropped all pretense of local involvement and used Northern cosmopolitans exclusively, both black and white. The "freedom riders" got on buses in the North and drove through the deep South, "integrating" Southern bus stations. Like other facilities, bus stations designated separate areas of the waiting rooms for blacks and whites.

The use of Northerners stimulated violence which the locally-based lunch counter sit ins never had. Southerners saw the CORE "freedom riders" as symbolic of an invasion of Yankee carpetbaggers, and old cultural memories were stirred. "Freedom riders" met mob violence in South Carolina and Alabama. A second bus ride caused a riot in Montgomery where the Alabama National Guard had to be called out to restore order.

Thus the movement, now with new players, used King's tactic of targeting a Southern social arrangement which maintained separate facilities for the races. Those informal arrangements were deliberately violated. Additional provocations were added until the angry response from whites was achieved. Meanwhile, the friendly television cameras whirred in the background. While the provocations were often intensified until violence was provoked, they were often dropped without resolution when the media lost interest.

It is difficult to see how the lives of black people were significantly improved by changing seating options. How much time did the average black person spend riding buses, sitting in bus stations and eating at lunch counters? It was said, of course, that these things were only "symbolic" of a larger problem and that the real issue was black pride, that separate facilities stigmatized blacks as inferiors.

Now we come closer to the mark. The civil rights movement never intended to improve objective conditions for blacks. It was always a movement concerned with psychology and attitude. Confrontations were chosen which provoked hostile white attitudes and inflamed black passions in response.

In fact the hostile black attitudes generated by the civil rights movement have worsened objective conditions for the race significantly. Unemployment among black youth was tracking white youth unemployment until the advent of the civil rights movement. Afterward, young-black unemployment numbers shot upward, doubling white rates, as young black men smolder in the resentment they had been taught.[96]

The same thing happened with crime statistics. A black crime wave rolled out of the civil rights movement, entrapping significant proportions of black youth in the criminal justice system. It now approaches 50% in some areas like Washington, D.C., with well over 70% of black males under 35 having been arrested at least once.[97]

Any semblance of the black family was also broken. Black illegitimacy rates now hover around 70% and the "welfare mamma" is becoming the norm. Single mothers raising children whose fathers are unknown and absent while living in a grueling poverty are scenes exactly paralleling the conditions of slavery as reported by Booker T. Washington in his autobiography *Up From Slavery*.

This is the second line of evidence which proves that the civil rights movement was actually an ideologically-led assault upon the dominant national culture, an assault which exploited black "shock troops" to redefine that culture in a more cosmopolitan direction. The civil-rights leadership was indifferent to the negative impact which their movement was having upon the blacks themselves. In the mid '60's, after ten years of racial violence and provocative demonstrations, it was clear that the black family was in the process of disintegrating. *Fidelity Magazine* issued a booklet entitled "The Beloved Community Gets Down" which documented what happened when the Johnson administration approached the civil rights leadership in 1965 with a proposal to make "strengthening the black family" the next phase of the civil rights movement. This proposal was totally rejected by the civil rights leadership, including Martin Luther King.

The publication identifies the reason for that rejection. The civil rights leaders were fundamentally more committed to cosmopolitan sexual promiscuity than they were to the welfare of blacks. The booklet states, "The civil rights movement grew up out of the desire for sexual liberation which was modernity's deepest aspiration and ... got absorbed back into it again." The book notes that black illegitimacy rates had grown to 20% during the civil rights movement of the '60's. When the civil rights leaders opposed any effort to strengthen black families and reverse these numbers, those figures grew to the contemporary "75% illegitimacy rate." This created a "permanent, welfare underclass" out of blacks.[98]

In any case, by 1963 King had dropped any pretense of finding an immediate "cause" for his confrontations. His Birmingham campaigns of that year were naked attempts to provoke police violence by the simple expedient of violating city parade laws. He continuously took the streets with the large number of people he could then command, while holding any requirement for parade permits or other city approvals in disdain and contempt. No longer were appeals made to immediate "insufferable wrongs," to segregated buses or lunch counters. The trivial justifications of the past could be dropped in favor of pointless defiance of city authority which would bring white cops into confrontation with black crowds and directly sell the made-for-television melodrama of innocent blacks brutalized by evil white rednecks. It would prove to be King's greatest production.

The historian Carson writes:

"The campaign opened in early April with marches. While those who headed the effort undoubtedly expected a violent reaction from police commissioner Eugene 'Bull' Conner, it was not immediately forthcoming. For the first few days, demonstrators were simply stopped by police, warned to disperse, and, if they did not do so, were arrested. Then Connor went into court and got a sweeping injunction against all demonstrations. King, with his usual contempt for local courts and law enforcement officials, could not wait to take to the streets. He and the other demonstrators were arrested and thrown into prison, King into solitary confinement. Mrs. Corretta King, his wife, then made strenuous efforts to contact President Kennedy to get him to do something about the situation. Whatever efforts were made on behalf of the President had little effect, for the jailed people remained in jail.

"The movement was about to collapse with nothing accomplished, so King posted bond to take charge once again. The decision was then made to use children in the streets to arouse sympathy for the protesters. The first day a thousand school children marched. The police arrested and jailed the children. The next day, 500 more children were sent into the streets. This time, 'Bull' Connor accommodated King and his cohorts with the police brutality they had been provoking. High-powered hoses were turned on the children, and as they were knocked down by streams of water under pressure, police waded in with dogs and nightsticks to break up the demonstration."[99]

Connor provided King with the searing television images

which seemed to permanently fix the American mind into a thought pattern which ultimately evolved into a novel type of fascism. Nearly every American living room witnessed white, southern "redneck" policemen assaulting black children with clubs and police dogs. Such images have a power of their own. They have an immediacy and no history. No one would remember that they were the end product of a pointless campaign of deliberate defiance of civil authority, a campaign which had exhausted the city's jails and was straining its police capacity. No one would remember that Martin Luther King had deliberately sent children into an increasingly tense confrontation with civic authority, sent them against an increasingly impatient police authority, to violate a court order. He had given America the television script, and now it was played as it had never been before.

King's career reached its pinnacle on the bloodied heads of black children and the flushed faces of Southern white cops whose sense of order had been flaunted to the breaking point. Five years later, New York City cops with impeccable cosmopolitan-liberal credentials would be provoked by Columbia University students in exactly the same manner and react with batons exactly as had the Birmingham police. It would not matter, however, for the faces of the New York "victims" would not congeal on the television screen into a single face, into the innocent face of an ethnic group needing protection.

Birmingham was a watershed, a place where the television images became more powerful than the alleged cause. Within days of the police assault, the Supreme Court met to overturn all Alabama segregation laws. It did not matter, for the images King had produced in Birmingham ignited a fire. The Birmingham police dogs had provided the fuel, but the fire required another small spark, one which was disturbingly familiar.

During the Montgomery "bus boycott" King had been propelled to national reputation when his house was bombed by "unknown persons." Soon after the confrontation with "Bull" Connor, the Birmingham house of King's brother, A.D. King, was bombed, again by "unknown persons." Within minutes of the news, a black mob had formed, and five hours of rioting ensued. It provoked the first of five "long hot summers." As black ghettos burned in riot that summer, King toured the country speaking to enthralled audiences, and ending the tour in a massive Washington rally during which he proclaimed to the nation his "dream" of universal brotherhood.

The problem we have with Martin Luther King is not simply his obvious hypocrisy, the inconsistency between his private morals and his public words, between his political conduct and his self-serving platitudes. Those things are obvious enough. He proclaimed a near religious commitment to "non-violence," but acted as if Southern authority didn't apply to him and thus inevitably provoked the violence which ignited half a decade of the worst rioting in American history. He said he wanted "a day when all God's children, black men and white men, Jews and Gentiles, Protestants and Catholics, will be able to join hands," yet he deliberately manipulated white Southerner authorities to act as "demons" before complicit television cameras, a theme which Hollywood has since reiterated hundreds of times in films.

King thus created a nearly pathological fear of and hatred for whites among American blacks. It is a hatred both races are suffering to this day, whites because millions have become victims of what an Australian newspaper called the "hidden crime war on whites," and blacks because the pathology has severely restricted their economic and social functionality.

The real charge which we level against Martin Luther King is that he is the father of social fascism. He is the destroyer of a nation, as well as a false prophet to his race. King's movement inevitably used the word "freedom" to described itself. The word was incessantly spoken and sung in the liturgy which was created for the movement. But what did these swaying chants of "freedom" at civil rights rallies really mean? Freedom to do what? Freedom from what? The only possible meaning of this usage was "freedom" from any claim by the dominant ethnic culture to private associations. Blacks would only be "free" if whites were restricted from making claims that their ethnic kinship and cultural heritage entitled them to exclusive social relationships within their own group. Whites were to be prevented from congregating in the public square as a visible and cohesive ethnic unit. By a succession of civil rights measures, all "whites only" signs were removed from law and from custom. All white ethnic consciousness was ruthlessly and systematically pilloried in film and on TV as brutish, ignorant, narrow-minded hatred of blacks.[100] The same treatment was not given black ethnic consciousness, however, which was portrayed as noble and elevating to an oppressed people.

The civil rights movement was designed by King to create this artificial perception of white consciousness as illegitimate and brutal. It was an artificial reality, sold the nation by cooperating television cameras. King knew that Southern whites held a strong ethnic consciousness reinforced by cultural memories of Reconstruction, the instinctive tribalism of the dominant Celtic stock and a religion which emphasized kinship loyalties. He knew how easily a Southern white defense of ethnic loyalty could be provoked. He also knew that white ethnic consciousness in the North was being undermined by a growing cosmopolitan fascination with sexual immorality. "Respectable" pornography had been successfully launched by Playboy in the early '50's, and movie goers were finding promiscuity titillating in such films as

God's Little Acre. The permissive sexuality invited a new "openness" to casual strangers and weakened kinship allegiances which were blamed for making people "suspicious towards outsiders."

The Southern white could be goaded by continuously violating his ethic boundaries. His inevitable counter attack would not be understood in the North where such kinship-based boundaries were increasingly considered "in bad taste" and "not nice." Reality would be manipulated—the "white-Southern beast" myth established—by carefully censoring out a significant fact to these confrontations. Southern violence was not against blacks in general. It was directed solely against civil-rights provocateurs.

The violence would not be perceived as against provocateurs, however, but as against the whole black population. Television images did not show personal backgrounds and political affiliations of participants. They showed only the color of the skin.

It would not occur to Northern audiences to ask why or if the violence was directed only against civil rights activists and not against local, uninvolved blacks. The Northern viewer would take it for granted that it was as presented on his television screen. He was led to believe that he was viewing "race relations" in the South, not a politically-inspired confrontation, and so he believed. The viewer who had bought the story line being fed him was incapable of recognizing when that story crossed the line from political theater to become reality; one of authentic broken "race relationships." The television images ultimately provoked significant segments of the uninvolved black community to join the political activists. King made it a "race relations" story with his Birmingham campaign, when the nation started burning.

Then we had a story which the media didn't notice, the story of a new "relationship" between the races, one in which blacks demanded that whites commit cultural and ethnic suicide and were themselves consumed by a nearly pathological hatred which blamed whites for all personal problems and short circuited confidence in their abilities to better themselves through their own efforts.

Seen objectively, the riots were a pathetic confession on the part of blacks. King and his television cameras had told them they were "perpetual victims" of whites, and they had begun to believe it. They lost all faith in their personal efforts, and unemployment figures began to skyrocket among black youth. They looked for some outside force to remove the media-imposed image of the "white devil" from their backs, and they rioted.

King and the civil rights movement inflicted an ideological wound upon American culture which required people accept imposed unreality in three areas. First, whites were forbidden to recognize ethnic bonds they held with one another. They were no longer allowed to cry "my kinsman, my brother." Starting with the contrived civil rights "confrontations," and later reinforced by fictionalized film and television, they were told over and over that such bondings were "racist" in character and would align them with the "brutal and dark past" of which an equally fictionalized history of white Europeans informed them. A hyper-individualism of cosmopolitan origins was demanded as a replacement for white ethnic bonds. Whites were to "invent" themselves as super-unique individuals with no alliance to past or people. They would only have a pastless future and an openness to everyone and anything.

The results of this hyper-individualism, this individualism without connection to a people, can be seen on any urban-influenced high school campus. For example, Boise, Idaho's North End is a trendy, white neighborhood heavily influenced by the political left. Lunch time at the local high school becomes a freak show. Clumps of students are easily recognized because they have done anything and everything to create a unique identity.

One is disturbed not merely by the nose rings, or the ears completely outlined in multiple rings or the purple or pink dyed hair or the half-shaved heads or the monk-like tufts left on top of an otherwise shaved head. One is disturbed by something in the eyes. They may be brazen and bold or anxious and insecure, but they are always the eyes of someone obsessed to discover if the social persona they imagined and constructed is the person who is being perceived. They are children who have lost substance and are groping for a substitute. Ethnicity is founded in history and biology. To deny its definitional power only leaves people stumbling in such low comedy.

The reality of ethnicity was forbidden whites by the victory of the "civil rights" movement. Such was not the case for blacks, however. Ethnic bonding is actually encouraged for blacks. We have already mentioned the "Afro-centric" school in Kansas City. Its very curriculum is dedicated to the purpose of cementing black ethnic bonds. We have discovered that even false histories are being constructed to further black "pride" and ethnic solidarity. "Afro-centrism" is not limited to one school. Its tenants are being manufactured on many university campuses and are currently being systematically implemented in many urban government schools serving large black populations. It is now the rage in metropolitan Washington, D.C. The point is that the civil rights movement created differential cultural "meanings" for blacks and whites, elevating black ethnic bonds to a virtue while condemning ethnic bonding in whites. Blacks became a "client" group whose interest must be served by opposing the dominant national ethnicity and its culture. This is our definition of social fascism which we can now clearly see was given power and direction by the civil rights movement.

The second unreality imposed by "civil rights" is related to the first. It is forbidden to recognize racial differences if the comparison reflects badly upon the client minority group. The strongest expression of this unreality is found in current federal "civil rights" law. The Civil Rights Commission considers racial imbalance in the workplace to be evidence that the firm is violating government employment mandates and will recognize no racially-linked differences in abilities. In dictating the racial composition of the work force the central government ignores innumerable studies which have shown that blacks as a group perform intellectual skills less efficiently than do whites. Comparison of I.Q. test scores between blacks and whites routinely give whites a 15 point advantage, even when factors such as housing, schooling and status are held constant.

Scholars who reveal these race-based differences have found themselves under brutal assault. For example, psychologist Hans Eysenck found himself physically threatened after releasing his book *Race, Intelligence and Education.* Eysenck said he wrote the book to make black education more efficient by revealing the biological factors which must be addressed. Eysenck, an expert in human intelligence, examined the known racially-based IQ differences as possibly explained by environmental differences. He studied white children from poor slum neighborhoods who went to slum schools, and compared them with black students from middle class households, good neighborhoods and good schools. He found that a difference of 12 IQ points in favor of the whites still existed. When he released his study, he found both himself and his family endangered.

In the U.S., the press censored coverage of the book. *The New York Times Book Review* refused to review it. In Europe, however, it received scathing reviews. Eysenck was prevented from speaking on British television and at several universities by near-violent student demonstrations. An Australian mob of students broke into a Sydney theater where the professor was speaking, beat security guards and forced the professor to escape to the roof. Eysenck's children were pointed out by teachers and received threats from other students. In order to protect them Eysenck changed his name to Evans.[101]

The recognition of racial differences is simply not permitted, and those who persist in doing so may be subjected to violence towards which the authorities are largely indifferent. The central government imposes such non-recognition with force of law. Social Fascism.

The third unreality imposed by "civil rights" concerns the dominant ethnic culture to which the client minority has now forcibly penetrated. The term "integration" means nothing less than giving full minority access to the culture of the dominant nationality, a culture which had previously been ethnically supportive. Not all elements of that culture make the minority comfortable, however. Those uncomfortable elements—especially if they put the client minority at a competitive disadvantage—are to be considered "racist" and suppressed.

Music is an obvious example. European music grew out of an increasingly sophisticated understanding of harmonics. A reality-based scale was invented which produced musical sounds containing partials of other musical sounds. This is the principle upon which chords are built. It ultimately led to the great symphonies of the classical composers.

African music, on the other hand, is primarily rhythmic and this ethnically-based understanding was continued in America by blacks, reaching its pinnacle in jazz. Jazz uses the harmonics and chords learned from the great Europeans and simplifies them to make clever plays upon rhythm. Jazz was pre "civil rights," and took European musical knowledge and applied it to African sensibilities to make one of the few contributions to "high culture" which this century has provided. Actually, the principles of jazz were even anticipated by classical European composers. Beethoven, for example, developed the "jazz tools" of syncopation and anticipation in his Scerzoes. These light pieces were considered humorous, as the meaning of scerzo is "joke." Beethoven was using these tools to *tease* the listener, as black jazz musicians use them to tease audiences today.

After "civil rights," however, it was European sophisticated harmonics which were expected to give way to African rhythmics. Post "civil rights" white music illustrates this exactly. The "rock and roll" which emerged during the mid-sixties deserted all harmonics for rhythm. "Rock and roll" uses only three simple chords to make a rhythmic beat. The full range of harmonics is replaced by what musicians call the one, four and five chords. Later, the four chord proved too difficult so the rhythms were built using only the one and five. Electronic special effects were used to cover the increasingly simplified music.

Today, the process has degenerated even further, as even minimalist music has been replaced by chants called "rap." "Rap" is a degeneracy for blacks as well as for the whites imitating blacks. It is a terrible fall from the elevated heights of classic jazz to this primitive barbarism. Since integration, the influence has been in the wrong direction. Jazz, arguably the greatest contribution blacks have made as a people to "high culture," was produced by "greats" who themselves sought influence from European greats. Scott Joplin, for example, wrote waltzes and an opera and is thought to have modeled himself partly upon Chopin.[102]

Almost intuitively, post "civil rights" white musicians came to believe that centuries, if not millennia, of musical discoveries were irrelevant because the practice of those discoveries largely excluded blacks. The French political philosopher, Jean-François Revel, identifies an even stronger example of a white suicide assault upon European cultural standards because those standards impose impediments to "racial integration." Revel points out that the great success of the civil rights movement has leapt the Atlantic ocean and has become the driving force of the European left. Although Revel does not recognize the full significance of the civil rights movement—that it has founded a new form of political totalitarianism by making racial minorities clients to be represented against the national dominant culture and ethnicity— he does object to its attacks upon reality. He recognizes that the ideology has "reduced a multiple reality to one phenomenon." He means by this that social fascism considers all forms of separation, from the accidental to a mere preference for one's own ethnicity, to be "racism" which is always equated with media-images of Nazism as the greatest racial murderers of all time.

According to Revel, the left must fight a perpetual war against a mythical Nazism in order to justify their own totalitarian impulses. Even though the authentic Nazi movement passed from existence in 1945, its ghost must be continuously resurrected by the left. They search for new incarnations and "civil rights" gave them a new name for the old enemy, "racism."

He gives examples of students in France and Spain turning on "competence" in education as creating "Nazi-like" exclusions. In other words, the principle of requiring preparation for advancement to university-level education—a principle which recognizes that Western knowledge is complex and requires skills and background to master—is to be abandoned in the interest of "civil rights."

Revel writes of student protests which broke out over the use of examinations to determine qualifications for university attendance.

"The rhetoric of the protesters was based upon antiracist metaphysics. It condemned the very principle of examination as being a *comportement d'exclusion* (behavior of exclusion). The dominant slogan was 'No to Discrimination!' In other words, a candidate for admission to a university whose degree of knowledge was to be tested was likened to a South African black or a Jew persecuted by Hitler....since selective admission, judged in terms of the racist paradigm, could only imply separation, exclusion, discrimination, and—who knows?—perhaps deportation as well."[103]

A rational element of white-European culture, the fact that the university exists for those who can actually master the offered knowledge, is considered an inhibition to minorities and must be eliminated. Much of the real knowledge contained in universities—knowledge of the authentic history of the ancient world, for example—is scheduled for destruction in the interest of "civil rights." Universities must become another thing.

The fact that the American civil rights movement leapt the Atlantic to become the foundation of the contemporary European left is instructive. There is a great irony in European leftists adapting what Revel calls the "antiracist metaphysic." In ethnically pure European nations, the social conditions didn't exist for the civil rights movement and had to be created before the ideology could be practically used. Following the example of Lyndon Johnson whose 1968 immigration bill reversed the ancient policy of favoring Europeans, the European nations themselves opened the floodgates to massive immigration by ethnic aliens. Great numbers of North Africans swept into France, Turks into Germany and Arabs and Africans into Britain. Only after European governments had created minorities via unrestrictive immigration policy could an American-style civil rights movement become viable politics. By the 1980's the civil rights movement was attacking not just Euro-American culture, but all of European culture in the lands of its origin as well.

What Revel, and presumably other European intellectuals fail to recognize is that this invasion, supported by a made-in-America ideology, is not politics as usual. The civil rights movement is not just the newest manifestation of Revel's "Great Taboo," the compulsive beating of the dead Nazi corps by European leftists. It is something new: a novel organization of power, and a new motive for its use. They fail to recognize the social fascist character of the civil rights movement, or more accurately, that the civil rights movement became the model for the emergence of a social version of fascism. The civil rights movement does not view the political landscape to identify the overlooked Nazi still lurking in the woods. It establishes sympathy for a minority social group and then practices advocacy for that group against the dominant ethnicity and its culture. It organizes power in the interest of this client and against the dominant national culture.

It is essentially an "anti-national" form of fascism which has begun to mirror the "great Satan" of the left, national fascism. The dual principles of minority clientism and hostility to the national culture are the definitional characteristics of the civil rights movement. It converts minorities into deadly organisms which are then used to attack and kill the host culture. Nations are not threatened by minorities, per se, but by the deadly poison of social fascism calling itself "civil rights."

Obviously, the principle of hostility to the dominant culture in the interest of a social client group is easily understood and just as easily transferred to new "clients." Over the years the principle was extended to additional clients: to women who reject their biological roles as bearers and nurturers of the next generation and want the dominant cultural patterns which support those roles attacked; to sexual deviants who want to suppress the attitudes in the dominant nationality which condemn their practices. In all cases, the historic nationality is attacked, its culture and its ethnic foundations, and in all cases that attack is conducted in the interest of a social minority group being treated as a client.

The environmentalist movement has proven that the "client" does not even have to consist of people. A pantheistic view of "nature" can become the "client" which is protected against the economic activities of the nationality, against the need to employ natural resources for the purpose of feeding, housing and clothing the nation. The principle of clientism, and the assault upon the dominant culture in the alleged interest of that client, is the same.

Where will it end? Where can it end? The social fascist demands that the nation "reform" itself in the desired image of the client. Those images, however, are seldom based upon reality. They are often neurotic sentiments, envies, feelings of inadequacies and rationalizations for unnatural conduct. Reality cannot be made to conform to such. Nations, however, can be destroyed by them.

8. The End of Reality; Its Consequences

In the Gannett-chain newspaper, *The Idaho Statesman*, the following letter to the editor appeared on July 13 of 1996:

"The recent editorial praising the wolf recovery effort demonstrates how out of touch *The Statesman* is with rural Idaho.

"Aerial surveys are so infrequent that wolves cannot be protected from poaching [livestock]. Ranchers and other rural citizens receive no warning when wolves are in their vicinity.

"The people of Baker [Oregon] had a wolf in their back yards for three days this winter before any action was taken.

"The Cascade [Idaho] ranchers lost three and possibly four calves before the wolf was trapped. If the wolf had not drowned, he would have been released and allowed to kill more livestock.

"Why has The Statesman *failed to report that a pack of wolves killed the biologist looking after them in a reserve in Ontario [Oregon] in May? Three wolves had to be killed to recover her body.*

"If wolves consumed newsprint or ate reporters, maybe the paper's wolf editorials would have a bigger bite of realism.- Ted Hoffman, Mountain Home." (Italics ours)

Mr. Hoffman's letter poignantly reveals that political unreality

184

can, and does, have serious consequences. No matter how cleverly "meanings" are manipulated, no matter how thoroughly contradictory fact is suppressed, no matter how touching the sentiments used to surround imposed unrealities, the ignored objective truth will always affect us. Cultures, no more than individuals, can desert the truth without suffering the consequences of madness.

Wolf recovery in the mountain states of the Northwest was sold by the *Statesman* and other social-fascist instruments by giving a new "meaning" to one of nature's most dangerous predators. During the last century and the early part of this, wolves had been eliminated from the region by ranchers and local governments because they had proven to be wanton killers. Not only were sheep and cattle threatened, but human beings as well. There had been multiple cases of children and wilderness sojourners killed by wolves.

Environmental reality managers and their patrons in the press, however, scoffed at the wolf's ancient reputation and sought to replace it with a new image. Using a "feel good" definition, the wolf was made to seem to be something it was not in order to sell wolf recovery. Pictures of "cute" and playful wolf cubs were circulated to associate them in the public mind with domestic dogs. The public was told that the wolves were a "missing link in the ecosystem" and would stay in the wilderness, providing the necessary function of thinning deer and elk herds. In this manner, a positive and desirable reputation was constructed for the animal, a new "meaning" to supplant what was historically known about wolves.

Mr. Hoffman points out, however, that the artificial reality, thus created for the wolf, really did not change the creature's nature. He still attacks livestock and, when given the opportunity, even attacked and killed an "environmentally-sensitive" biologist. The wolf's new "reputation" apparently did nothing to save her.

Hoffman also reveals that the *Statesman* acted as we would predict. They enforced the new artificial reality for the wolf by suppressing contradictory fact, in this case, news of the biologist's death. However, the woman was, bluntly speaking, still dead. The "reality managers" could not change the "fact" of the wolf any more than they can change the "facts" in the multitudinous other areas they have imposed artificial "realities." To ignore factual reality by believing it to be otherwise does not mean you are removed from that reality. It only means you suffer it ignorantly.

One does not desert reality with impunity. Negative consequences, however, are no longer reserved only for true believers in artificial meanings. Not just biologists mentally imposing a "kinder reputation" upon real killer instincts are at risk. Increasingly, social fascism is using the force of law to compel everyone to risk artificially-imposed realities.

For example, the hard-left Board of Supervisors for San Francisco made a law requiring that pizza companies deliver to crime-infested ghetto neighborhoods. Pizza delivery services had begun "red lining" certain neighborhoods after a 22-year-old deliverer for Domino's Pizza was shot and killed in 1994. Delivery personnel had been robbed on multiple occasions in such neighborhoods, and, in one instance, the windows of a delivery vehicle were shattered by an attack with bricks. The policy of refusing to send deliverers into dangerous neighborhoods was called "racist" since many of those neighborhoods were predominantly black. The Board of Supervisors unanimously voted to compel companies to deliver in these areas.[104]

The perception of neighborhoods as "too dangerous to service," a perception independently confirmed by many companies, was redefined as an "act of racism." The redefinition occurred after the relative of a black Board of Supervisors member was offended by two pizza companies refusing to deliver to his neighborhood. The perception of a neighborhood as "dangerous" will no longer be tolerated if that neighborhood is composed of members of a client group. The "client viewpoint," in this case the pretense that ethnic minorities cannot, by definition, be more criminally inclined than whites, will be imposed by force of law. Delivery people will be forced to act as if criminally dangerous black neighborhoods are not criminally dangerous.

The just-enacted San Francisco law is currently under intense pressure from those it is trying to force into harms way. It may ultimately be modified, but whatever its fate, the attempt has already set a political precedent, judging by the national media attention it has received. It was called a "national model" by the *New York Times*.

The principle has been established. Pizza-delivery people must set aside their ability to recognize and avoid authentically-dangerous situations. Even if that appreciation of objective reality has survival implications, that appreciation must be set aside in favor of an artificially-imposed "meaning." The recognition of danger must be seen as implicitly "racist" and the avoidance impulse must be suppressed.

This mental distortion is to be enforced by law. Thus, damaging personal consequences are being imposed by an artificial reality upon people who know they are not acting as the artificial reality claims. They *know* that they are not "racist," but the law compels them to *act* as if they are. They are not biologists walking into a wolf pen under the delusion that wolves are gentle and harmless. They are being compelled to walk into that pen.

The San Francisco law is something of a watershed since it shows that social fascism is now willing to compel innocent bystanders to act in self-destructive ways. Actions dangerous to them personally are being dictated by imposed, artificial "meanings." Political unreality does not damage only the mind, and its practitioners are not only comic figures stumbling in absurdity. Increasingly, there are flesh-and-blood victims, but of course they will never be acknowledged as such.

Gannett's *Statesman* suppressed news of the death of a biologist from wolves because the newspaper had recently helped "cleanse" the wolves' reputation. Both consciously and unconsciously, and by a variety of methods, the media tends to turn all victims of political unreality into "non persons," and the damages caused into "non-events."

We have already considered how this is being done in at least one instance. We have seen how elements of the "media elite" conspired to obscure the human faces of those damaged by "affirmative action." Cries for justice were redefined and given a new "meaning." The victims were never allowed to speak for themselves and were described as collectively composing a dark and impersonal force which was threatening "civil rights gains." In other instances, victims are simply buried in obscurity *a la* the *Statesman*.

There is a third way, however, which is used to obscure public recognition of the damage caused by political unreality. It may be even more dangerous because it tends to multiply the original harm. To disguise real causes, "voodoo" or mysterious explanations are given which must be accepted on faith and which essentially short-circuit the rational mind. Unreality is compounded upon unreality, and the public mind becomes primitive and superstitious. People are made to lose their capacity to address events with reason.

To obscure the connection between the policies of social fascism and the resultant harms, artificial and mostly irrational "alternative" explanations are given. This method might be called "imposed ignorance and deliberate stupidification." In this instance, the "fact" of the damage is acknowledged; but experts are trotted out who give obscure, largely-incomprehensible explanations which are accepted on the basis of "faith in authority." We have already considered how a politicized "authority" was used to overcome scientific fact in ozone depletion. In the same way, "authoritative" obscurantism hides clear connections between some damage and the political unrealities of social fascism. The public loses the capacity to focus on real causes and accepts inanities as a substitute.

A prime example of this "censorship by stupidification" occurred in early July of 1996. On two successive days, parts of Western states suffered total electrical power failure. The disruption was massive as traffic snarled from failed traffic lights, businesses closed due to darkness, factories shut down and sent workers home, foods melted and spoiled in the accompanying heat wave and travelers were stranded by inoperative gas pumps. In the first reports following the chaos, details were included which identified the real cause of the shut down. In later stories, however, these details were quietly dropped and/or obscured as reporting became more managed.

On the day after the first electrical failure, the Associated Press reported that the darkening occurred because a huge electrical power delivery was being attempted from Canada to California across the Western power grid.[105] Enough electrical power to service 1.2 million California households was shoved through the power lines of Washington, Oregon and Idaho. At the same time, generators in the Northwest were at near-record output to service the region's hottest day of the summer. The lines simply could not take the load of the California delivery, and power "escaped" into the power grid.

The intense surge caused automatic safety equipment in great numbers of power plants throughout the West to shut down. Every generator in the state of Idaho shut down simultaneously. In the early reports, it was said that power lines in Southern Oregon could not deliver the whole of the Canadian power to California, and the excess was backed up.

The system was painfully restarted from scratch, with some rural communities off-line for 24 hours. The next day, another massive failure, again shutting down the state of Idaho, was experienced at nearly the exact same time of day. Presumably, the California delivery was again responsible, but this is not known for sure because reporting of the story had become completely managed.

The local press, which had covered the first blackout with screaming 72-point bold headlines, barely mentioned the second occurrence.[106] The reason? The earlier, uncensored reports may have endangered one of the media's clients. Implications could have been drawn from the earlier reports which suggested that environmentalism might be threatening the power system.

For the last thirty years, every attempt to build a power plant in California, as well as the West in general, has been inhibited by environmentalists. The Diablo Canyon nuclear project was attacked by hysterical, media-fanned "safety concerns" which ignored the perfect safety record of nuclear power generation in the U.S. The cry of "Three Mile Island" suppressed the fact that that "disaster" released less radiation than one experiences naturally while flying in a plane at 30,000 feet.

Hydro-projects were stopped by feigned concerns for trivial sub-species alleged to be harmed by the building of dams across rivers and streams. Such claims were accompanied by gross politically-inspired unrealities such as the continuously-used absurdity that the supposed "endangered specie" could not live anywhere else but the proposed dam site.

Unknown to the public, power generation in California was even reduced further by environmentally inclined state regulators in 1995. Using the threat of denying a needed rate increase, the regulators pressured the state's utility to shut down one of the three nuclear generators at San Onofre, located south of Los Angeles. Regulators allowed the utility a significant rate increase so they could purchase power outside California, if the utility would shut down the San Onofre plant.[107] In July of 1996, we saw the result of that "deal."

Environmentalists and their friends in the media managed to stop power project after power project by shifting focus away from the current and future needs of Californians to some alleged environmental concern. Every project was redefined by the environmental viewpoint, and power requirements of the state were simply forgotten. The state's utilities were thus prevented from planning and providing for the growing needs of its residents. Ultimately, the shortfall reached 1.2 million residences during a summer peak which had to be supplied by a foreign nation nearly a thousand miles away and across multiple intervening states.

Although the early Associated Press reports had not asked why California needed to transship power for 1.2 million residences across 1000 miles and the whole Northwest, those reports did reveal that such a shortfall existed. Further, those reports revealed that the California shortfall had put the whole Northwest power system at risk, that California's immediate neighbors—themselves subject to environmental restrictions—could not make-up California power shortfalls, and that California was being required to go further and further afield for its needs. These were not "good" facts to be let out by a media continuously sensitive to the impact of their reporting upon certain client groups (see Chapter 3). The story was simply dropped from their radar screen, even though the next day another massive blackout occurred.

The story wasn't resurrected until July 21, this time with the offending details eliminated and another "explanation" in place. The Associated Press reported that The Western Systems Coordinating Council had discovered that the blackout was caused by "a flashover between a southeastern Idaho transmission line and a tree that had grown too close."[108] In that AP report, the massive California delivery was called one of the "other factors," and the details which had threatened environmentalism were completely eliminated. Descriptions of the massive California delivery were reduced to the single phrase: "high transfers on lines between the Pacific Northwest and California." The cover-up, however, was partially undone when one of the Northwest's utilities, Idaho Power, announced that it would restrict power transfers through its lines to prevent another blackout. Press coverage of the Idaho Power announcement still eliminated all mention of the California delivery and still gave prominence to the "flashover" as the cause.[109]

There is a rational problem with this reductionism, this attempt to attribute a huge effect to a trivial cause. The AP used "authoritative" sources to allege that 14 Western states and parts of Canada and Mexico were darkened by a power line shorting out to a tree. That explanation was used to supplant an earlier and less "politically-considered" one which had a greater ability to satisfy the reason. The blackout occurred because of a power surge threatening to damage power generators which had to be cut off-line to be protected. How can a short, which draws power into the ground and away from the lines, be accused of sending increased power through those lines? It was obviously, at best, a catalyst which may have diverted the California delivery into the grid by making a sudden demand. The cause was still the

California delivery since it was that which provided the surge.

We are not trying to make a tedious exercise in logic, only to point out that rationality has been short-circuited by media reports of the event, reports designed to obscure facts which are potentially damaging to environmentalism. The real factual causes were hidden and replaced by a trivial but "authoritative" explanation. People accepted this explanation on faith and with the belief that it was too "deep" for them to understand. Cause and effect were made to seem "mysterious" and "unknowable." In fact, the causes are eminently comprehensible by people of average intelligence but were reduced to "mysticism" in order to protect environmentalism.

The western blackout is instructive in several ways. The initial, pre-managed reports gave us a brief glimpse of the risk which environmental successes are placing upon our power-supply system. Prevented from building plants locally, under-producing utilities are forced to import power from great distances, and the "grid system" was initiated to accommodate these transfers. Power lines have been converted to long distance highways and are being strained to the point that a trivial incident, a flashover to a tree, can initiate massive disruptions. Environmentalism, and the artificial "meanings" it has imposed upon power-plant constructions, may have serious consequences for great numbers of people.

The blackout was instructive in another way, for it showed how the press "managed reality" to keep the public from identifying the source of their risk. The consequences of formerly-imposed political unrealities were obscured by eliminating "sensitive" facts and substituting a trivial and largely irrational "cause" for the authentic one. Incidentally, the method worked. People in the affected region generally believe that the blackout was purely "accidental" and are ignorant of any strains upon the system which provides them with a necessary commodity.

It is clear that a media dominated by social fascism currently has a tremendous power to "define reality." It is using that power to great harm, but it is also using that power to hide its damage and its victims. When the mask of unreality is stripped away, it can be seen that the list of victims is reaching impressive numbers. Well over 2000 people were injured or killed in the 1992 "Rodney King" riot in Los Angeles. The media portrayed the riot as "caused" by an all-white jury which failed to protect an "innocent black man" by refusing to convict white police officers who had beaten him. In fact, the riot was caused by a media which had deliberately hidden King's provocative and violent behavior leading up to the beating (see Chapter 2). The rioting black mob acted upon an unreal image provided by the media.

Two thousand casualties not yet a significant enough number to indict political unreality as a serious threat? How about the 25,000 range? That's more or less the number of timber jobs eliminated by closure of the Northwest forests due to "Spotted Owl" environmentalism.[110] A southern-Oregon newspaper counted over 200 rural timber-dependent communities which it said were "on the brink of economic collapse." Yet an actual owl survey, AFTER THE FORESTS WERE CLOSED, revealed that the Spotted Owl was not actually a threatened species and had a much greater range of habitats than environmentalists had claimed. It doesn't matter. As one Oregon environmental activist told the current writer, the owl was only an "excuse" to get the loggers out of the forest. The loggers themselves were the target. They "desanctified holy nature" with their "profane" cutting of trees. The media simply made the victims of forest shut-downs into "non-persons" by giving little or no coverage to their economic plight. They also obscured the significance of a hefty increase in lumber prices following the shut-down.

Sometimes it is helpful to put a human face upon the raw statistics. The following letter was found in a mail drop in Port Angeles, Washington, a community hard hit by the forest shutdown. Local police believed it genuine. All grammatical and spelling errors are in the original.

"Dear Santa Clasc: Please help my mom and dad this Christmas. My dad is not working anymore. We don't get many food now. My mom gives us the food she would eat. Please help m mom and dad. I want to go to Heven too be with the angels. Can your bring me to Heven? My mom an dad would not have too by things for me no more. That would make them happy. Please bring my dad a job an some food. I live in my house like last year. We got candils. A city man took the lights away. It looks like we don't live heer no more. We do. I will wate for you too come in my room. I will not slep. Wen you give my dad a job and some food too my mom I will go with you and the rain deer. Merry Christmas too you Mrs. Clas too the elfs too. Thad."[111]

Twenty-five thousand still not a significant number? How about in the millions? How about over 25 million unrecognized victims of political unreality? The Australian journalist Paul Sheehan, wrote of one of the three unrecognized impacts of the "civil rights movement" upon American blacks. "[I]n the mid-1960's...there was a sharp increase in black crime against whites, an upsurge which, not coincidentally, corresponds exactly with the beginnings of the modern civil rights movement."[112]

Martin Luther King's campaigns were carefully orchestrated melodramas which presented a willing media with images of "innocent" blacks being brutalized by "evil" whites. Confrontations were continuously provoked between white authorities over petty Southern segregation practices. Finally, in Birmingham, Alabama, King dropped the pretense of reforming petty Apartheid and conducted a grueling campaign the only issue of which was King's "right" to take-over city streets without a parade permit. For days, police tried to enforce a court injunction against the illegal demonstrations and tempers flared. At the height of the tension, King sent children into the streets, daring police to sully their reputations by attacking these symbols of "innocence." Police broke-up one of these demonstrations with night-sticks and dogs, sending searing images into the nation's living rooms via television. King's media "success" ultimately provoked the first black "civil rights" riot which occurred in Birmingham that summer. The myth of systemic and continuous brutality by whites against blacks was born. It was reinforced by a barrage of fictionalized films which showed innocent blacks brutalized by "red necks." Michael Hoffman documented over 200 such films released in a 20-year period.[113]

During the height of the civil rights tension, white violence did occur against civil rights activists but never extended to the black community in general. It was presented, however, as if it did. This was the origins of a political unreality which provoked a massive retaliatory crime wave which Sheehan describes as a "hidden war on whites."

In film after film, white "heavies" were portrayed as gratuitously brutalizing innocent and likable blacks. Because such artificial images continuously irritated black resentment, a quite different phenomenon was beginning to occur in the real world.

As the nation was taught to believe the "brutal white" myth by the media, blacks began attacking whites in record numbers. For every single white attack on a black, nearly twenty blacks attack whites. Since these figures began their acceleration during the post "civil rights" period, 25 million whites have suffered, have become victims of political unreality.

Neither the fact of this phenomenon nor its extent have been reported in the American press. Sheehan notes that to do so would expose an American journalist to sanctions as a "racist." Numerous lines of evidence, including the firing of a Vermont journalist for reporting a black manhandling of a white woman at a public event, reveal that Sheehan is correct. The 25 million have been turned into "non-persons" by a press which refused to disclose either the source or the motive of the assaults.

The artificial "racial crime" formula invented and furthered by King and the film industry, is now being imposed upon fact by use of Wittgensteinian "meanings." The actual state of inter-racial crime is disguised and the artificial formula *"blacks are perpetually victimized by white racism"* is substituted in its place.

In the summer of 1996, largely unconnected events were lumped together into an artificial category and given a Wittgensteinian "meaning," that is they were made to "mean" that a "white-racist crime spree" was being inflicted upon blacks. In point of fact, nothing of the kind was happening.

In the first part of 1996, it was noticed by the media that 73 black churches had burned since 1995 in Southern states. The King-media formula was imposed, specifically that these fires "meant" that a campaign of racist terror was being conducted by the latest incarnation of the "brutal white Southerner" myth. After all, that's the way it was continuously portrayed in Hollywood films. This "meaning" was imposed without evidence, without noting that as many white churches had burned during the period, without considering what the normal rate for church fires is, or that other explanations were being discovered for many of these fires.

A fire in a black church was made to "mean" that it had been torched by a "white racist." The "civil rights leader" Jesse Jackson, for example, charged that the fires proved that the "white sheets" of the Ku Klux Klan had been recently converted into the "blue suits" of respectable Southerners. Both President

William Blythe-Clinton and the National Council of Churches railed against the "criminal racists" attacking black churches.[114] Blythe-Clinton held a news conference with selected black "church" leaders who expressed angry outrage at this newest assault on their "civil rights."

The phenomenon they were attacking, however, simply did not exist. Reluctantly, the press revealed that the fires were not exclusively a black problem. In fact, more white churches had burned than black. In a five-year survey, it was discovered that arson was up against churches in general but had only "random links" to racism.[115]

Nonetheless, Federal agents were rushed to the South to protect black "civil rights," and congress passed hurried legislation to broaden federal powers to fight "church property burnings" after two black churches were "torched" on the same day in a small Mississippi community. Associated Press coverage of the burnings, however, also revealed, with no detail and in passing, that a white church had also been attacked in that community and on the same day.

A case of "racist arson" in North Carolina was discovered to be an electrical fire, and one in Texas had been caused by two small boys playing with matches. A "racist attack" in Shreveport, Louisiana, was discovered to have been caused by a black church member who was a pathological arsonist.[116]

A spokesperson for an insurance trade group which tracks fire statistics said that "the number of arson fires that have broken out this year [in churches] are within the norm." Of the 73 fires at black churches between January 1995 and July of 1996, only 16% (12 fires) give strong evidence of "racist" motivation. The spokesperson for the Insurance Information Institute implied that this was in the expected range of what she termed "a crime which has been going on for a long time."[117]

It might be noted, that none of the press coverage even bothered to consider the motives for arson attacks upon white churches. The presumption of "white suspect, black victim" was sustained throughout all coverage. The perception that blacks were the victims of a white-racist arson spree was immunized from the discovery that the great majority of the fires had another explanation.

Further, the few "racially-motivated" fires were accounted for by a very small number of individuals. They were a small group, heavily composed of serial arsonists.[118] Despite the revelation of the true facts, elements of social fascism continued to impose the "racist torching" unreality and continued to insist that it was endemic to American white society. For example, three weeks after the Associated Press revealed that "racist motives" represented a small number of the black church fires and were the work of an even smaller number of serial arsonists, a solemn event to condemn the "racist burnings" was held by civil rights activists at the Capitol building in Boise, Idaho. It was held in conjunction with other "memorials" being held across the nation.

Governor Phil Batt, who prides himself on having furthered the state's "civil rights" laws, told the crowd that they must oppose the attempts of church burners to "drive another wedge of division into our society." A list of the burned black churches was read, without noting the cause of the fires. The state's director of "Human Rights" called the church burners "cowardly" and said they "need to know when they are doing this, they are doing it to all of us." The director is white. Thus she affirmed her solidarity with the "black victims." A "collection" was taken for the "black victims" of three churches which had burned in the Northwest (cause unknown) and the solemn assembly ended with the singing of the civil rights anthem, "We Shall Overcome." This was all dutifully reported by the local Gannett newspaper.[119]

In this manner, "victimhood" was once more officially conferred upon American blacks. It didn't matter if most of the "racist crimes," for which they were being offered "holy martyrdom," hadn't actually occurred. The image, the Formula, is all that matters. The Formula is ennobling–blacks are always the victims, and we stand with them against their "white oppressors." The Formula confers "reality," not the facts. There is no place in the minds of these True Believers–or their consciences –for the 25 million white victims of black assault nor the 45,000 dead in post-civil-rights America. Such facts are without ennobling sentiment, are outside the "civil rights" Formula.

This pretense at victimization is not just an exercise in unreality. As a practical matter, it will harden the attitudes which produced Sheehan's "hidden war on whites." When resentment is produced by artificial images and has no real cause, it is the kind of resentment that needs no cause. It is irrational and free-floating and can descend upon a target without provocation. Thus great evils have and are being perpetrated, and the reality of those evils is suppressed by people who pretend to great virtue. The level of hypocrisy is more than the stomach can bear.

9. Political Unreality and a
Criminalized Presidency

The damages inflicted by social fascism, and its version of "client-sensitive reality," are not limited to individuals. Our very political institutions appear to be suffering from the practice. Specifically, a media-enforced public relations screen is being used to shield a president from serious criminal allegations. These charges are not trivial. Evidence has been brought forward that William Blythe-Clinton has converted elements of government, on both the state and national level, into resources for a criminal syndicate. In at least one instance this included a for-profit criminal operation which allegedly netted millions of dollars.

Very little of this information has reached the American public, however. The American media adopted a censorship policy evidenced by the fact that information with criminal implications for Blythe-Clinton was given prominent coverage in major European newspapers but never saw the light of day in the United States.

But why would the press protect a politician from such allegations? Consider this. A president who has shown himself willing to take strong action towards the clients favored by the media, towards homosexuals, civil rights, feminism and environmentalism, is discovered to have less than desirable ethics in other "non-sensitive" areas. The media have already shown themselves to be indifferent to the victims of clientism. They have let many many people suffer in the dark and in silence. They already possess a warped sense of justice. In their minds, "justice" consists of anything favorable to their clients.

Such a president would be favorable to their clients. That he may have committed crimes in other areas could be a matter of indifference to an ideologically uniform media, for you see, social fascism is itself a form of criminality. Knowledge of the possible illegal acts of such a president must be ruthlessly suppressed. Such knowledge could bring him down and eliminate the "good" he is doing for favored groups. After all, this is the president who attempted to force homosexuals on the military in 1993 and vetoed the partial-birth abortion ban in 1996. Blythe-Clinton is a shrewd man who knows that the clients of social fascism are the only groups with which one needs to keep unswerving faith, if he desires media protection.

The president known as William Clinton grew up under Mafia influence in Hot Springs, Arkansas. This is not the charge of Clinton's enemies, but the description of Clinton's mother Virginia in her book *Leading with My Heart*. Clinton was born Willie Blythe, the illegitimate son of a traveling salesman whom his mother later briefly married. Willie Blythe became William Clinton when his mother married Roger Clinton.

Hot springs was a town of police-protected whore houses and gambling dens. It was a town of retired mobsters, like Owney Madden, who were treated as celebrities. According to Virginia

(Clinton) Kelly, it was a town where "gangsters were cool, rules were meant to be bent, and money and power—however you got them—were the total measure of a man." [120] Virginia Clinton stated that Roger was heavily involved in these activities. "Roger Clinton and his friends had a long history of getting away with crimes and acts of drunken violence." She taught her son the skills of a con artist. In her book, Virginia says that she taught Bill Blythe-Clinton that what one did in the past didn't matter because a person could "reinvent" himself each day. The boy Blythe-Clinton was thus schooled in the principle that one could escape from the consequences of misdeeds by a clever manipulation of one's image, by simply "reinventing" oneself.[121] One did not repent wrong deeds. One merely "reinvented."

This, then, is the background of the man who was elected president in 1992. He had not come to that office free of scandal. As the governor of Arkansas, allegations had been circulating which questioned his moral fitness and his honesty. Most of these had been suppressed during the campaign by a media which favored Blythe-Clinton's politics—suppressed with one exception.

A former mistress, Gennifer Flowers, had produced a tape recording of a conversation with Blythe-Clinton which gave evidence of their illicit relationship. This scandal was defused when Blythe-Clinton was allowed to go on CBS television and, while holding the hand of his wife, admit that they had suffered some marital difficulties in the past but were now reconciled. CBS executives would later claim that they had saved Blythe-Clinton's candidacy with this broadcast.

It would be nearly a year after the election before serious criminal allegations surrounding the Blythe-Clinton governorship would come rolling out of Arkansas and be given a ruthless cold-shoulder by the nation's media. It would be more than a year and a half before a very limited audience would know that Blythe-Clinton was accused of running a money laundering operation for a drug smuggling ring and that Arkansas state resources were allegedly used for this purpose. It would be longer than that before knowledgeable people would begin using the term, "Arkancide" for suspicious deaths of potential witnesses against Blythe-Clinton, which were officially ruled "suicides."

From the time that Blythe-Clinton and Hillary marched into the White House, however, there was evidence that something was wrong. The people he brought with him to staff the presidential residence seemed to constitute something of a criminal sub-culture. Extensive drug use was admitted. Staffers wouldn't, or couldn't, pass background checks for security clearances. Petty larceny, running to the hundreds of thousands of dollars, was reported. Within six months, Commerce Secretary Ron Brown was investigated for soliciting a 3/4 million dollar bribe from the Vietnamese for helping them get normalized trade relations with the U.S.

Recently, more detail of this criminal atmosphere in the early Blythe-Clinton White House has been revealed in a book by a former FBI agent who had been assigned there. The treatment of the book and its author by the media is instructive.

In the book *Unlimited Access* Gary Aldrich tells what he saw and learned as he tried to conduct background interviews of White House staffers for the FBI in the early part of the Clinton regime. In explaining why he wrote the book, Aldrich said, "I left the Clinton White House thinking that I'd spent more than two years back on the streets, fighting a new Mafia—this one from Arkansas."[122]

Aldrich tells that on inauguration day, the Clinton mob stormed the White House, coming without official positions, resumés or any paperwork indicating what particular job they

might be performing. They took over the government with little
in the way of formality—more like pirates storming the ship of
state. Later, the Personnel Office was ordered to construct phony
paperwork and to back-date retroactive appointments for the
Clintonistas. When the career director of that office objected to
this as illegal, he was replaced by a Clintonista, and the phony
paperwork caper began in earnest.

Using this new power to manufacture paper positions, favored
staffers were assigned two "jobs" which gave them two separate
government salaries. There seemed to be little concern for either
accuracy in job descriptions or respect for function.

From the very first, some Clinton staffers displayed a
larcenous inclination to convert governmental authority to their
private use. After the inauguration, federal employees attempted
to find $150,000 worth of equipment which had been appropriated
by the Clinton mob. The Clintonista to whom this equipment had
been entrusted, and who never adequately explained its
disappearance, was Craig Livingstone. For his diligence,
Livingstone was appointed White House director of security.

It should be noted that the position of "director of security"
has a hidden and private significance in the Blythe-Clinton view
of governmental operations. In Arkansas, the security detail had
become a kind of personal Pretorean Guard for Blythe-Clinton,
loyal to his person rather than the government. He converted
them to his private ends and convinced them to act illicitly for
him. Arkansas security men acted as sexual procurers for Blythe-
Clinton, and the chief of security became a kind of private
enforcer for the politician. Livingstone would carry on this
Arkansas tradition in the White House. He would later be accused
of expropriating FBI files on Clintonista political enemies and
using them to defend Blythe-Clinton.

Livingstone was one of several "sensitive" Clinton

appointments whose required FBI background check would be short circuited. Since a security chief has other "functions," a heavy dose of ethical straight-lace might be, uh, "constricting." Prior to Livingstone's appointment, Aldrich was asked by White House counsel what the "FBI might think" if there were "a character issue in [Livingstone's] background." When told that the security director must be clean, Aldrich was told "it doesn't matter...Hillary want's him."

When college interns were invited to the White House, Security Director Livingstone demonstrated that he wasn't inhibited by an overactive sense of righteousness in his job. He advised the students to "have fun," and then verbally winking at what that "fun" might be by closing his briefing with, "I know what some of you guys are going to do, but don't get caught."

Livingstone was not the only Clintonista whose background check would be preemptively eliminated because it would disqualify him. David Watkins, an intimate friend of the Clintons, similarly forbad FBI investigations into a known character issue in his background. Watkins had been accused of sexual harassment during the campaign and made a $37,000 payoff to his accuser with Clinton campaign funds. Both parties signed an agreement to keep quiet about the affair. When Aldrich tried to investigate the incident, he was told by a White House lawyer that the document which committed the parties to silence also prevented the FBI from investigating the matter. When Aldrich protested to his superiors, he was told the Watkins case was to be closed "without an interview."

When many other Clinton staffers began resisting background investigations, Aldrich complained to higher Clintonista officials. He was called into the office of White House Counsel William Kennedy and told that the Clinton staffers "don't like telling strangers about their personal business." Aldrich replied that the investigations were required by law and supported by traditions going back to Eisenhower. The confrontation ultimately resulted in a deliberate dismantling of the White House security system by Kennedy. The Secret Service was denied access to the background files on staffers for the purpose of reviewing them before issuing passes and security clearances. Aldrich was told that the Secret Service was ordered to issue permanent passes, "even though the a staffer might still have a history of theft, drug use, or even mental problems."[123] After publication of Aldrich's book, the Clintonistas issued a statement claiming they are forcing staffers with drug histories to take random drug tests.

At one point, Aldrich accuses Clinton staffers of "having too much to hide" to work in the White House. His book can't reveal what that might be since, as a former FBI investigator, he is restricted legally and ethically from revealing all that he obviously knows. Other sources are not so restricted, however. *Washington Dateline*, an independent newspaper column out of Baltimore, Maryland, reported in April of 1994 that the FBI was investigating a "drug courier" who was allegedly operating in the Clinton White House. The column identified an unnamed "Capitol Hill source" as giving the information. The source also indicated that the staffers were being provided with a "safe house" located away from the White House proper. The obvious purpose of such a "safe house" is to allow activities which might be inhibited in the highly-scrutinized White House "fish bowl." The existence of this "safe house" was independently confirmed by another unnamed source inside the office of Democrat Senator P. Moynihan of New York. While Moynihan's office officially denied the report, a White House staffer told the *New York Post* that such a "safe house" did exist and was in nearby suburban Virginia.[124] The Clintonistas obviously feel threatened by public scrutiny.

Further, there are persistent reports of pilfering in the White House. Everything from lap-top computers to food from the cafeteria have allegedly been taken. At least two instances of homosexual activity being conducted in White House offices have also been reported.

This, then, is Aldrich's portrait of the people William Blythe-Clinton brought with him to Washington. They are kinky dressers, casual to a fault and with backgrounds which cannot bear scrutiny. They brought with them levels of immorality and unlawfulness previously unknown in the American presidency. Pilfering, drug use and sexual immorality are apparently endemic in the Clinton White House, and a "safe house" has been provided at government expense, quite possibly for such "recreations." How is the American media handling this exposé? How is Aldrich's "reality" being "managed?"

The book hit at an opportune time, in the midst of the latest Clinton scandal, for which it has obvious relevance. The Blythe-Clinton regime has been accused of expropriating several hundred FBI dossiers on Republican operatives in which they hoped to find political dirt. Aldrich's "insider" book covers several of the principals in that scandal, notably Craig Livingstone, and Aldrich was invited by the *Wall Street Journal* to make comment upon what is tiresomely known as "filegate." This gave him a high profile, and he began receiving invitations to be interviewed by the major media.

Enter White House damage control. Presidential aide George Stephanopoulos and Press secretary Mike McCurry became a two man hit squad. Their success in suppressing Aldrich's exposure and redefining the book indicates the intimate relationship which exists with Blythe-Clinton and the media. It also reveals how willing the media is to shield the regime from allegations of criminality, a willingness which will prove very significant as we probe more serious criminal charges.

The White House hit squad managed to get scheduled Aldrich canceled outright on all three networks. Further, the networks began providing "reality management" for the White House to discredit Aldrich's witness. This former FBI agent, whose strong sense of morality and justice was offended by what he confronted when the Clintonistas took over the presidential residence, was "redefined" as something malevolent and evil. The now familiar media techniques of imposing artificial reality were applied to him.

The attack against Aldrich began on June 30, 1996, when Leon Panetta, the Blythe-Clinton chief of staff called ABC news VP, Robert Murphy to complain about a scheduled Aldrich appearance on *This Week with David Brinkley*. Also contacted by various Clintonistas were an associate producer and the Executive producer of the show, the president of ABC, the president of ABC's parent company, and ABC's Washington bureau chief. The message delivered to these ABC officials was the same. "Drop the Aldrich appearance." Clintonista press secretary Mike McCurry even threatened ABC bureau chief Robin Sproul's "access" to the Clinton regime should the Aldrich appearance be carried out.[125] While Aldrich's *Brinkley* appearance was not canceled outright, George Stephanopoulos was allowed to appear, after Aldrich had left the studio, and slander the author and his book. Stephanopoulos characterized *Unlimited Access* as "lies" and motivated by a right-wing desire to "damage" Blythe-Clinton.

It would be the last appearance allowed Aldrich on major television. The shows *Larry King Live*, ABC's *Nightline* and NBC's *Dateline* withdrew invitations to Aldrich. CBS also refused to put him on the air. The book and its author were discussed, however, on regular news programs. Following the

Clintonista line, Aldrich was called "irresponsible" and "mentally unbalanced."[126]   The censorship and trashing of Aldrich's reputation by the major media was so complete that George Stephanopoulos would brag that the regime had "killed" the book's threat to them.[127]

Stephanopoulos created a political unreality for the book by a very simple expedient. He had members of the Blythe-Clinton regime write "sworn affidavits" that they did not say the things to Aldrich which were reported in his book. For example, White House counsel Lloyd Cutler "swore" he did not tell Aldrich that he had convinced Hillary Clinton to stay with her husband after the public revelations of the Blythe-Clinton affair with Gennifer Flowers. By a multiplication of such "sworn statements," Stephanopoulos was able to make the claim that the book was "a fabrication," and the press repeated the line.

Of course, there is no possibility that Blythe-Clinton has staffed his regime with people willing to lie, even "swear" to a lie, in their own self interest. There is no possibility, that is, unless objective standards of evidence are applied. In that case, at least one of Stephanopoulos' "sworn affidavits" has been proven to be less than factual. In a 67 word statement, Clintonista William Kennedy denied telling Aldrich that Hillary Clinton had ordered the hiring of Greg Livingstone as Chief of Security. Unfortunately, another FBI agent in the Blythe-Clinton White House has supported Aldrich's recollection. Dennis Sculimbrene told a Senate Judiciary Committee on June 9, 1996, that Kennedy had also told him that Livingstone got his job at Hillary Clinton's insistence.[128] It is obviously not Aldrich who is lying, but the press has chosen to use Stephanopoulos' stack of phony affidavits to declare Aldrich "unreliable" and "mentally unbalanced."

It is another case of unreality being imposed for political motives, but in this case, to protect a criminal cartel in the highest seat of power. What kind of man is it who collects to himself thieves and druggies, people who are willing to lie without conscience and who are willing to destroy the reputations of honest witnesses with ruthless deception? As we shall see, Aldrich hasn't even begun to tell the story.

Drugs, Sex and the Money Roll

A July 19, 1996, *New York Times News Service* story written as part of the "damage control" in the Aldrich affair, quoted Clintonista press secretary Michael McCurry as saying, "The president is very clear: He has an absolute zero-tolerance standard for drug use at the White House." This must be one of Virginia Clinton's famous "reinventions" by her boy, since drugs and illicit sex have been a very big part of Willie Blythe-Clinton's behind-the-scenes life during his political career.

This interest in drugs has not been limited to what might be called "recreational use." There are indications that the persona, packaged as "likable Bill Clinton" by the media, was knowledgeable of, participated in and facilitated a major money laundering operation for drug smugglers. Further, it is alleged by witnesses that he developed and converted state resources to this end.

Finally, state and federal resources were used to bribe, intimidate and possibly assault witnesses to this and other Blythe-Clinton crimes and acts of immorality which threatened his political image. All the evidence has been carefully censored by the same social fascist media which trashed Gary Aldrich on command from the Clintonista White House.

The *London Sunday Telegraph* revealed that, while governor of Arkansas, Blythe-Clinton had both a personal and political relationship with a man implicated in drug trafficking. Dan

Lasater was ultimately convicted of distributing drugs and spent six months under a "sweetheart" sentence, incarcerated in his own home. He was then "pardoned" by Governor Bill Clinton. Lasater employed Clinton's half-brother Roger and paid off a drug debt for him. A corporate apartment was "donated" to Roger in the Vantage Point complex in Little Rock. It was used primarily by the Clinton brothers and Dan Lasater to conduct drugs-and-sex parties.

The London paper picked up this trail of Blythe-Clinton's drug involvement from the Vantage Point manager.[129]   The complex was managed by Mrs. Jane Parks, wife of a Little Rock detective. Her office shared paper-thin walls with the "donated" apartment and Mrs. Parks discovered the second-term Governor of Arkansas conducting sex and cocaine parties with his brother there. Mrs. Parks says she saw Blythe-Clinton enter that apartment and, on multiple occasions, listened as he and brother Roger discussed the merits of the cocaine and marijuana they were using. She also heard and saw young, under-age women join the party at times, one of whom was shared sexually by the two men.[130]

The *Telegraph* confirmed Mrs. Parks story with another woman who also observed Blythe-Clinton entering the apartment and heard the activities. The article identifies another witness to Blythe-Clinton's sex and drug habits in the early '80's. Sharlene Wilson, one of Lasater's "party girls" turned drug informant, said she saw both Blythe-Clinton and his brother at Lasater "toga parties." These were orgies where cocaine flowed freely and participants wore nothing but sheets and shared sexual partners.[131]

Mrs. Parks alerted her husband Jerry to the governor's activities. The detective began keeping a file on Blythe-Clinton, a file which would ultimately prove fatal to the detective. Jerry Parks was gunned down gang-land style several months after the

Blythe-Clinton White House discovered the existence of that file. Two Little Rock police detectives were reported to have prepared an indictment against a Blythe-Clinton operative in the murder, an indictment which was ultimately squashed.[132] None of this, of course, was reported in the establishment press.

So who is the real Blythe-Clinton? "Likable Bill" of the media package or "wild Willie" of the hidden witnesses? Is it Bill telling a national radio audience that he "shared the pain" with the "black victims" of church burnings? The media smiled upon "sensitive Bill" when he said, "I have vivid and painful memories of black churches being burned in my own state when I was a child." They did not report that both the Arkansas state historian and the president of Arkansas' NAACP said that there were no church burnings in Arkansas during Clinton's boyhood.[133]

But we now know that facts are irrelevant to this media which believes "reality" is only a politically-desirable perception. This is the reason that other facts were irrelevant to them; facts which documented "wild Willie;" facts which indicate that his interest in drugs may have extended beyond the use of cocaine at kinky sex parties.

The media were told by the White House, for example, how they should view the affidavit of Arkansas State Trooper J. D. Brown and why they should not report what he said. Brown's information set them on the trail of one "wild Willie," a trail which could only lead one to conclude that Willie was as close to mobster as a politician could get.

In July of 1995, the White House gave Brown the infamous "Aldrich treatment." When ABC inquired about Brown's information. A White House counsel —who had obtained a copy of the death certificate of Brown's mother indicating she had died in a gun accident in 1971—told ABC that Brown might have been "implicated" in his mother's death.[134] Thus, allegations without evidence were used to slander a witness and give a willing media a reason to censor his testimony. It would not be the last time the technique was used.

What did Brown say which required "media management" by the Clintonistas? Brown was assigned to the security detail in the governor's mansion during the period Blythe-Clinton was governor of Arkansas. He was one of the four state police officers who had earlier revealed that they had provided illicit sexual liaisons for Blythe-Clinton during that governorship. Brown's second revelation, however, was more serious. It would implicate Dan Lasater in a bizarre drug-smuggling ring and identify Blythe-Clinton as protecting that operation.

Brown said that while serving in the Blythe-Clinton governor's mansion, he had applied for a spot with the CIA, and that Blythe-Clinton had helped facilitate this application. Brown said that he was contacted by a CIA operative and assigned the task of helping fly arms to the Contra anti-communist rebels in Nicaragua from an airport in Mena, Arkansas.

From several independent sources, the *London Telegraph* learned that Barry Seal, a known narcotics trafficker, was contracted in 1984 to fly guns to the Contras from Mena until his death in 1986. Seal had convinced the feds that he had "turned over a new leaf" and would help the Drug Enforcement Agency conduct a sting upon the Medellin cocaine cartel, which he, in fact, did. Seal never quit running his own cocaine operation, however. The *Telegraph* reporter, Ambrose Evans-Pritchard reports an unnamed "Seal associate" as saying, "The CIA didn't realize that Seal had synergised their covert operation with the Dixie Mafia. They didn't figure it out until they were in the quicksand, and by then it was too late. In the end you had a situation where the Dixie Mafia was blackmailing the CIA."[135]

Brown said he took two flights with Seal, and, after making

air-drops at prearranged points in the Honduran jungles, Seal would land at Tegucigalpa, Honduras, to refuel for the return flight. Seal took advantage of these stops to load duffel bags. At the end of the second flight, Seal showed Brown what was contained in those duffel bags. In an attempt to bribe Brown, The Blythe-Clinton security officer was shown packets of cocaine taken from one of the bags. Since the flights had been cleared by the CIA, they were unhampered by federal drug interdiction efforts. A "free pipeline" for cocaine had been opened into the U.S. Seal was ultimately gunned down by agents of the Medellin cartel while hiding in Louisiana.

Disturbed that he had uncovered a smuggling operation which was seemingly being protected by the CIA, Brown took his fears and his concerns to his mentor and the power which he served, governor Bill Clinton. Brown describes arriving back at the governor's mansion after suffering Seal's bribery attempt. It was night, but he found Blythe-Clinton still up. Brown related the cocaine story, but the governor's reaction was not at all what he expected. After hearing the details, Blythe-Clinton showed no surprise. He simply told Brown, "That's [Dan] Lasater's deal," with the clear implication that Brown was to leave it alone.[136]

In what sense was it "Lasater's deal?" Unfortunately, Blythe-Clinton's reported conversation with Brown gave us no more detail. We do know that when the cryptic comment was alleged by Brown in 1994, Blythe-Clinton responded by calling the former security agent a "pathological liar" and arranged to have Brown's taxes audited by the IRS.[137] Other lines of evidence indicate what the "deal" might have been, and Blythe-Clinton is intimately involved.

Larry Nichols is a kind of lighting rod drawing the evidence and witnesses together to expose Blythe-Clinton's "hidden activities" to public opinion. He is a man obsessed as only

someone who feels himself betrayed can be obsessed. He has
paid dearly for this obsession, both in his personal life and by
suffering an unwarranted arrest, beatings and what appears to be
a subtle poison attack which nearly killed him.

Nichols, you see, had once been a Clintonista "insider" who
was pushed out and his reputation trashed after he discovered
something which gagged him and threatened to go public with it.
Nichols' discovery may be the key to "Lasater's deal."

Nichols had provided publicity services to Blythe-Clinton,
helping hush up the seemingly continuous potential sexual
scandals created by Blythe-Clinton's "alley cat" morals.[138] In
1988 Nichols was made the "marketing director" for a state
agency which Blythe-Clinton had initiated in 1985. It was called
the Arkansas Development and Finance Authority (ADFA).
ADFA was supposed to help Arkansas small businesses by
selling state secured bonds and providing loans to worthy
enterprises. According to Nichols, it didn't exactly work that
way.

Nichols soon discovered two things as marketing director of
ADFA. First, ADFA president Wooten Epes didn't want him to
do his job. He thought his purpose was to publicize ADFA
opportunities throughout the state and solicit new business. No
such thing. Nichols writes, "After pushing Epes, saying that we
should hustle more loans, he said to me, 'You don't understand.
Your job is not to get loans. It's damage control.'"[139]

Second, he found out why that was true. Many of the loans
were going to friends and associates of Blythe-Clinton: to people
like Seth Ward, father-in-law of Hillary Clinton's associate,
Webb Hubble. The application process was a joke. It consisted of
"a simple set of documents to which Clinton supporters attached
a profit and loss statement. ADFA never bothered checking out
these applications." These phony applications were "reviewed"

in the morning and voted upon in the afternoon. Everything had already been decided. If the loan didn't go to a "friend of Bill" it went to those who "donated" $50,000 to the Clinton political coffers and/or paid expensive "consultation fees" to law firms associated with Blythe-Clinton.

The chairman of the ADFA review committee once told his members, conducting business in a public dining room, to hold up an application because the applicant had yet to put his $50,000 "donation" into the campaign chest. A reporter for the *New Republic* was allowed to see only about a third of the records for ADFA loans. The rest, Nichols alleges, have been "shredded."[140]

Nichols discovered the reason the loans were "attractive" enough to warrant $50,000 "donations" and to bring in Blythe-Clinton's circle like flies to honey. "After two months of putting together the annual report, it became apparent that *no one was paying interest on these loans.* The question arose, 'Where are the payments from these companies on their loans?' After checking with everybody concerned, it became apparent that there weren't any." Nichols says he discovered something very shocking: that these loans to the political friends of Blythe-Clinton were being "zero balanced" with no record of a payment coming in. He copied the paperwork to prove these allegations.

But if repayment schedules were not being met, this left a very serious problem. Bonds, guaranteed by the state, had been sold to make these loans. Nichols puts the problem this way. "Another thing really piqued my interest—and led to trouble galore—was, 'Who bought these bonds?' because it made sense that whoever it was, they were going to be looking for blood when they didn't receive their payments. Problem was, you couldn't locate even one owner of ADFA bonds." Money seemed to just "appear" with no one waiting in line to reclaim it. Where were the "defrauded" bond holders?

The solution to this mystery had to await another revelation. A large number of ADFA bonds were brokered by Dan Lasater. It has been discovered that Lasater set up a phony bond account at about the time that ADFA was initiated. The account has all the marks of a money laundering front, and Nichols says as much as $50 million of ADFA bonds were purchased through that account.[141] In 1985, a Kentucky county court clerk named Dennis Patrick was enticed by an employee of Lasater & Company to allow a bond account of questionable purpose be opened in his name. For allowing this, the account was immediately credited with $21,000, a pretty profit for just opening an account.[142] He would discover it might not have been such a good deal. First, the IRS wanted to know why $107 million worth of bond purchases had been run through Patrick's account during a short period in 1985. When Patrick asked that same question of Lasater's company, he found himself in even more trouble. Three separate attempts were made on his life. One of the would-be assassins told police he was to be paid $20,000 for the job. Officials accused Patrick of being in the drug trade because the assaults fit the pattern. Patrick uprooted his family and went into hiding. Only recently did he connect the assaults with the bond account to which he had lent his name.

If the Kentucky court clerk didn't make those purchases, where did the money come from which Lasater funneled through the man's account into ADFA and other bonds? The most likely source of such a huge cash infusion was "Lasater's deal."[143] Could monies be infused into ADFA through phony bond purchases? Could these bond holdings then "disappear" from the ADFA books and equally phony "loans" to co-conspirators be "zero balanced" by the now non-accounted cash infusion? Who would complain if such bond purchases were "forgotten" on the ADFA books? The court clerk in Kentucky in whose name the bonds were held but who had no investment in them?

Bonds purchased fraudulently can be made to "disappear," leaving an unaccounted cash reserve in the bonding agency. This reserve can either be made to "pay back" phony loans, or, perhaps, be "transferred" to an off-shore bank on a largely unregulated island where it might be quietly put in the account of a hidden owner. A curious ADFA "coincidence" brings some suspicion as far as the latter possibility is concerned. An account for deceased drug-trafficker Barry Seal was discovered in Fiji Bank in Cayman Islands holding $1.6 billion. That's with a "b." In December of 1988, ADFA wired $50 million to this same Cayman Islands bank. There is no evidence that the money was returned to Arkansas, nor why an off-shore bank closely associated with smuggling profits was chosen.[144]

The kick-in-the-head came when Nichols went to Blythe-Clinton to report his finding accounting irregularities in ADFA. He reveals that he assumed the governor knew nothing of the problems, and Nichols demanded an immediate auditing of the ADFA books by an independent source. Blythe-Clinton responded not with the audit, but by firing Nichols and announcing to the press that the former ADFA marketing director had been discovered converting state resources to illegal use. He was accused of using state time and resources to work and raise funds for the Nicaraguan Contras. The press thus used a fashionable left-wing "cause," support for Nicaraguan communism and hatred for its enemies, to suppress a whistle-blower. Nichols writes, "Every day brought a supposed new revelation about my 'wrongdoing'–TV, front pages of newspapers, the radio, you name it."[145] Thus began a long slander campaign against Larry Nichols whose "crime" consisted of stumbling into what appears to be a Blythe-Clinton money-laundering scheme for "Lasater's deal."

A little detail is needed to update the story to the time that Blythe-Clinton appeared on the national scene. During the year Our Hero was running for president, ADFA still apparently held excessive cash from the alleged money laundering scheme. To clean things up a bit, ADFA monies were put in a shadowy off-shore account which refuses to produce records for the transfer. According to the *New York Post*, the money was placed with Coral Reinsurance of Barbados and no records have been produced to show if the money was ever repaid or who ultimately received it. A salesman for the company told the *Post* that Barbados law does not require them to divulge that information.[146]

Larry Nichols' response to being fired and having his reputation publicly destroyed by a crooked politician protecting a criminal enterprise was to fight. His campaign for the redemption of his reputation became a crusade to reveal the true Blythe-Clinton. Nichols is the author of the *Clinton Chronicles*, a video and book which tells his story, as well as documents other crimes committed in the defense of Blythe-Clinton.[147]

The story is a sordid one. A pattern of crime is revealed which is worthy of a Mafioso. Not only was a state agency allegedly built for the express purpose of conducting a money-laundering operation, but crimes of violence were committed to protect the author of that scheme. State policemen assigned to protect the governor were converted into a type of private mob. They acted illegally as sexual procurers for a man not above using his power to coerce young women to compromise their integrity. Their chief was taken by Blythe-Clinton into the federal government where he became a type of "enforcer" who offered bribes to former subordinates for their silence and may be implicated in more violent ways of assuring silence. Other state offices were also allegedly converted to criminal purposes, to cover up the murders of potential witnesses.

The pattern of violence surrounding Blythe-Clinton is unmistakable. It is the mark of a hardened but successful criminal. Some murders benefit Blythe-Clinton, but there is only circumstantial evidence that such was the motive. This was the case of detective Jerry Parks who collected a file on Blythe-Clinton's sexual immoralities—including pictures, names, dates and places—after his wife alerted him to the governor's sex and cocaine parties held at the Vantage Point apartments. Coincidentally, Parks had also done security work for the Clinton presidential campaign, but had not been paid by the summer of 1993. He called the White House and told them of the existence of this file, threatening to release it to the public unless he got his money. A short time after alerting the regime to the file's existence, Parks' house was professionally burglarized with only the file being taken. Two months later, Parks died in a hail of bullets.[148] In a speech in Boise, Idaho on November 12 of 1994, Larry Nichols said two Little Rock police detectives wanted to indict Buddy Young for this murder, but prosecutors had refused the indictment.[149] Young was Blythe-Clinton's chief of security as governor of Arkansas and was given a job in the federal government afterward.

Some violence, however, has been directly linked to the protection of Blythe-Clinton's public reputation. The *London Telegraph* reports that attorney Gary Johnson was beaten and left for dead because his security camera inadvertently taped William Blythe-Clinton letting himself into the apartment of his mistress Gennifer Flowers. Johnson's apartment is located across the hall from Flowers'. Johnson said he revealed the existence of the tape in a Little Rock night club. Several days later, three men appeared at his door and physically intimidated him into giving them the tape. Once they had secured the tape, they beat him severely, leaving him unconscious and apparently dead. The beating shattered his arm, caused severe head injuries and perforated his bladder. His spleen was removed because of the beating.[150]

Other crimes have also been committed which were designed to remove evidence of Blythe-Clinton corruption. After the White House became aware that the conservative publication, *The American Spectator,* was working on a Blythe-Clinton sex scandal based on the confessions of two of his former security officers, the offices of the magazine were burglarized and the files rifled. Both the *Spectator's* Washington and New York offices were broken into and the files searched diligently.[151]

Further, reporter L.J. Davis of the *New Republic,* who was covering ADFA and other elements of the corruption story in Arkansas, was mugged and left unconscious. His notes on the Blythe-Clinton affair were stolen.[152]

Intimidation attempts were also made against the state police officers who revealed to the magazine that Blythe-Clinton had ordered them to procure women for his pleasure. The officers were called by Blythe-Clinton's former chief of security in Arkansas, Buddy Young, and warned to discontinue talking to the *Spectator.*[153]

Young, who is currently enjoying a $100,000-a-year job in the Blythe-Clinton regime as a FEMA head, has had his name linked to three suspicious deaths which benefited the cover-up. He is alleged to have been on the verge of indictment by Little Rock police in the Parks murder. His name has also come up in reports on the strange death of Kathy Ferguson and her live-in boy friend, Bill Shelton.

Ferguson has worked in the Arkansas governor's mansion and claimed she had been sexually assaulted several times by Blythe-Clinton. Shelton called Young and tried to blackmail the regime into giving him a federal job by threatening to go public with Ferguson's accusations. Several days later, the body of

Ferguson was found in Shelton's apartment with a gunshot to the head.

The death was ruled a "suicide" by Arkansas coroners, but medical experts viewing the body disputed the official version. They found a cosmetically disguised bullet hole behind Ferguson's left ear, indicating she had been shot behind the head execution style, and not through the massive wound in her temple as claimed by Arkansas coroners. Four weeks later, the body of Shelton was found laid-out on Ferguson's fresh grave. He had also been shot behind the ear and the death ruled a "suicide."[154]

The Media Make the Charges "Unreal"

The national press has been restrained in its accounts of Bill Clinton's private life, and with good reason. Most of those who have made charges against him have been despicable people; jealous, stunted sorts." Newsweek, May 1994

In their coverage of William Blythe-Clinton, the left-dominated media have proven they not only tolerate the private crimes of favored politicians, but are complicit in the cover-ups of those crimes as well. They are nearly accessories after the fact. They *politicize* Blythe-Clinton's private crimes, and they *politicize* the victims and witnesses as well.

To the degree that criminal allegations threaten Blythe-Clinton's reputation, they are damaging to him politically. Those witnesses and victims who make these allegations are, therefore, defined as "political enemies." This politicized viewpoint of the allegations tells us several things about the media. They have a distorted sense of decency and a rather ruthless indifference to unjust suffering.

Thus we find the *Newsweek* of May 1994 treating the facts

which identify a criminal pattern in the activities of Blythe-Clinton and associates as if they were illegitimate "opinions" of social pariahs and detested outsiders. The ideologically-conformist media defends Blythe-Clinton by ignoring the substance of the charges—the checkable facts—in favor of a continuous and brutal attempt to tarnish the public image of the witnesses. They are dismissed as "despicable people" as "jealous, stunted sorts." Nothing which people of this "sort" says can be "true." Their evidence must be dismissed out of hand, their facts completely ignored. The criminal is made to seem the "victim" of the witnesses testifying against him.

"Attack the witnesses" has been a vicious little game which Blythe-Clinton and his media supporters have played since the first stench started to ooze out of Arkansas. When four Arkansas state troopers came forward and confessed that they had acted as procurers and facilitators for Blythe-Clinton's promiscuous sexual habits while acting as his security force in the governor's mansion, they were characterized as unreliable witnesses by major elements of the press. Editors and bureau chiefs at the *Wall Street Journal*, *U.S. News and World Report* and the *New York Times* used this characterization to justify why the troopers' revelations were censored.[155]

When a female employee of the state of Arkansas told of being summoned by Blythe-Clinton to a room in a hotel at which she was manning a state-sponsored booth, and there being sexually manhandled by Blythe-Clinton who also exposed himself to her, the press attacks against the witness became even more severe.

Paula Corbin-Jones tells of feeling virtually imprisoned in the room by a state policeman posted outside the door as Blythe-Clinton lunged and grabbed her. Only after she had resisted three such attempts did he agree to let her go, but not before threatening reprisals against her job if she should report the incident.

She says she was propositioned on two more occasions by state police officers for Blythe-Clinton and was informed that the state police officer was monitoring her private life.[156]

Journalist Scott Wheeler reports what happened after Corbin-Jones made her allegations. "But in typical form, instead of focusing on Paula's startling allegations, the reporters lost no time in going out and attempting to dig up some dirt on her."[157] The media not only implied she was a "liar," but accused her of being a "dupe" of conservatives, and characterized her as a lower class hick and a theatrical fraud. Editor-in-chief Mortimer Zuckerman of *U.S. News & World Report* said her story "didn't pass the smell test."[158] *Time* magazine mocked her, characterizing her appearance in a documentary as being "dressed in a little girl costume" and speaking "in a high pitched voice."[159]

It appears that the more serious the allegations against Blythe-Clinton, the more severely the media trashes the witness. The strongest character assassinations were reserved for the participants of the *Clinton Chronicles* video, and especially the driving force behind that video, Larry Nichols. The explosive video explores the full range of evidence and allegations against Blythe-Clinton and the syndicate he has gathered to himself. Reviewed are the ADFA/Mena drug smuggling and money laundering operations, suppression of investigations of the same; the sex scandals; and the violent deaths of potential witnesses.

The video began to have a major impact in 1994 even though its distribution was limited to "unorthodox" channels such as talk radio shows and underground newsletters. The media took notice of the video when it was offered by high profile leaders of the "religious right" who are considered the primary domestic enemy by social fascism.

An attack on Nichols began in earnest. He was slandered by

Time, U.S. News & World Report, the *Philadelphia Inquirer* and the Knight Ridder news service. Most of these attacks were pure deceptions designed to blacken Nichols' reputation.

For example, the *Philadelphia Inquirer* reported that Nichols was a "dead beat dad" and was several thousand dollars behind in his child support. This was not true. Nichols was paying the money into a court-ordered trust fund because his ex-wife was in violation of a custody order.

Arkansas officials also cooperated in the press assault. With great publicity, Nichols was arrested for several bank overdrafts which had occurred six and eight years previously and which had been covered at the time. The charges were quietly dropped for lack of substance and the fact that the statutes of limitations had expired, but not before major stories appeared in the *Arkansas Democrat* and elsewhere, implying that Nichols was a felon.[160] An illicit arrest was made for the sole purpose of creating negative press coverage of Nichols.

The *Clinton Chronicles* video, itself, as well as many of the witnesses who appeared in it, also came under media assault. Journalist Scott Wheeler reveals that *U.S. News & World Report* published an attack on the video, but with information only "based upon a one-minute phone call to one witness in the [*Clinton Chronicles*]..."[161]

The tone of the *U.S. News* article was one of mocking satire. It implied that anyone who would believe the evidence in the *Clinton Chronicles* would just as likely accuse Blythe-Clinton of being part of the alleged conspiracy which killed John Kennedy or of having a part in the assassination of Julius Caesar in 44 B.C. The video and its supporters were satirically presented as paranoid and irrational. The attempt to create this impression of "irrationality" used the standard political-unreality techniques which we have previously examined.

Suspicions that the death of Kathy Ferguson was not "suicide" were made to seem "irrational" by suppressing evidence. Suspicions that Ferguson was murdered were made to seem an "irrational belief" by eliminating from the article such information as the blackmail attempt of Blythe-Clinton by Ferguson's boyfriend days before her death; the discovery of another bullet wound by medical witnesses which was unreported in the "official" coroner's report; and the testimony of neighbors that they heard sounds of a possible struggle from the apartment in which Ferguson's body was discovered.

In the case of detective Jerry Parks' murder, *U.S. News* trashes the testimony of the surviving Parks family members in order to obscure a possible motive for Blythe-Clinton in the death. The Parks were made to seem like "liars" in alleging the murder was connected to a stolen file which Jerry Parks had kept on Blythe-Clinton.

A standard political-unreality technique was used to discount the existence of this file which surviving family members said was burglarized from the family's residence prior to Jerry's murder. "Authoritative pronouncement" was used to make the existence of the file seem unbelievable. A Little Rock police lieutenant was quoted as saying that he had "no evidence for such a file."

What he was actually saying, and saying with all the authority of a police official, was that the Parks family was lying in their testimony. The only "evidence" for that closely-guarded file was the Parks family and the history they gave of it. That history, of course, was never mentioned in the *U.S. News* article.

The file began in 1984, when Mrs. Parks encountered Blythe-Clinton, his brother Roger, and Dan Lasater conducting sex and drug parties in Roger Clinton's donated apartment. These encounters included such incidents as the open delivery of a bag of cocaine in the hallway fronting the apartment; the bringing of 14 to 17-year-old girls to the parties; and discovering participants, both female and male, running nude from the apartment into the complex's communal courtyard surrounding the pool.[162]

Jerry Parks became concerned for the legal safety of his wife who, as manager, might be held responsible for these brazenly illegal, but "politically protected," activities. He began taking detailed notes, including times, places and people. This was the origin of the Blythe-Clinton file.

Jerry's son Gary Parks says the Blythe-Clinton surveillance was continued after Roger Clinton gave up the apartment for a federal prison cell on a drug conviction. Gary said his father was hired, Gary believes, by some unknown person of wealth who desired influence over Blythe-Clinton, through a local politician by the name of Tom Robinson.[163]

In any case, Gary reports that as a boy he accompanied his father on several surveillances of Blythe-Clinton at places Parks knew Blythe-Clinton frequented. The governor had established habits, arriving, for example, at the Quapaw Towers at around 11:30 at night. The Quapaw Towers were home both to Blythe-Clinton's mistress, Gennifer Flowers, and his "business associate" Dan Lasater. Gary's last surveillance with his father was in 1988.

In late July of 1993, right after the White House had given Jerry Parks the payment he had demanded for the security services provided the Blythe-Clinton campaign, the Parks residence was burglarized. The burglary appeared professional. The phone and power lines were cut, eliminating the burglar alarm.

According to Gary Parks, "The burglars went in and took only Dad's file on Bill Clinton from the bottom drawer on his bedroom dresser. They were several inches thick with photos and notes.

"Dad never even told me about it; Mom told me after his death. They never reported it to the police either. As my mom said, 'you can't call up the police and say someone just stole the investigative file on Bill Clinton.'"[164]

There you have it. The way the press has twisted guilt and innocence to protect a politician whose policies service the clients of social fascism. They are indifferent to the reality of those crimes–only concerned that the charges might undermine the political effectiveness of Blythe-Clinton.

The criminal allegations are of a very serious nature. It is alleged, with the support of multiple witnesses, that in 1984 William Blythe-Clinton as the Governor of the state of Arkansas was being entertained at lavish sex and cocaine parties by Dan Lasater and was seen to participate in the same by at least two witnesses.

In that same period known-drug-runner Barry Seal was conducting Contra rearmament flights for the CIA from Mena, Arkansas and carrying cocaine back into the country. Seal was discovered doing this by a Blythe-Clinton security officer who had been hired by the CIA through Blythe-Clinton influence.

When informed of this, Governor Blythe-Clinton appeared unconcerned and said the operation was affiliated with his friend and political associate Dan Lasater.

In 1985, Blythe-Clinton established ADFA, a semi-private state agency whose board was appointed solely by himself, and which was removed from oversight by state auditors.[165] Lasater, who was known by Blythe-Clinton to be affiliated with a drug-smuggling operation, was given the authority to sell a large percentage of ADFA bonds. Lasater was discovered to have established one false account by means of a $21,000 bribe through which bonds were purchased, thus disguising the origin of the money.

By 1988, ADFA was found to have a surfeit of cash by a recently-hired executive, Larry Nichols. This cash was being siphoned out of ADFA by the cancellation of interest and payments on "loans" made to Blythe-Clinton associates.

Blythe-Clinton was, himself, personally profiting by requiring a $50,000 donation to his political campaign chest from those participating in the ADFA "loan" program.

ADFA also placed cash into two separate off-shore financial institutions, one of which held an account in Barry Seal's name for $1.6 billion. No record of these funds returning have been forthcoming.

Many ADFA records have been discovered to be missing or have been withheld from public scrutiny. One reporter found that two-thirds of the "loan" records were no longer available.

Witnesses to Blythe-Clinton sexual irregularities have suffered violence and death. Lawyer Gary Johnson was beaten and left for dead by thugs who took a security-camera video tape showing Blythe-Clinton letting himself into the apartment of his mistress Gennifer Flowers.

Detective Jerry Parks was gunned down after revealing the existence of a file documenting Blythe-Clinton's sexual immorality.

Kathy Ferguson was shot behind the ear after what witnesses said sounded like a struggle in her apartment. She had just threatened to go public and reveal Blythe-Clinton sexual assaults against her unless her boyfriend was given a federal job. Arkansas authorities declared the death a "suicide," but hid the existence of a bullet wound which medical experts were able to identify. These events occurred after Blythe-Clinton became President of the United States.

While there may not be enough evidence to convict, there is surely enough evidence to investigate, if not indict Blythe-

Clinton for major felonies. This will not likely occur, however, for the media has created an "atmosphere of terror" by slandering and destroying the public reputation of anyone who dares bring forth witness. They have made Blythe-Clinton into a client and are willing to impose artificial reality in his defense. They make the accused seem like the "victim" by throwing slimy and deceitful dispersions upon the characters of his accusers.

FBI agent Gary Aldrich, who identified White House protection of moral and legal defects in the staff, was characterized as dishonest and a tool of the opposition party by national news programs.

Arkansas State Trooper J. D. Brown, who testified of Blythe-Clinton's knowledge of the Mena/drug/Lasater connection, was accused of complicity in his mother's death and his story thus discredited by ABC.

Larry Nichols, who witnessed financial irregularities in ADFA —who copied records to support his charge, by the way—was inaccurately accused in negative press accounts, first of illegally supporting the Nicaragua Contras, then being a "dead beat dad" and, finally, of being a "check fraud."

Paula Corbin-Jones suffered Blythe-Clinton sexual assault and extended harassment and was later the target of raw political muscle in order to extort her into silence. When she came forward, she was portrayed as a "hick," a "gold digger," and a "tool" of conservatives by the media.

Gary and Jane Parks were characterized as liars by a major news magazine.

The media's ability to slander and destroy anyone's credibility with ludicrous charges has made any attempt to investigate and prosecute virtually impossible. What witness would be willing to risk his reputation and economic well-being by coming forward, especially when he knows the "fate" of other witnesses? What law will protect him from physical harm?

The media has imposed a reign of terror on those who "know" and invites everyone else to believe in the "smilin' Bill" image of their carefully-constructed PR campaign for Blythe-Clinton. It appears to be working admirably. At this writing, it seems a near certainty that Blythe-Clinton will be reelected in 1996.

What can be done? Is there any solution for the individual when a media-imposed unreality dominates the public consciousness while a multiplicity of its victims are simultaneously buried in the darkness beyond? Certainly one need not be personally victim to it. One may determine that truth consists of what the facts dictate, not what the media proclaims truth to be. One can understand that the media of twentieth century totalitarianism—whether it be Communist, Nazi or social fascist— are the most successful sustainers of lies the world has ever known. This is especially true of social fascism since they possess even more powerful tools than did their predecessors. The image of television has more power to convince than either the spoken or written word.

The purpose of this book is to reveal that the lie is *systematic*. It is not accidental or occasional. The contemporary mass media lies because that is the purpose for which it was built in the first place. Huge networks and centralized newspaper chains were created to persuade and evoke a uniform opinion among the masses. To operate that way, however, the media must itself be unified by an ideology and this has recently been accomplished. Social fascism has been forged as the chains for the American mind. It is appointing an end for the American people, erasing their history, and dissolving their culture. It has set a criminal over them. Individuals might escape the mind-prisons being prepared for them. That will do nothing for the nation, however. The tyrants of the mind must be completely overthrown and cast down before that can occur.

Notes

Chapter 1
[1] *Environment Betrayed*, June, 1994, Box 1161, Winona, MN 55987
[2] *Ibid.*
[3] *Environment Betrayed*, July, 1994, p. 1
[4] *Environment Betrayed*, June, 1994, p. 6
[5] *Environment Betrayed*, Aug., 1994 p. 8
[6] *Environment Betrayed*, March 1994
[7] *H du B Reports*, Oct. 1995 p. 6

Chapter 2
[8] *AIN White Paper: The L.A. King Trial and Its Aftermath; What the Establishment Media Isn't Telling*, Aug. 1992, The Paradigm Company, Boise, Idaho
[9] *Ibid.*
[10] *The Reaper*, May 12, 1992, Box 84901, Phoenix, AZ 85071
[11] *AIN White Paper:* Op. Cit.
[12] *Ibid.*
[13] *Ibid.*

Chapter. 3
[14] Carson, Clarence, *The Flight From Reality*, The Foundation for Economic Education, Irving-On-Hudson, New York, 1969, p. 29
[15] *Ibid.* p. 38
[16] *Ibid.* p. 46
[17] *Ibid.* p. 36
[18] *Ibid.* p. 36
[19] George Boas, *Rationalism in Greek Philosophy* (Baltimore: The Johns Hopkins Press, 1961), p. 8. As quoted in Carson
[20] "Flower Child of Fascism," *The New American*, Appelton, WI, March 18, 1996, p.27
[21] *Ibid.*
[22] *Ibid.* p. 23
[23] *Ibid.* p. 24

[24] *Ibid.* p. 27

[25] Ludwig Wittgenstein, *Philosophical Investigations* (New York: Macmillan, 1971)

[26] Ludgwig Wittgenstein from *Culture and Value* as quoted in *Wittgenstein and Derrida*, Henry Staten, University of Nebraska Press (Lincoln, NB) 1984, title page.

[27] As quoted by Noem Chomsky in *Language and Mind* (Harcourt Brace Jovanovich: New York) 1972. p. 25

[28] *Philosophical Investigations;* p.10

[29] *Wittgenstein and Derrida, op. cit.* pp. 66-67

[30] *Language and Mind, Op. cit.* p. 25

[31] *Ibid.* p. 1

[32] See Khun, *The Structure of Scientific Revolutions* (University of Chicago Press, 1962)

[33] Personal experience. Columbia University, 1968-70.

[34] See Carlos Castaneda, *The Teachings of Don Juan,* University of California, Berkley (1971)

[35] Quoted in *A Layman's Primer to Whole Language Foolery;* unpublished manuscript by Lawrence Dawson, 1995

[36] *National Right to Life News,* April 12, 1996 p. 23

[37] *Ibid.*

[38] *Ibid.* p. 23

[39] *The New American,* Appleton WI, May 27, 1996. p. 3

[40] "Abortion foes take the low road in attacking late-term procedure" Goodman, Ellen, *Idaho Statesman,* June 7, 1996

[41] "Flower Child Fascism" *op. cit.*

Chapter 4

[42] *The Media Elite; America's New Power Brokers* by S. Robert Lichter, Stanley Rothman and Linda S. Lichter; Adler & Adler Publishers, Inc. Bethesda, Maryland, 1986 p. 22

[43] *Ibid.* p. 29

[44] *Ibid.* p. 41

[45] *Ibid.* p. 55

[46] *Ibid.* p. 19

[47] *Ibid.* p. 64

[48] It should be noted that Lichter and Rothman do not report raw percentages of journalists distorting the retelling towards their ideology. They give only left-leaning vs. right-leaning as a percentage of all alleged

bias. The actual percentage of journalists distorting the retelling toward
their shared ideology had to be calculated from the figures the authors
did give.

Ibid. p. 67
The Journal of Social, Political and Economic Studies, Summer 1991,
6861 Elm St., Suite 4H, McLean VA 22101
The Wanderer, June 4, 1992
Herbert Gans, *Deciding What's News*, (New York: Pantheon Books,
1979) p. 201
Gans, "Are American Journalists Dangerously Liberal?" *Columbia
Journalism Review* , (Nov./Dec. 1985), p.p 32-33
Op. cit.
Dispatches, Aug. 16, 1993, 7095 Hollywood Blvd., Suite 627, Holly-
wood, CA 90028
The Pathfinder Dec. 1003 Box 291, Spokane , WA 99210
Jubilee, Jan./Feb. 1996 p. 3, Box 310, Midpines, CA 95345
The incestuous relationship between government educrats, especially the
left-of-center National Education Association teacher's union, and the
media must be reserved for another effort.
The Wanderer, June 3, 1993, 201 Ohio St. St. Paul, MN 55107
The New York Guardian July, 1993, 3316 Great Neck Rd., Great Neck,
NY, 11021

Chapter 5
"Conversations" *Otto Scott's Compass* March 1, 1996, Box 69006,
Seattle, WA 98003 p.1
Access To Energy, Feb. 1996, Box 1250 Cave Junction, OR, 97523 p. 1
Environment Betrayed Dec./Jan. 1995/96 op. cit.
The Kansas Intelligencer, June, 1993, 211 W. Elizabeth Ave.,
Morganville, KS 67468

Chapter 6
Telling the Truth, Simon & Schuster, New York 1995, pp 16-17
Ibid. p. 36
Ibid.
Ibid. p. 27
Patai, Daphne and Koertge, Noretta, *Professing Feminism: Cautionary
Tales from the Strange World of Women's Studies* (New York: Basic
Books, 1994) p. 178

[70] "When The Truth Yields to Political Pressure" *Campus Report*, Jan./ Feb. 1996, 4455 Connecticut Ave., NW, Suite 330, Washington, D.C., 20008

[71] The Encyclopaedia Brtannica, New York, 1910, Vol 9 p. 43

[72] *The Washington Times*, March 6, 1996, Washington, D.C.

[73] *Ibid.*

[74] *Not Out of Africa*, Basic Books, NY, NY, 1996 pp. 4-5

[75] *Ibid.* P. 46

[76] "We Win as a Team or We Lose as a Team," *Issues & Views*, Fall/Winter 1996, Box 467, NY, NY 10025

[77] Schultz, Roger "PC Historians Agitate in Atlanta," *Campus Report*, March 1996, *Ibid.*

[78] *Ibid.*

[79] "When The Truth Yields to Political Pressure"*Campus Report, op cit.*

[80] *Imprimis*, March 1996, Hillsdale College, Hillsdale, MI, 49242, p.2

[81] Lefkowitz, Mary, *Not out of Africa; How Afrocentrism became an Excuse to Teach Myth as History*

[82] Berger and Luckmann, *The Social Construction of Reality*, Anchor Books, Doubleday, 1966, New York, P. 3

[83] *Ibid.* p.1

[84] *Ibid.* p.22

Chapter 7

[85] *Anti Shyster*, Vol 5, No. 4, Dallas Texas, and *Media Bypass*, Oct., 1995, Evansville, IN

[86] Hoffman, Michael, *Independent History and Research*, Box 849, Coeur d'Alene, ID 83816

[87] The black journal, I*ssues & Views* (Summer, 1995) says that elite all-black schools in Washington, D.C., North Carolina and elsewhere were forcibly replaced by inferior "integrated" versions by the Brown decision. This effectively destroyed state-supported rigorous intellectual college preparation for young blacks. Box 467, New York, NY, 10025

[88] See *Birth of a Nation*, the early silent film by D. H. Griffith

[89] *Issues & Views* (Spring 1996?), *op. cit.*

[90] *Issues & Views* (Summer 1995) *op. cit.*

[91] *The Welfare State, 1929-1985*. American Textbook Committee (Wadley, AL) 1986 p. 236

[92] *Ibid.*

[93] "Afro-centrism" consists of historic unrealities being imposed to inculcate "black pride." It has already been discussed at length in an earlier chapter.

[94] *Time*, April 29, 1996, pp. 44-45

[95] Charles S. Hyneman, *The Supreme Court on Trial* (New York: Atherton Press, 1963), p. 199

[96] *Yale Free Press*, Box 6574, Yale Station, New Haven, CN 0652, Feb. 1994

[97] *Straight Talk*, 128 Lighthouse Dr., Jupiter, FL, 33458, Dec. 5, 1992

[98] *Fidelity Magazine*, 206 Marquette Ave., South Bend, IN, 46617, March 1992

[99] The Welfare State, *op. cit.* p.p. 238-239

[100] Hoffman, *op. cit.*

[101] *The Journal of Social, Political and Economic Studies*, Summer 1991 6861 Elm St., Suite 4H, McLean VA 2210

[102] The musical information I owe to my wife Meg who deserted her career as a musician for the greater calling of motherhood.

[103] *The Flight from Truth*, Random House, New York, U.S. edition, 1991, p. p. 69-70

Chapter 8

[104] New York Times News Service, July, 14, 1996

[105] Associated Press, July 3, 1996

[106] *Idaho Press Tribune*, July 3, 4 1996

[107] Personal communication from Dr. Arthur Robinson.

[108] Associated Press, July 21, 1996

[109] *Idaho Statesman*, July 23, 1996

[110] *The American Information Newsletter*, July 1993. *op. cit*

[111] *Straight Talk*, Jan. 21, 1993, 128 Lighthouse Dr., Jupiter, FL, 33458

[112] *Sydney Morning Herald*, May 20, 1995

[113] *Op. cit.*

[114] *Human Events*, July 5, 1996 p. 8

[115] Associated Press, July 5, 1996

[116] *Idaho Statesman*, July 11, 1996

[117] Associated Press, July 5, 1996

[118] *Ibid.*

[119] *Idaho Statesman*, July 23, 1996

Chapter 9

[120] American Research Foundation, Aug. 15, 1994, Box 5687, Baltimore, MD 21210

[121] *Ibid.*

[122] *Human Events*, July 5, 1996

[123] Gary Aldrich, *Unlimited Access*, (Regnery, 1996)

[124] *The Spotlight*, March 28, 1994, Washington, D.C.

[125] *The Weekly Standard*, July 22, 1996, 1150 17th St., N.W., Suite 505, Washington DC, 20036-4617

[126] "Home Run: L. Brent Bozell", *The Wanderer*, July 18, 1996

[127] *The Weekly Standard, op. cit.*

[128] "Aldrich's Chief Charge Is Still Intact" *Human Events*, July 19, 1996

[129] *London Telegraph*, July 17, 1994

[130] *Human Events*, July 29, 1994

[131] *London Telegraph*, July 17, 1994

[132] *American Information Newsletter*, op. cit., Dec. 1994

[133] "Who Benefits from Torching Churches?" *The Spotlight*, July 1, 1996, *op. cit.*

[134] *The American Spectator*, Oct. 1994, Arlington , VA

[135] *London Telegraph*, Oct. 9, 1994

[136] *The American Spectator*, Oct. 1994

[137] *Ibid.*

[138] Larry Nichols, "Clinton's Circle of Power-The Epicenter," *The Clinton Chronicles Book*, Jeremiah Books, Hemet, CA 1994

[139] *Ibid.*

[140] *Ibid.*

[141] *Ibid.*

[142] *London Telegraph*, May 8, 1994

[143] *Dispatches*, June 5, 1995, Hollywood , CA with *For the People Radio*, Feb. 1995, White Springs, FL

[144] *London Telegraph*, Oct. 9, 1994

[145] Larry Nichols, *op. cit.*

[146] *Strategic Investment*, Jan. 18, 1995, Baltimore, MD

[147] *Clinton Chronicles*, Jeremiah Films

[148] *Issues and Strategy Bulletin*, March 31, 1994, 450 Maple Ave. E., Vienna, VA 22180

[149] *The American Information Newsletter*, Dec. 1994, *op. cit.*

[150] Also see *Clinton Chronicles*

[151] *The New American*, Feb. 7, 1994, Box 8040, Appleton WI 54913

[152] Larry Nichols, *op. cit.*

[153] *The New American*, Feb. 7, 1994.

[154] "Clinton Connection Found in Deaths of Alleged Witnesses to Scandal", *The American Information Newsletter*, Dec. 1994, op. cit.

[155] *Accuracy in Media Report*, Jan. A 1994, 4555 Connecticut Ave., N.W., Washington DC 20008

[156] A review of Corbin-Jones vs. Clinton suite in the *American Information Newsletter*, July 1994

[157] Scott Wheeler, "Media Bias in Politics-Truth 'Left' Out," *The Clinton Chronicles Book, op. cit.*

[158] *U.S. News & World Report*, May 23, 1994

[159] "The Clinton Hater's Video Library," *Time*, Aug. 1994

[160] *For the People Radio*, Aug. 3, 1994, White Springs, Fl

[161] *Op. cit.*

[162] Gary Parks, "Hit and Run Execution," *The Clinton Chronicles Book, op. cit.*

[163] *Ibid.*

[164] *Ibid.*

[165] Larry Nichols, *op. cit.*

ABOUT THE AUTHOR

Lawrence Dawson is an autodidact whose science department has become the internet. His formal academic training had ended in the political convulsions which deconstructed Columbia University in the late 1960s. As a student Fellow of the Faculty under the tutelage of Robert K. Merton, one of the founders of the sociology of science and perhaps the nation's best "meta-scientist," the author had watched the university recomposed by a radical epistemology which undermined the scientific method.

Prior to the 1960s student uprising, the linguistics of Ludwig Wittgenstein had begun to dominate the department. Wittgenstein taught that language could never test reality since all linguistic meaning was only a social consensus. Wittgensteinianism was compatible with an emerging scientific corruption which was replacing empiricism with a non-tested consensus. Only a few years previously, Hubble's constant, which had provided the foundation for the popular "Big Bang" theory and an expanding universe, had been revised downward by consensus even though the revision was incompatible with Hubble's original data set. The revision occurred because the "consensus" needed a longer age for the universe than Hubble's original constant had provided.

The author found himself intellectually paralyzed in the recomposed university which was replacing data and hypothesis testing with a Wittgensteinian generated social consensus as the means of determining scientific truth. That paralysis excluded him from an academic career.

It was 25 years later when, as an editor for a small academic publisher which was monitoring scientists who had lost employment due to unapproved research directions, that the author found the indisputable evidence for the damage that Wittgensteinian consensus had done to science. The 1995 Nobel Prize in chemistry had been given for a set of equations which had been disproved prior to the award. However, the disproving data had been completely suppressed in a consensus dominated scientific press and this suppression had allowed the Nobel to go forward. This discovery led to the book "The Death of Reality" which documented the damage which Wittgenstein had done to science and to the culture in general.